DRAWING FOR PRINTERS.

CHAPTER I.

INTRODUCTORY—DESIGNING OF VALUE TO THE PRINTER—NA TURAL ABILITY VERSUS INSTRUCTION—SMALL DESIGNS AS DIFFICULT AS LARGE—READER NOT TO BE DISCOURAGED BECAUSE HE CANNOT BE A FULL-FLEDGED ARTIST —"HOW SHOULD I BEGIN TO LEARN TO DRAW?"—LEARNING TO SEE— INSTRUCTION DOES NOT CONSIST OF NAMING MATERIALS—THE STUDY OF A HAT SEEN IN DIFFERENT POSITIONS—THE V ALUE OF OBSERVATION.

THERE has been in recent years a marked change in the character of the printing done in this country; plain printing has been superseded by decorative printing; the typographer of a few years back was only a compositor and pressman, today he should be a designer as well. In view of that requirement this little treatise is written, in the hope that, though its advice may not make an illustrator out of its reader, it will at least acquaint him with some principles of design that he may apply in his daily practice.

The reader will not be deceived, the writer not misunderstood, if at the outset it is put on record that great success in art is dependent much more upon natural ability, aye, genius, than upon study, and that these chapters can only tell you how to study—they cannot guarantee you success. A man of fifty, a master printer, may study our advice thoroughly and then attempt to {18} draw an elephant chasing an African, and the result may be conspicuously inferior to the treatment of the same subject by little eight-year-old Johnny Green who is yet in the primary school; but Johnny Green may have "an eye for drawing" and our master printer be as devoid of it as is a cow of melody in her voice.

Not only is it true that without talent you must not expect to succeed in producing important pictures, such as full-page illustrations, double-column portraits, poster designs and large work in general, but it is almost more unlikely that you will succeed in designing the most simple tailpiece or initial letter. It is quite natural that you should suppose it a very easy task to design an initial letter or a tiny silhouette of a leaf or flower, a branch or wreath or two forming a "printer's mark"; every artist in Christendom thinks the same—until he tries it; but you would be surprised if I filled this chapter with the history of certain initial letters and devices, and tracing them to their fountain head, we found that in nine cases out of ten they were designed by the very greatest artists of the time.

You can take it as an undisputed fact that should some publishing house wish an ordinary full-page illustration for a book, and at the same time a simple "publisher's mark," a device about an inch square for the title-page of that book, they would find ten artists who could execute the former to one who could design the latter so that it would be up to the standard of the best "marks" in history.

Is it then, you ask, our intention at the very start to discourage you, and advise you to attempt nothing because you cannot excel in anything? Not at all. A {19} country editor need not refrain from studying rhetoric so as to improve the style of his editorials, just because he knows that without genius he may not expect to equal the diction of Macaulay. The rhetoric may not give him wit to put in his editorials, but it at least may teach him to cast his sentences properly. So this treatise may not supply you with "art feeling," but it will, we hope, show you how to make a design in a more workmanlike way than you would without our advice; and we most sincerely advise you to try.

Everyone in asking the question, "How should I begin to learn to draw?" expects that the answer will direct him to use certain materials in a certain way, and that by the manipulation of these materials in this certain way, he will get the desired result. So far as this treatise is concerned, the reader will be disappointed in this regard; it is true that the writer is particularly interested in the technic of the different graphic arts, and later on will have something to say about the best methods for pen drawing, for chalk-plate, for wood engraving; but in these first chapters on drawing it must be distinctly understood that our advice is that the student should not worry about what pencil or what paper he should use, or about how his lines should look, but should realize from the outset that his principal study should be the education of his eye. The reason that we do not draw well in infancy is because we have not learned to see. You may take it as a positive fact that the untrained eye of every man sees things in an absolutely incorrect manner—or rather he does not know how he sees things. Let us take, for example, an immense factory-building with over a hundred windows

{20}

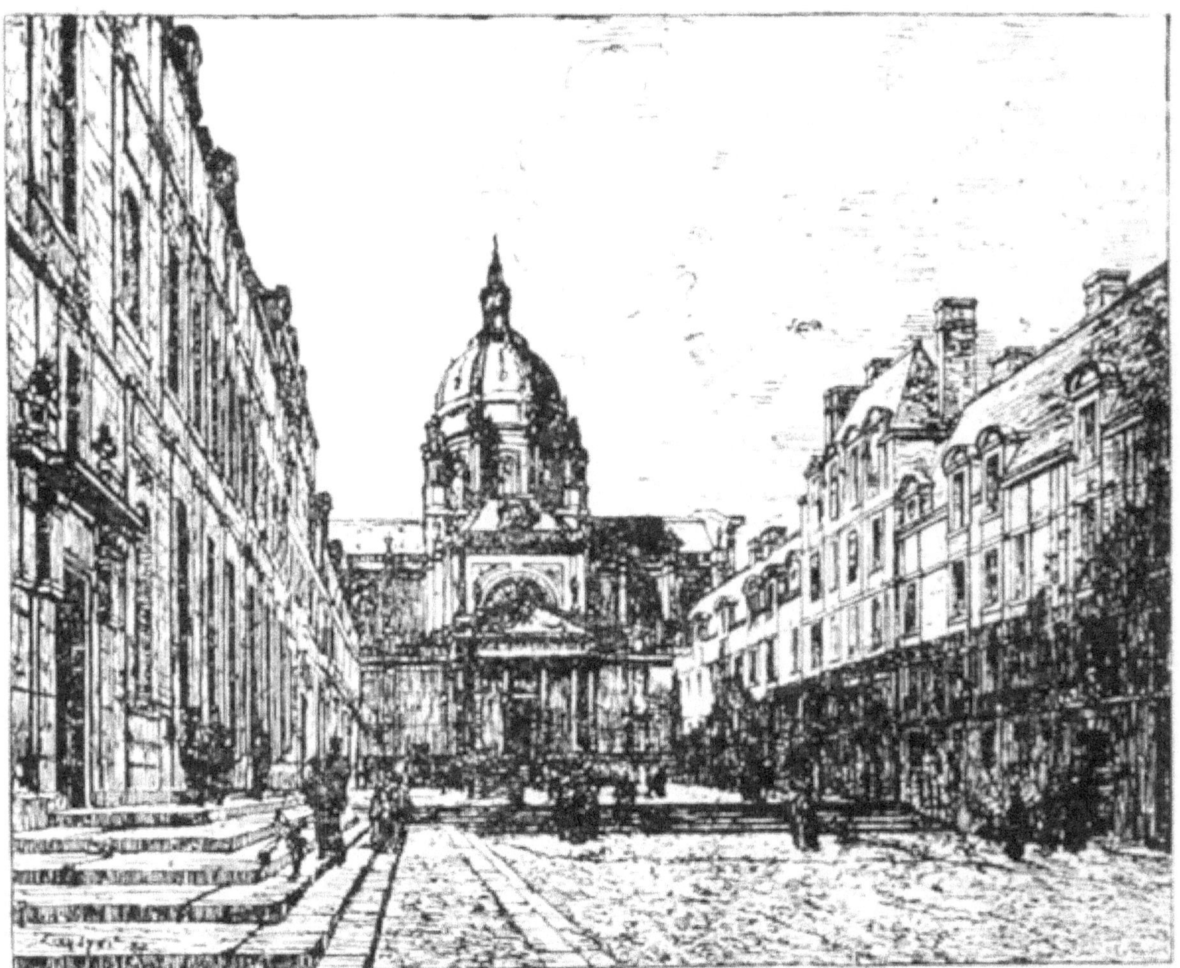

THE COURTYARD OF THE SORBONNE IN 1886.
Pen drawing by E. Lansyer.

Looking at these buildings as in this picture, an artist knows that a doorway or a window in the building with the dome would appear as a perfect rectangle, as we see in the case of the main doorway, because seen "in front view"; but the windows in the buildings at the sides are not perfect rectangles because, being seen "in perspective," or at an angle, their sills and lintels seem to tip downward. The uneducated eye, however, knowing them to be rectangles, sees them as such, not realizing that each receding window is narrower than its predecessor; and that, moreover, the lintels and sills of a window in a higher story have a greater tip than those of one below, and that every lintel has greater tip than its corresponding sill. This knowledge, however, should be known to all artists through the study of perspective.

{21}

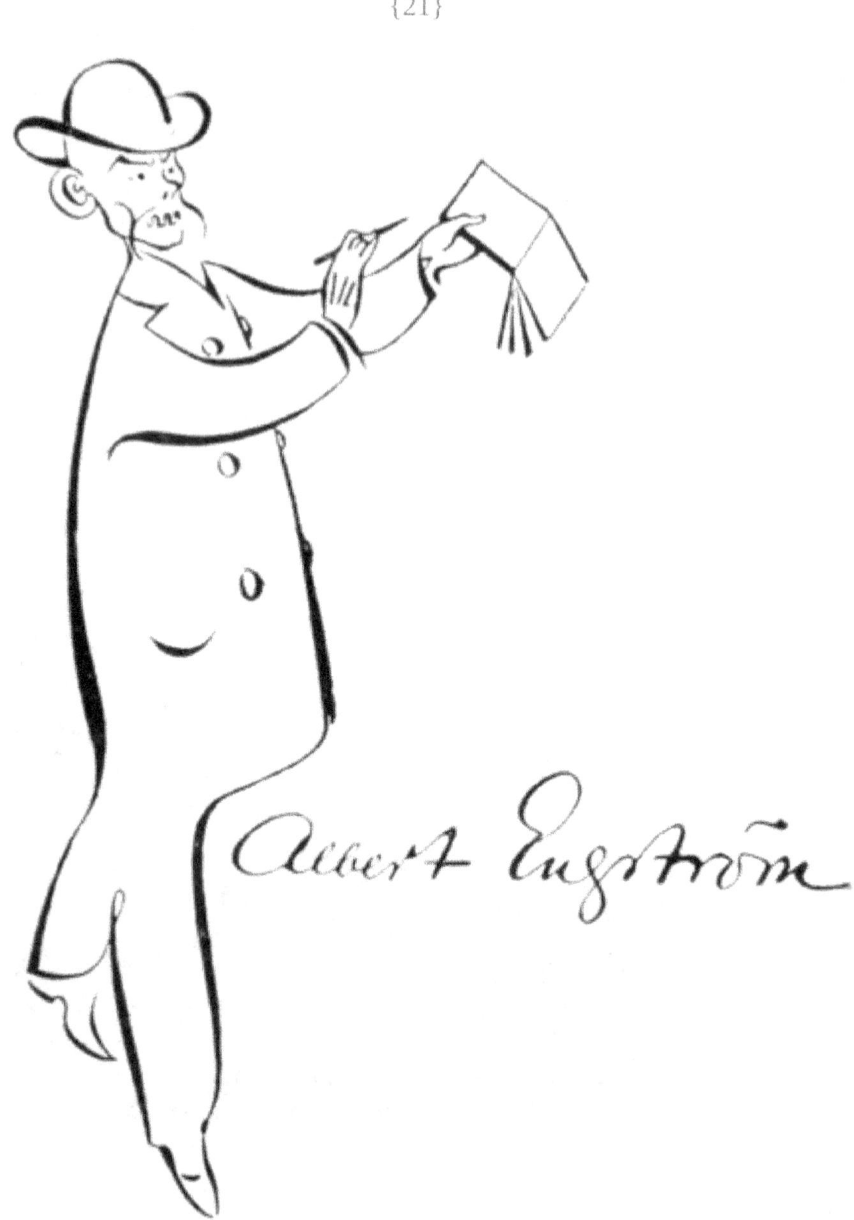

CARICATURE OF THE ARTIST HIMSELF.
By Albert Engström.

{22} on its front and on its sides. Let us presume that a man is standing directly in front of the building; the chances are that he sees every window in a tolerably correct manner. He sees that all the windows are alike, etc.; that each is a certain distance from the other, etc. Good! But now let him walk to the end of the building and look at it diagonally; he still sees the building as he saw it in the front view; depend upon it, that he sees each window as a perfect rectangle, and each window the same distance from the other; he would be incapable of going home and showing you on a piece of paper the "direction" of every window line. Let an artist step in his place and he sees every window *different* from the other! You probably do not realize the full truth of this statement at present, but you will after we have our chapter on perspective. For the present please take my word for it, and bear in mind that you must first learn to see.

Let us take the caricature by Albert Engström for our first lesson. We have selected it for two reasons: first, because it is a caricature, and we wish our readers to realize that this treatise is going to be of use to printers from the beginning, and that we are going to study drawing in an interesting manner. Many a printer is as well the publisher of a newspaper and feels that from time to time he would like to publish a caricature to enliven his pages, or at any rate he is interested in the cartoons in the illustrated press, and would like to know how they are done, and the best way to acquire this knowledge is to practice a little one's self. Besides, the practice of caricaturing is most beneficial to every draftsman; there have been but few great painters who {23} have not indulged in it. Another reason for using this cut is that it is drawn in a very simple manner in a few strong lines. While the students at the art schools usually begin to get effects with light and shade, the printer will do well to master outline sooner than light and shade, for it is the most quickly executed and the most easily engraved, and, I need not add, last but not least, most easily printed. I should advise you then to take commonplace objects that are about the house and make innumerable sketches of them in the manner of this drawing. Take a derby hat for example, place it a little above the eye and endeavor to draw it as Engström did his. Do not worry much about your style of drawing, do not complain that your pen will not work and that you cannot get a line varying in thickness like this one; or if you do succeed, do not ask your friends to admire your handsome pen line; do not think about your drawing at all, but solely about learning to see. Place the hat above you, notice that you see the under part of the brim nearer you, and the inside of the brim on the far side; if there is not a head under the hat endeavor with a single curved line to indicate as much of the lining as you see; if you see anything else that is *not* given in Engström's drawing and you try to express it as he expresses things you employ an excellent method of study. Next place the hat in the same position but below the eye, on the seat of a chair, and notice that you no longer see under the brims but inside of them; then place the hat on its crown upon the chair so that you see the oval of the inside of its crown, and endeavor to express that oval with two semi-circles, as simple as the one which Engström uses in drawing the {24} crown of the hat. Again, put the hat on the mantelpiece and draw a side view of it; this will be more simple than any of the other views. I think that an hour's practice of this kind will soon convince you that the casual glance of the uneducated eye does not take in a complete or perfect view of an object, but that after you have studied an object with a view to drawing it, you begin to see with more thoroughness. You will, I think, notice, as you walk home in the evening, the contours of the different hats that you see in the hatter's

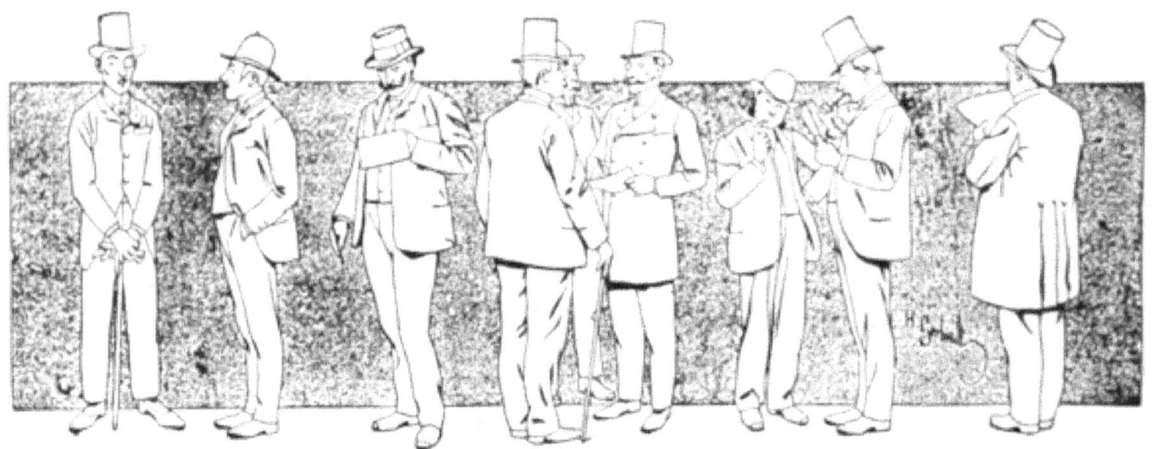

PEN DRAWING WITH MECHANICALLY STIPPLED BACKGROUND.
By H. Gerbault.
Showing different kinds of hats in various positions.

window, and upon the pedestrians; you will begin to guess how you would draw such a hat or cap, and from time to time you will see headgear that "lends itself to drawing," as it were; you will say, "When I go home I will try to draw that hat." We print on this page an interesting drawing by Gerbault. To the casual observer a drawing of this kind simply represents some men with their hats on, and he enjoys looking at the hats collectively, while he may enjoy the individual {25} faces; but the illustrator, with his practiced eye, finds enjoyment in examining the way each individual hat is drawn. You will find the same enjoyment if you practice drawing hats as we have recommended, and it is needless to say that your enjoyment will be profitable, and, moreover, that your practice need not be limited to the drawing of hats, but may embrace coats, gloves, and shoes as well.

If such is the influence upon your mind made by this chapter, we feel sure that you will never regret having read it and given the time to the practice we recommend, and we think that the first step in the study of drawing will have been made, and that you will feel it has been a successful one.

CHAPTER II.

MORE ABOUT HATS — PERSPECTIVE MAY BE LEARNED FROM THEM — DRAWING MORE A MATTER OF SEEING PROPERLY THAN USE OF PEN — TEXTURE — SILHOUETTE DRAWINGS USED BY EGYPTIANS.

WE TRUST that you followed the advice of our former chapter, that you tried to draw a hat in several positions, and that you then found, as we prophesied, that you were led to observe the hats that you saw in the street with a new sense of discernment; if that is true, you will appreciate this chapter, we think, though it be very short.

We select two more caricatures for you, in which we find hats that are very similar. Now we can tell you quite positively whether you have an eye for drawing or not. Stop a moment, and before reading the next paragraph, look at these hats, pages 28, 29, and argue out the reason why they are drawn as they are; if your reasons are somewhat like the following, your chances for learning to draw are good; if not, you have much study ahead of you, even before you can make a start.

Your observation is good if you realize that in drawing almost anything you may represent it as a silhouette. The Egyptians did much of their writing in hieroglyphs, using silhouette pictures of thousands of different objects; helmets and crowns, hands and feet, men and animals, tools and utensils were employed as characters in their alphabet; and if you see plainly how a silhouette is made by outlining an object as it is seen from one point {27} of view, usually a perfect side view, the object on a level with the eye, and that the outline is filled in with black, you may be sure that you have been observing correctly. You will notice then that these two hats are (1) on a level with the eye, for if (2) below the eye, you would see the top of the crown and into the brim; if (3) above the eye, you would see underneath the brim. You notice also that the "Hedin" is the true silhouette, which is made by leaving out the lights on the side, the suggestion of the band, and the upper edge of the brim. You will also notice (4), particularly in the "Jörgen," that the feet are as though the gentleman were walking on a chalk-line on a table and the spectator sitting on a low chair, so that the feet were on a level with his eye; this is a characteristic feature of Egyptian hieroglyphs. If the feet were drawn realistically they would not only not be on a line one with the other, but we would seem to look down upon the shoes, as ordinarily a man's feet are below the spectator's eye.

We think that this is enough for one lesson, and if you find that the propositions that we have numbered are not clear to you, you would better work out the problems on a sheet of paper. We take it for granted that Nos. 1 and 2 are clear to anyone who drew the hats according to our last chapter; but Nos. 3 and 4 may not be so evident; if not, get a pair of shoes and put them on the mantel on a level with your eye; next place them upon the floor in the position in which one ordinarily walks or stands, and our propositions will be clear to you.

It is most important that you should understand all these matters of optics, though it makes little difference

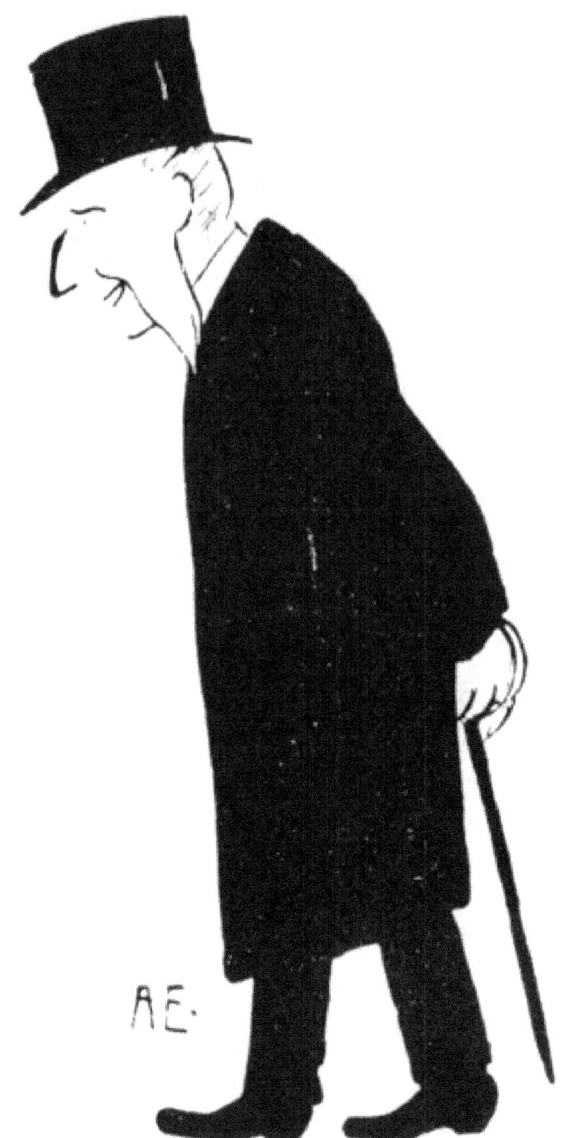

"HEDIN"—A CARICATURE.
By Albert Engström.
The hat and coat are pure silhouette, the face "suggestive outline."

{29}

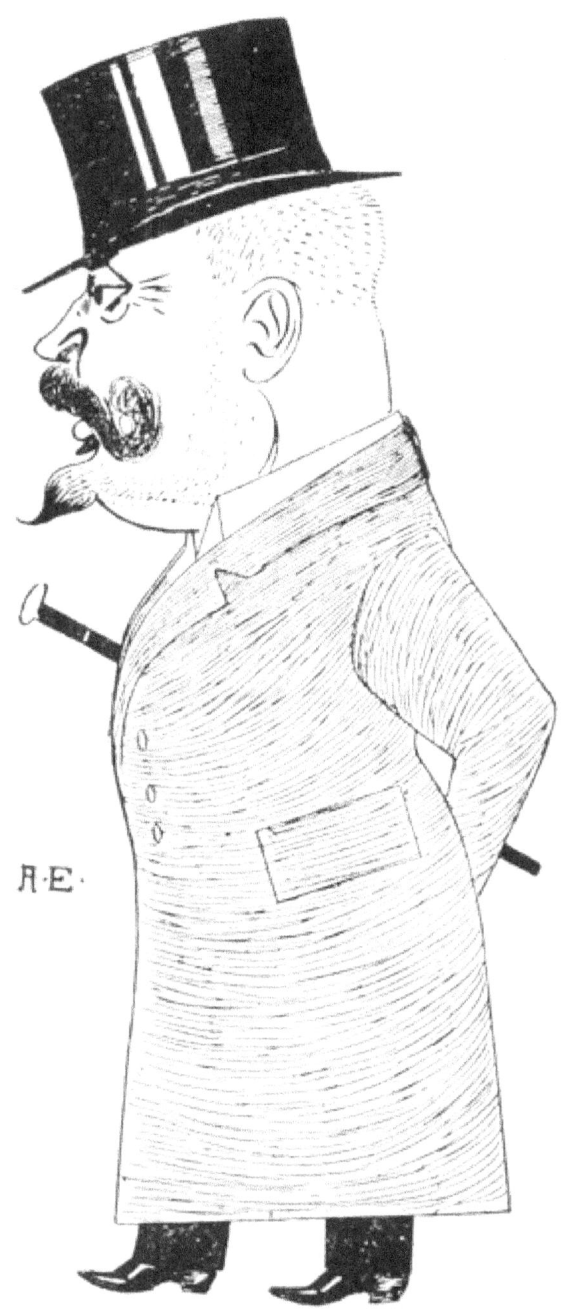

"JÖRGEN"—A CARICATURE.
By Albert Engström.
The hat and shoes are partially silhouette; but the high lights upon them are connected with finished work.

{30} with what kind of a pen you may make your drawing. Having mastered these principles, you would then understand such a criticism on Engström's work as the following: Mr. Engström sometimes employs the pure silhouette, as in the "Hedin," and sometimes silhouette in a modified form, as in the "Jörgen"; in the former case an artist sacrifices rotundity, detail and texture (the white streaks on the "Jörgen" hat suggest the surface of the beaver; this we call texture; a felt hat has no such white streaks upon it, and might be adequately represented by a set of lines such as are used on Jörgen's coat, but no silhouette can suggest texture); in his caricatures Engström unites with the silhouette effect the single-plane effect of the Egyptian hieroglyphs. (The hieroglyphs were mostly painted on walls and the feet represented as though flush with the wall, and not one farther from us than the other, hence we say that they are on one plane.) Many caricaturists have effectually burlesqued the Egyptian method of drawing and the placing of their figures. The trousers and the cane in the "Jörgen" drawing are the only objects in one plane; the coat collar is distinctly rounded. In the Moloch illustration we see also silhouette treatment. You can easily imagine how Hedin's hat, if the proper size, would fittingly rest on Crispi's head.

{31}

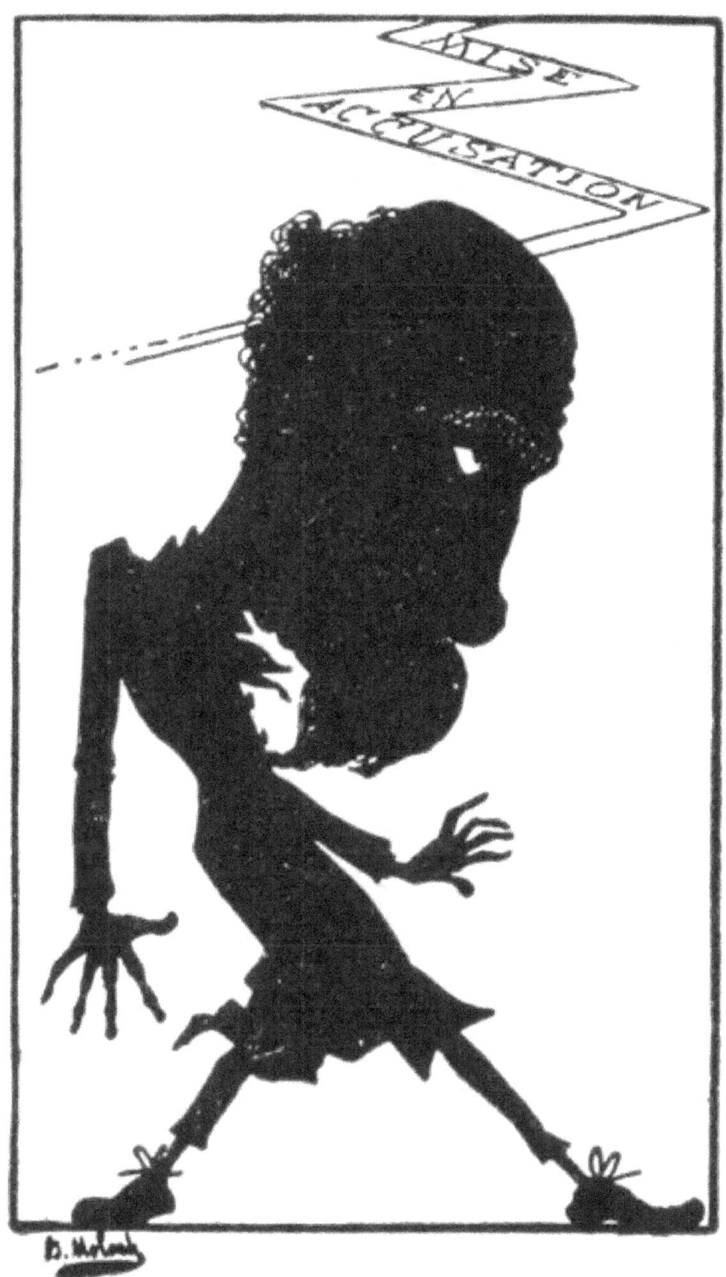

CRISPI UNDER HOSTILE LIGHTNING.
Caricature by B. Moloch.
An example of silhouette drawing.

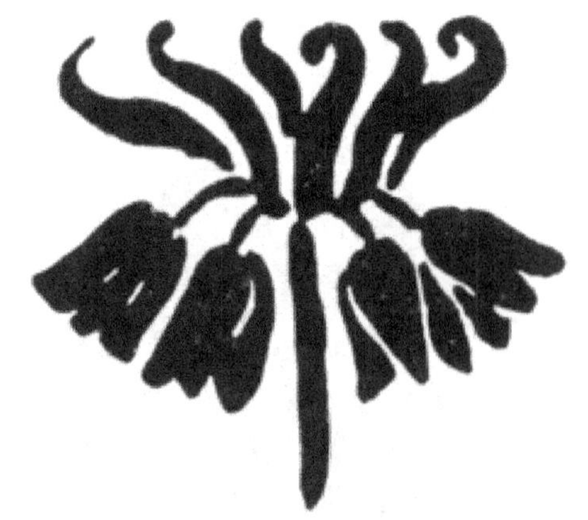

TYPOGRAPHICAL ORNAMENT.
Designed by Eugene Grasset.

CHAPTER III.

HIEROGLYPHIC DESIGNS OR SILHOUETTES — THEIR USE AS TYPOGRAPHICAL ORNAMENTS — OBJECTS SEEN AS ON ONE PLANE — PLACING YOUR OBJECT — HORIZONTAL LINES PARALLEL TO THE EYE — HORIZONTAL LINES NOT PARALLEL TO THE EYE.

WE PUBLISH two kinds of drawings with this chapter, which many be classified as follows: The Grassets are hieroglyphic-like designs or silhouettes; the Crispi, in his *robe de chambre*, which for want of the artist's name we shall call the *Don Chisciotte* cut—"Don Chisciotte" you no doubt suspect is the Italian for Don Quixote, and it is the name of a cartoon paper—is a pure outline drawing.

Now let us take them in turn. Every printer will recognize that the Grasset designs are excellent, for they may be printed with greater ease than shaded drawings, and their simplicity is in perfect harmony with the solid black of type. Now, not only would it {33} be pleasant for you as a printer to begin making some such silhouettes, but it is very good practice in drawing for you to search the house for objects that you can put up against the window pane and draw their contours, filling them in with black. A whisk broom, a pair of scissors, a pair of eyeglasses, a leaf, a feather may be put up against the glass and its silhouette copied, and you then realize how many objects may be represented by their contours. Later you learn how to silhouette objects less flat; you may try the ink bottle with a pen in it, the glue pot with the brush in it; this leads you to such a thorough understanding of Grasset's flowers as pages of writing would never give. In walking in the streets after such an exercise you will notice not only the "block" of a man's hat (which we spoke of in Chapter I), but you will notice what kind of a silhouette it makes against the sky; then the shape of the birds, the weather vanes, the church steeples as they are "etched against the sky," as the poets say, will have a new interest for you.

In this practice of silhouetting objects you learn something that is most important in more advanced work. You learn *to see objects as on one plane*. We fancy your knowledge of geometry is sufficient for you to understand what we mean, but let us go over the ground slowly so that it may facilitate our future explanations of perspective problems.

By a plane we mean a plain, a flat surface. A table top is a plane. But the plane the artist draws upon—say a sheet of paper—though he may let it lie horizontal on a table, is always considered a *vertical plane*, corresponding to a pane of glass in a window. Now, if {34} we are looking across the street, through the window, we know that each receding cobblestone in the street (though in one horizontal plane) is in a different *vertical* plane from the others. If we wished to make the plane a tangible one we could set up a pane of glass in front of the nearest cobblestone, and then another pane in front of the cobblestone across the street, then it would be evident to anyone that these stones were in two planes, would it not? Good! Now, if you should go to the window and trace with a paint brush a picture of these two cobblestones on the glass, you would draw your picture on one plane, and that a *vertical* plane. Well, that is just what the artist does when he draws a picture by the eye. He may lay his paper horizontally on a common table, or obliquely on a tipping drawing table, or on an easel, but he does not draw the objects as though seen through a horizontal or oblique plane (except sometimes when he sketches from a church-steeple or a hilltop), but on the contrary, the ordinary drawing always represents objects as seen through a vertical pane of glass and as they would be traced on that pane, hence *reduced to one plane*.

Having read the foregoing two or three times we will ask you to turn to the *Don Chisciotte* caricature. Has it not a new interest to you? Do you not see immediately that the legs of the bureau, though in reality some few feet apart and so in different planes, are drawn on a sheet of paper on one plane? Well, the second step after you have learned to draw a simple form in outline is to learn to "place" your objects and their receding parts—as the legs of the bureau. It would be impossible for me to overestimate the trouble this gives the {35} beginner—such as the man who sees the factory viewed at an angle as though it were seen from the front (see Chapter I). But if perchance you can get it into your mind that you must draw as though tracing on a window pane, nay, better still, if you will dip a brush in the ink and actually draw on the pane for several days, you will soon have little need of puzzling over perspective, and when you look diagonally at a rectangular object—as the windows in a factory—you will see at a glance that they are no longer rectangles, as in a front view, but the lintels and sills actually seem to *tip* (in an upward direction if below the eye, in a downward direction if above the eye). Then you suddenly realize that certain laws of optics come into play in making the very simplest of views. You look at such a simple interior as in the *Don Chisciotte* room and you recognize at once that the lines in it which were horizontal in nature are governed by three laws; the portière rod and the side boards of the couch are drawn horizontal because the artist sees them in a front view—they are parallel to his eye—but the lines of the front of the bureau and the floor line behind it run up because they are lines seen not in front view, but seen diagonally, and they are below the artist's eye; but the top line of the mirror runs down because it is above the artist's eye.

From this chapter any reader with a mathematical mind will have already deduced the facts of the following rules of perspective, even if he has not formulated them in precise language; but you might as well learn them by heart, as they are applied every time you draw a box, a table, a room, a railroad track, a street, etc.

1. All horizontal lines in nature that are parallel to

{36}

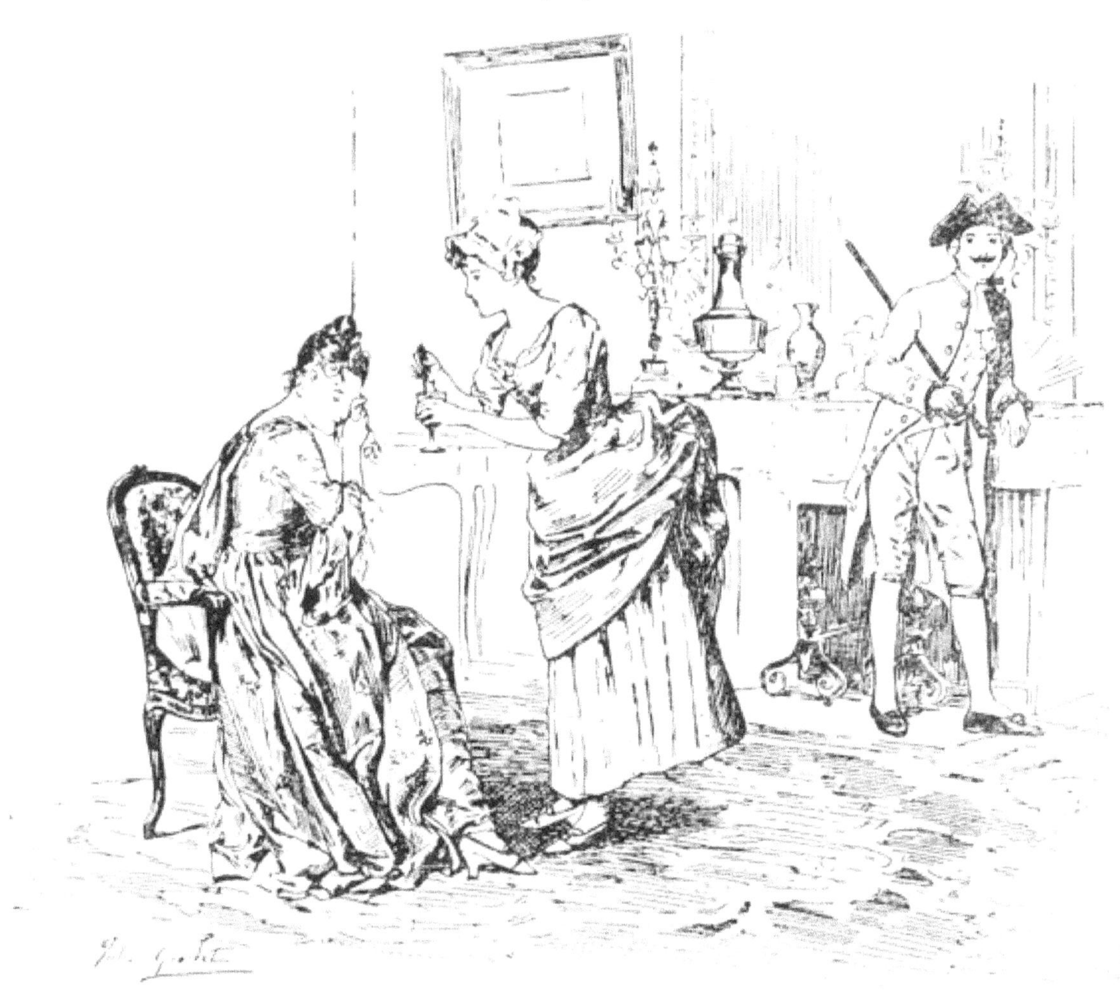

PEN DRAWING.
By Jules Girardet.

Showing a mantel a little below the eye.

The student should practice drawing interiors with the purpose of learning the theory of perspective from every object drawn. The horizontal lines of the picture frame, for example, tip in the opposite direction to the mantel, because they are above the eye. Had the mantel been a few inches higher it would have been drawn as a perfectly horizontal line.

{37}

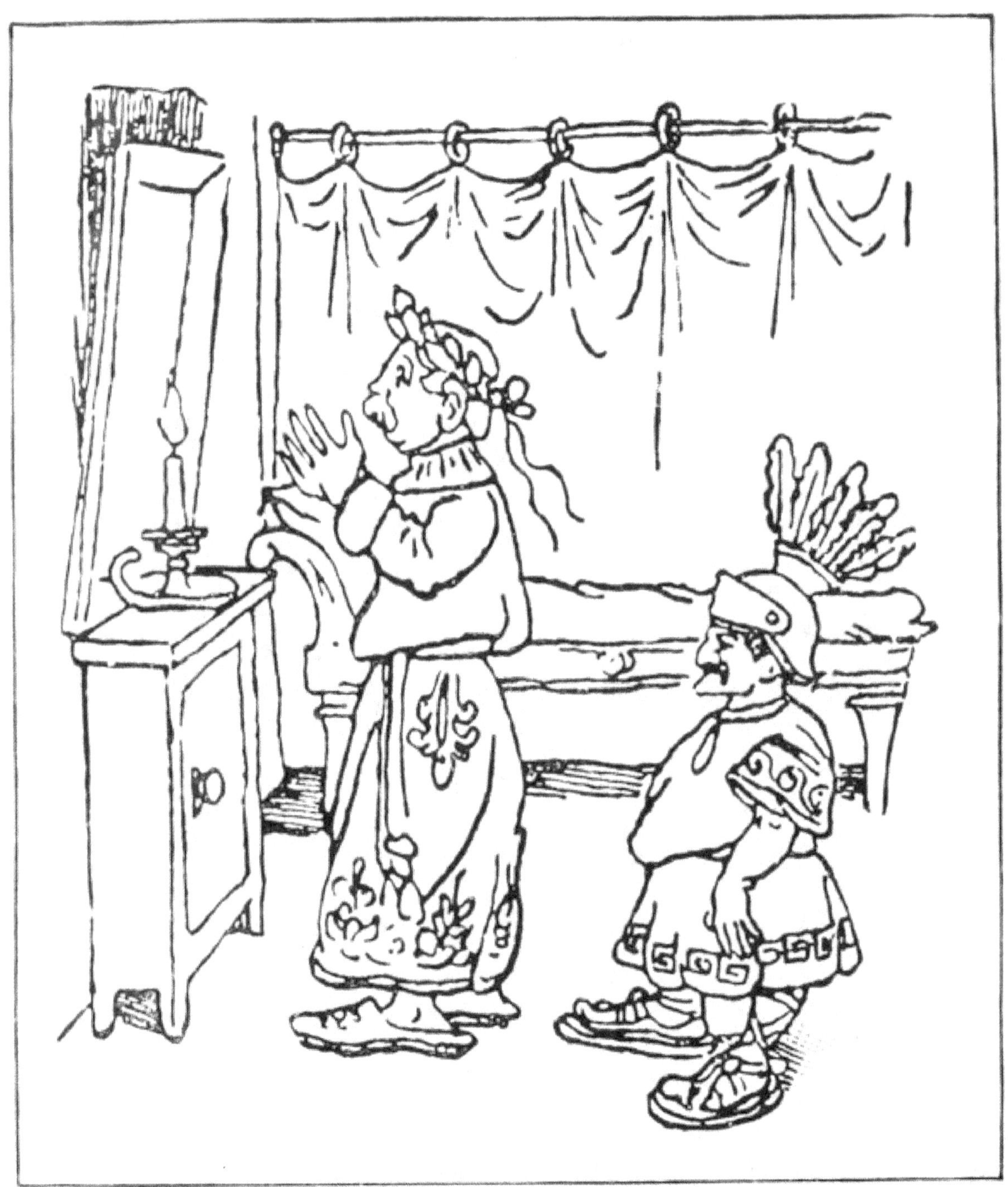

CRISPI AS CÆSAR IN HIS ROBE DE CHAMBRE.
A political caricature from *Don Chisciotte*.

{38} the eyes of the spectator (like the portière rod and the bed part of the couch in the *Don Chisciotte* caricature, like the lintels and sills of the Sorbonne doorway), that is when one is standing directly in front of them, appear as horizontal lines and are to be so drawn, they do not tip either up or down whether below or above the eye.

2. But when a horizontal line is no longer parallel to the axis of the eyes, that is when it is seen diagonally, as the floor line, the front of the bureau and the top of the mirror, then it follows this law; if it happens to be just on a level with the eyes, that is on the horizon line, then it *is* horizontal to the sight and is so drawn; if the mirror were hanging where it is in the *Don Chisciotte*, but were cut off just on a level with Crispi's eyes, and the draftsman of the picture were just Crispi's height, then the base of the mirror would be drawn horizontal. But when the lines are below the eye, as the floor line and the bureau lines, then they seem to run up to the horizon and are drawn slanting upward; while if they are above the eye, as the top of the mirror, they tip down to the horizon and are drawn slanting downward—the end farther away from the artist lower in the picture than the end nearer him. (See the side buildings in the Sorbonne courtyard.)

It is advisable for the student of perspective to cut a rectangular opening, not too large, say the size of this page, in a piece of pasteboard, which he may hold at arm's length in front of him and look through as he would through a small window. This will not only frame his picture for him, but it gives him two horizontal lines and two perpendicular lines, and he can hold his pencil or his ruler against the face of the frame {39} so that it just covers any straight line he wishes to draw; and he will readily see that all vertical lines in nature make his pencil run parallel to the sides of his frame, while horizontal lines if in nature parallel to the axis of his eyes, or if on a level with his eyes, make it run parallel to the base and top. And then, best of all, he can hold his pencil parallel to oblique lines which run away from him, and they will appear parallel to the face of his frame, or in one plane, as they would be in a drawing. This is very helpful, as there is nothing so confusing to the beginner as the lines which run away from him. (In looking up a railroad track the rails seem to run away. You know they are actually parallel, but to your eye they converge. Not only that, but you know they are flat on the ground, whereas, in a picture, you draw them standing up. All this is at first very confusing.)

{40}

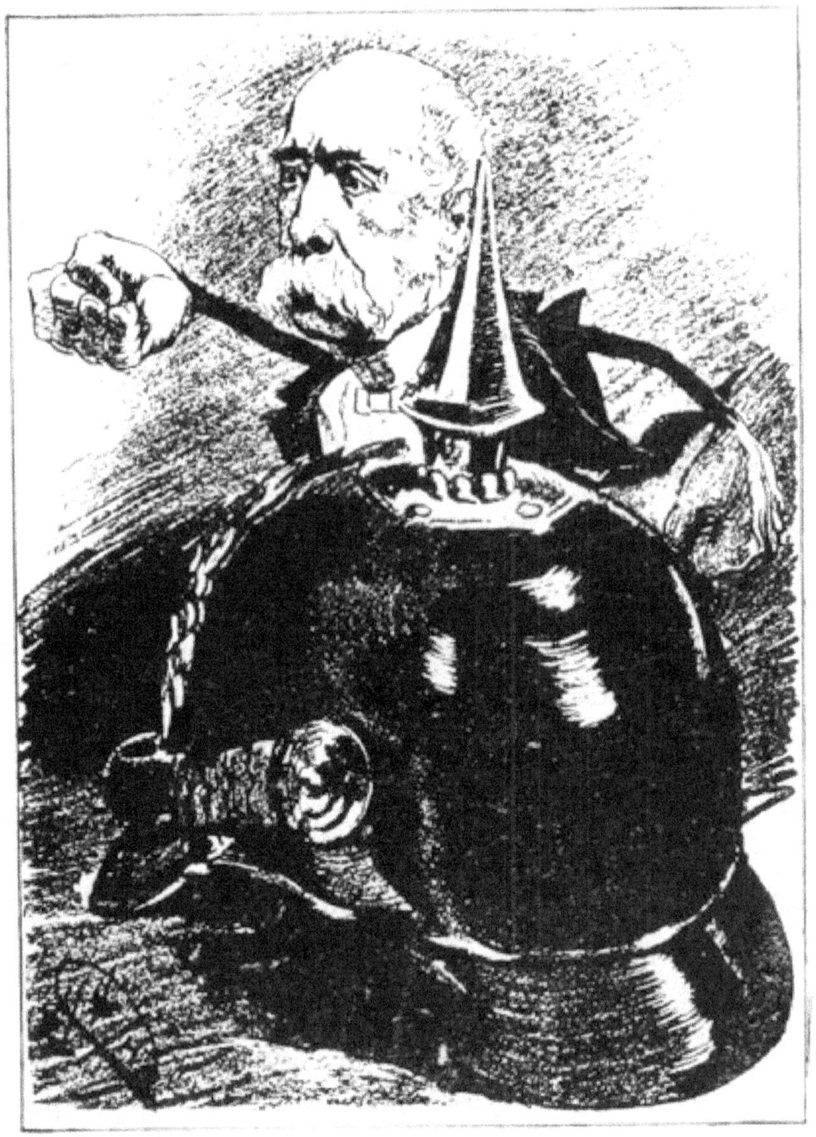

MEN OF THE DAY—CRISPI.
By Luque.
From *La Caricature*.

TYPOGRAPHICAL ORNAMENT.
Designed by Eugene Grasset.

CHAPTER IV.

POWER OF OUTLINE — SHADED DRAWINGS — TEXTURE — LOCAL COLOR AND VALUES — THROWN SHADOW AND MODELING SHADOW — MANNERISMS OF A CARICATURIST — BEGINNER ADVISED TO USE OUTLINE ONLY, BUT HE MAY PRACTICE IN SHADING.

IF I have been successful in making every point clear in my foregoing chapters the reader now has such a knowledge of the art of drawing as will enable him to understand, (1) the power of an outline, and (2) to realize that one may become a tolerable draftsman if he will train his eye to see the outline of an object as if marked upon a pane of glass—that is, reduced to one plane; and to realize, moreover, that (3) this learning to see things in one plane involves some knowledge of perspective, of which more anon; but for the present let us leave outline and take up another branch of the subject. In the Luque cartoon the helmet is represented {42} in a new form. The careful observer will see instantly that it differs materially from the helmet in the *Don Chisciotte* cartoon, shown upon page 37.

Let us make an analysis of this difference. I contemplated no pun when I wrote of a *material* difference. Yet that is the main point of contrast. We guess that the helmet of the major domo in the *Don Chisciotte* is metal, but we only guess it. We argue that the Romans wore metal helmets, hence we fancy this is one; but outline rarely indicates texture (we mean by texture the material of an object—wood, wool, stone, linen, etc.) or color. But in the Luque we are very sure that the helmet is of black leather. True, we surmise this only, because we know that modern helmets are apt to be either metal or black patent leather, and this one is too dark for metal, and the high light upon it is just like the white light on a black patent leather helmet. (When the light falls on a rounded object there is nearly always one place upon it where the light strikes, creating a white light—no matter what the color of the object—which artists call the high light. This is always more apparent upon highly polished objects than upon rough objects.)

Now, you see in the Luque we have a very different kind of drawing from a pure outline like the *Don Chisciotte*, or a silhouette like the Grasset. In such drawing the outline is only the framework; after it is put in, the labor is by no means over; to the contrary, every bit of surface has to be covered with an appropriate tint, and two different considerations decide how light or how heavy this tint shall be: first, the consideration of light and shade; secondly, local color. When the artist put a {43} dark mass under Crispi's mustache he did not mean to suggest that Crispi had been eating blackberry jam, or that he had a negro's lower lip, but he meant to represent the strong shadow that a thick mustache throws upon a lower lip when the light comes from above; in doing this he noted a "thrown shadow." When, however, he made the dark line on the lower part of the chin he did not mean to suggest that the upper part of the chin threw a shadow on the lower part, but he represented the part of the chin that rounds under the jaw; this is called a "modeling shadow." (A circle may represent a ring, or a disk—as in the medal inscribed *Literis et Artibus* in the Fallström (page 44)—or a sphere; but without shading it is said not to have modeling; and if it is intended for a sphere, it can only suggest a sphere; to make it fully represent one, we shade it; then it is positively not a ring, nor a disk, if the shading is properly done. This shading gives it rotundity, or bulk, and this effect we designate as modeling.) When Luque makes the part of the visor of the helmet to our right darker than the part to our left and leaves a light between, he also models—that is, represents modeling or rotundity; but when he makes both the shaded side and the lighter side dark, and also makes Crispi's coat black, then he is said to represent local color.

Here you see we have a very advanced form of drawing, and a form I should not advise you to employ in your early efforts to do professional work; if you essay to make a cartoon for your paper, I should advise you to confine yourself to outline or silhouette. But in order that you may fully understand a drawing which at first appears to be outline, but which upon examination turns

{44}

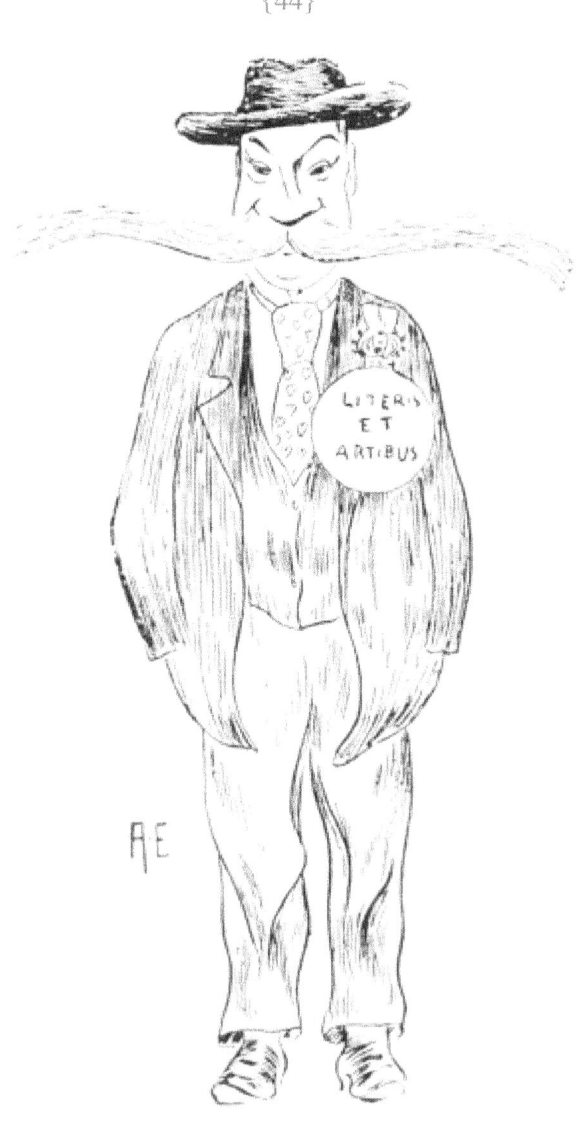

DANIEL FALLSTRÖM.
A caricature by Albert Engström.

{45}

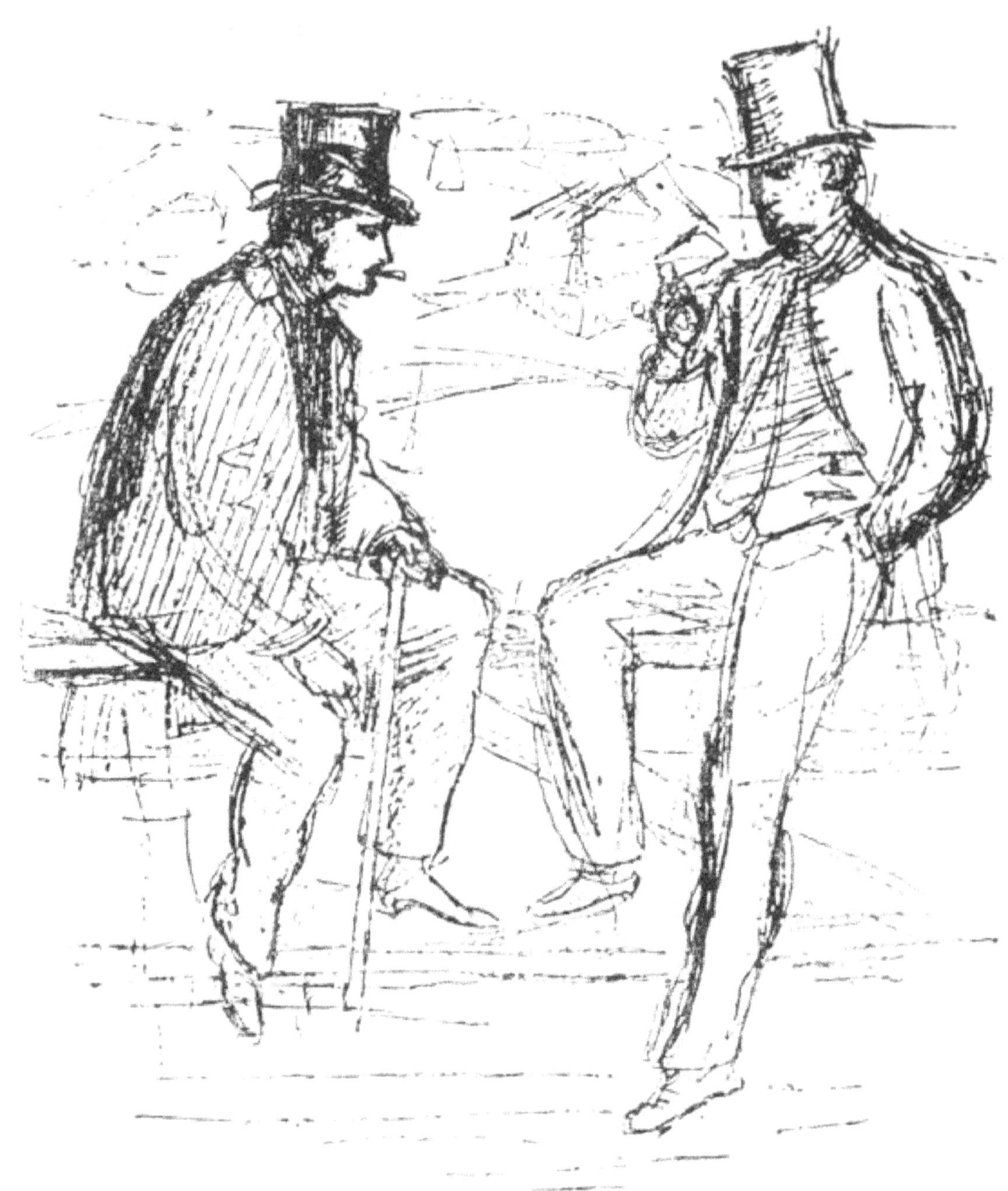

PENCIL SKETCH.
By John Everett Millais.

This is not a careful study, but shows an artist's method of "placing" objects. The right-hand figure is evidently that of a minister, and the artist at first intended to have his coat fall over his left thigh but afterwards changed it. The gray lines which thus place the skirt of the coat are those referred to in Chapter V. In the left-hand figure the head was drawn first and the hat added. It is interesting to note how low upon the head the hat rests. The mistake of the beginner is usually to put a hat too high on the skull. (Or perhaps the artist's first intention was to draw a derby hat, which was afterwards changed to a high hat.)

{46} out to be partly shaded, we have introduced in these first chapters this question of modeling and local color. We have pointed out (Chapter II) that Engström sometimes uses pure outline, sometimes outline and silhouette, and sometimes outline, silhouette and shading. His "Fallström," given with this chapter, is without silhouette effect, but is in outline, shading and local color. The medal referred to is a piece of pure outline. Ordinarily, when an artist draws a thing of this kind—a button, a policeman's badge, etc.—he makes the lower line a little heavier than the rest so as to suggest the shadow the object throws upon the coat; but Engström has omitted this. In the nose, however, we have not pure outline, but a distinct broadening of the line under the nose giving the same suggestion of its protruding and of its throwing a shadow as does Crispi's mustache in Luque's drawing. In the hat, moreover, we have both modeling—very good modeling, too,—and local color.

You should be reminded that Engström is a caricaturist, and takes liberties with the art of drawing as well as with his subjects. The example we gave in Chapter I, his own portrait, was a perfectly consistent drawing, all pure outline; so was the "Hedin" (Chapter II), because silhouette goes perfectly well with outline. But to model a hat as fully as in this "Fallström" drawing, so that under its rim is a shadow, and yet not have it throw a suggestion of a shadow upon the man's head, is most inconsistent drawing —permitted the caricaturist only. If you were making such a study from nature you would surely see a *thrown* shadow on the head and you should put it in. {47}

While I say you should not employ shading and local color to any great extent in your early work, yet you may study the theory of it so as to use it sparingly, and that study is best pursued by putting on a table a group of objects of different colors and textures; put a white box beside a brown book, an ink bottle beside a glass, a teacup beside a brown stone jug, and draw each object in relation to the others. Make your ink bottle blacker than your brown jug, but note that both have distinct high-lights upon them. The white box will probably not have a high-light upon it, but one side of it may be all light, while the corresponding side of the brown book will be darkish, though lighter than its side in shadow. (We suppose that you place your table near a window so that the light from it falls on one side of the objects, the other side being in shadow; this is the best arrangement for objects studied for their light and shade. Do not have light come from other windows.) You, therefore, in your drawing, have white paper to represent the light side of the box, but you put on a slight tint to represent the light side of the brown book. The ink bottle you will treat very much like Luque's helmet; black as it is there will be streaks of white upon it— sometimes high-lights, and sometimes reflection of the window as seen in a mirror. If the cover of the box, because it projects a little, throws a line of shadow upon the side of the box, you will instantly recognize that this is the same kind of a thrown shadow as that which Luque put under Crispi's mustache and Engström put under Fallström's nose. Some study of this sort will soon train your eye to see the reason of *spots of light and dark* in artists' drawings. {48}

One of the points we admire in an expert's drawing is the use he makes of black spots. The Japanese have rules of composition, governing this distribution of spots, which they follow, balancing a black here with another there in an admirable manner. In our chapter on wood engraving we shall give some specimens of well distributed blacks. In our tailpiece by Grasset you will notice how on the right-hand side five petals and two buds balance a tri-parted leaf on the opposite side. One of the problems for the designer of printers' devices is to balance them properly. It is much easier to copy a spray from nature and fill it in with black ink than it is to make that spray balance so that when placed at the end of a chapter or used to divide paragraphs it will balance as perfectly as the letter V or A. It is needless to note that every printer realizes that paragraphs might be separated by the letter I or A or V, but not properly by the letter B or D or E.

CHAPTER V.

HOW TO BEGIN A DRAWING — EDUCATION OF THE EYE THE FIRST THING — MANTELSHELF SEEN FRONT VIEW — SIDE VIEW BUT EXACTLY ON A LEVEL WITH THE EYE — TIPPING DOWNWARD IF ABOVE THE EYE — UPWARD IF BELOW THE EYE — PLACE THE BIG PROPORTIONS OF OBJECTS BEFORE ATTEMPTING DETAIL — THIS SHOULD SHOW PROPORTION AND DIRECTION — SEPARATE COMPLEX SUBJECTS INTO ELEMENTS — MEANING OF ELEMENTS — EVERY OBJECT HAS ITS AXIS — BEGINNING OF EVERY FIGURE SHOULD ALWAYS SHOW ITS ACTION — GENERAL PRACTICE TO PLACE ALL THE OBJECTS IN A PICTURE WITH PENCIL LINES FIRST — SOME EXAMPLES FROM MUNKACSY.

I HEAR some of my readers ask, "Is there not something a teacher should tell us that will help us whether we are drawing in outline or whether we are shading—something that will teach us *how to begin* any kind of a drawing?" The reply is "Yes," and I propose to give such help in this chapter; but it has purposely been delayed till now, because I wished to emphasize the fact that the principal thing is not for me to tell you how to draw, but for me to help you to learn to see so as to know what to draw. For example, I will ask the printer to insert a rule here in a horizontal position, thus:

This represents a mantelshelf seen in front view, or one seen in side view exactly on a level with your eyes. Now, it stands to reason, does it not, that anybody can {50} draw such a line? What you need to be taught, is that the mantel is to be drawn that way only under the two circumstances mentioned. The moment you have a side view of it when it is below or above the eyes, you must draw it tipping. Tipping downward (away from you) if above the eye; upward, if below. Thus, if above the eye:

B ⎯⎯⎯⎯⎯⎯⎯⎯⎯⎯ A

(A, the end nearer spectator.) Thus, if below:

B ⎯⎯⎯⎯⎯⎯⎯⎯⎯⎯ A

This difference in the direction of line according to the position of the spectator is something the novice does not see, and it is the business of the teacher to point it out. Hence the many references to seeing and the few to drawing which are found in our foregoing chapters.

But there is a suggestion about drawing which I will give you that will help you at the first stage of your study. It is this: Accustom yourself to place something on your paper—some form having a height and a breadth—that resembles the big proportions of your subject, before you attempt to finish any single part of it.

Our illustrations clearly show the working of this method. In the Herkomer study the lower parts of the tree trunks are not finished, they are merely placed. The outlines of the trunks show (1) the relation of the two trunks to one another, (2) their size, and (3) their direction. With the same simple means the artist could have shown contrary facts; for example, that (1) the trees were nearer together, (2) that the left one was

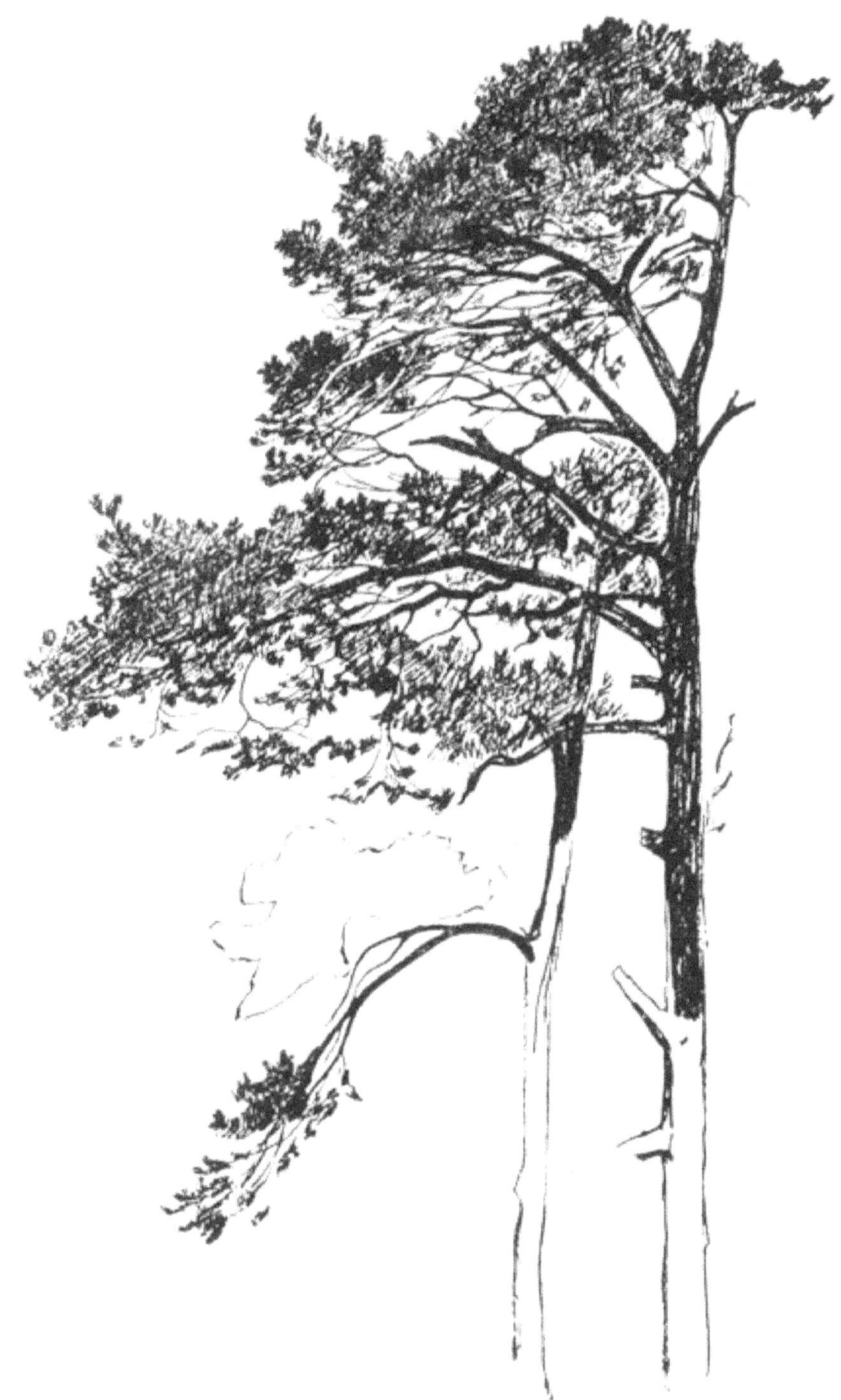

STUDY OF PINE TREES BY HUBERT HERKOMER.

The form above the lowest branch, which looks something like a cloud, shows us the artist's method of "placing" a branch before finishing it; also the lower parts of the trunks show their placing. All objects should be thus outlined before they are shaded.

{52} wider than the right, (3) that they tipped at an angle of fifteen degrees to our left.

Again, the mass that at first glance looks like a cloud, is really the "placing" of a branch. Now, before the artist put any of the black in his picture, which suggests the dark colors of a pine, he placed all the principal branches, limbs, and the trunks of the two trees, just as you see them in the unfinished places we have pointed out. The reader should need very little more help than this to fit him to go out to nature and begin a landscape.

Almost any element you may see can be begun in this manner. (I use the word element to cover either one object or a group of objects; we say of some picture that it has four elements: a foreground, a pine tree, a clump of trees and distant hills.) For example, without the line representing the limb below Herkomer's outline for the unfinished branch might almost stand for a cloud—its outline would then simply be a little less toothed. Its upper part might also stand for a group of distant trees. Now, this branch, no less than the trunks, has its big proportions; it is almost twice as long as it is high, and no amount of pretty drawing of details would ever represent *that* branch if you should start out with a form twice as high as it is wide. Always look out for these dimensions at first. The branch also has a *direction*—the direction of its axis—which is downward to our left, and no amount of pretty drawing of its details would ever represent *this* branch if it were represented with a horizontal axis. (The axis of the lowest branch is at a still greater angle; this downward tip is characteristic of the lower branches of the pine, larch, elm, beech, willow, etc.) Now, a cloud has its

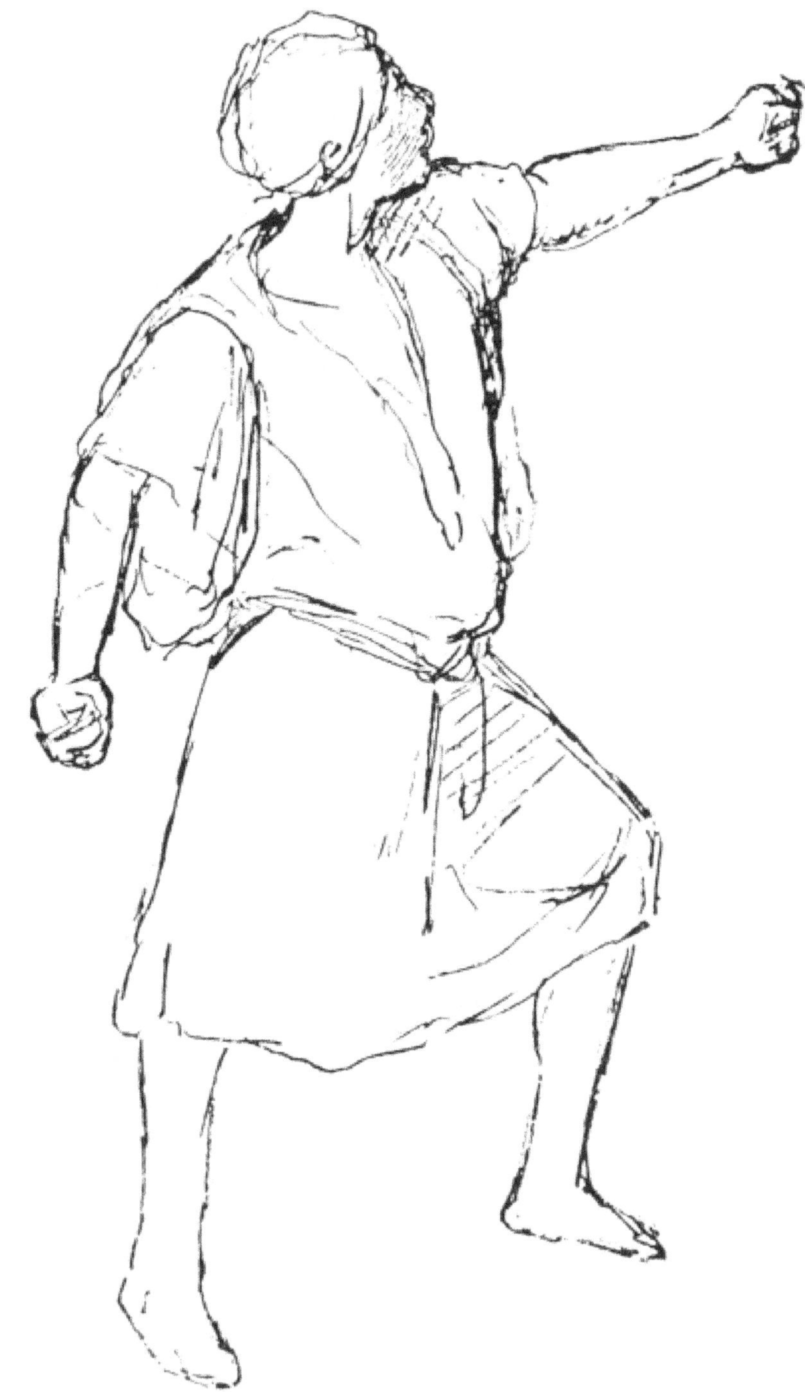

STUDY FOR A FIGURE IN A PAINTING.
By Michael Munkacsy.
This shows the placing of the parts of the figure so that it shows *action*, though there is no finish.

{54}

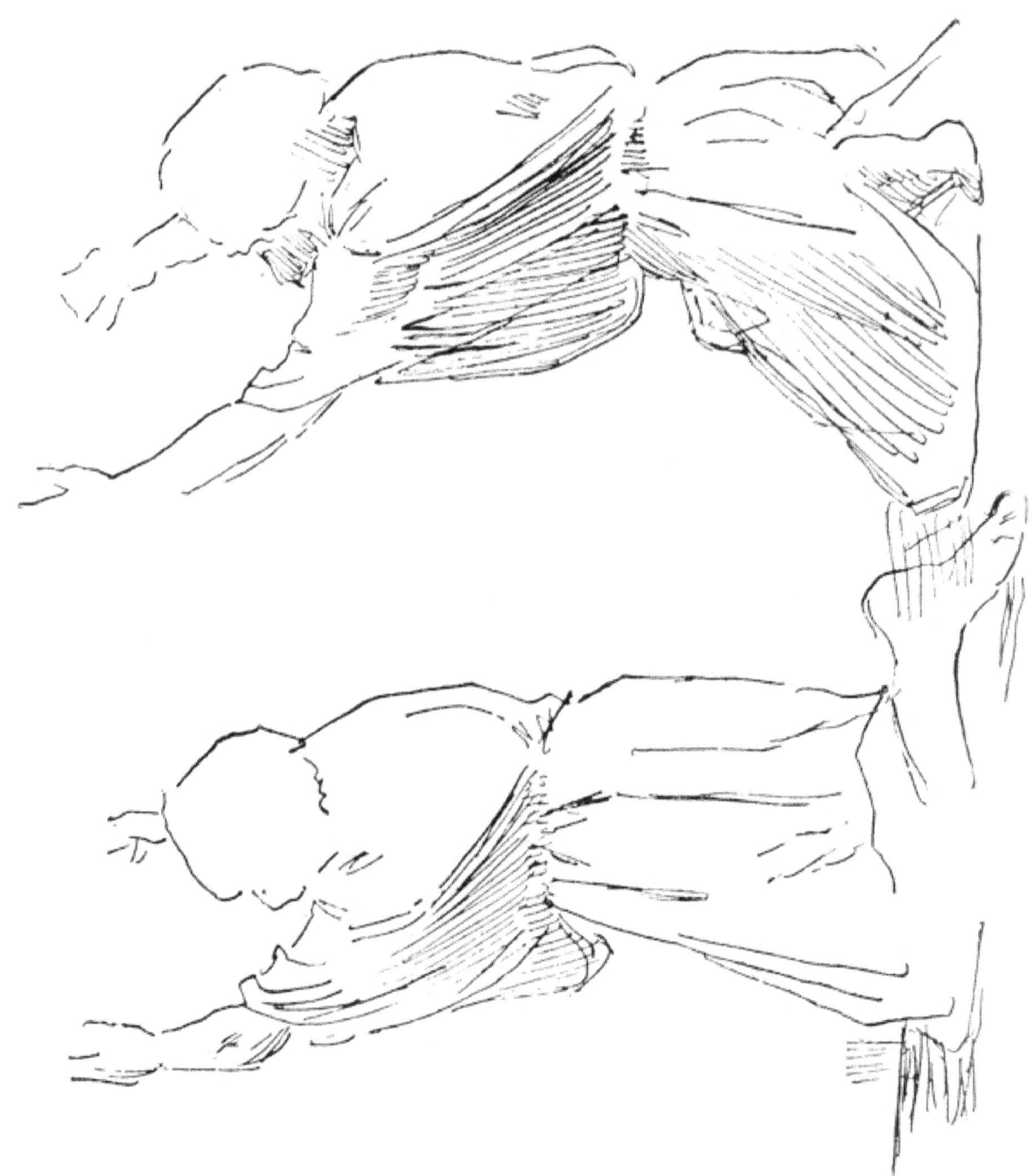

STUDIES FROM A MODEL FOR FIGURES IN A PAINTING.
By Léon Bonnat.
These studies show the placing of the parts of the figures so that they express *action*, though there is no finish.

{55} axis, a group of trees, and you must not draw a stratus cloud which lies horizontal as though it were a cirrus or a cumulus cloud blown upward by a contrary wind. In the placing of an element, then, it is not the margin of the outline we think of, but the positions of objects, their general bulk, and the direction of their axes.

In the figure studies we reproduce by Bonnat and Munkacsy, you can plainly see that the action of the figures is graphically portrayed without any attempt at detail, simply by "placing" the parts of the figure in the right place. A good beginning in the case of figure drawing should always show the action; that is to say, show that the man is stooping over, leaning back, standing upright or sitting down, long before the drawing shows that his coat is black or has four buttons on it, or that he has finger nails on his fingers.

It is nearly always the practice with artists to place objects in this way with a pencil line, even if the subsequent drawing is to be in pen or wash. Let your lines be light, and then you can erase them after your ink lines are put over them. Do not be afraid of feeling your way with lines; put down several until you get the right one. Do not expect to get your work right at first. If you get in a branch of a tree and think it is correct, leave it till the tree is complete; but if in the end you see it is too large for the rest of the tree, rub it out and make it smaller. Every artist has to do this many times if his subject is at all complicated.

{56}

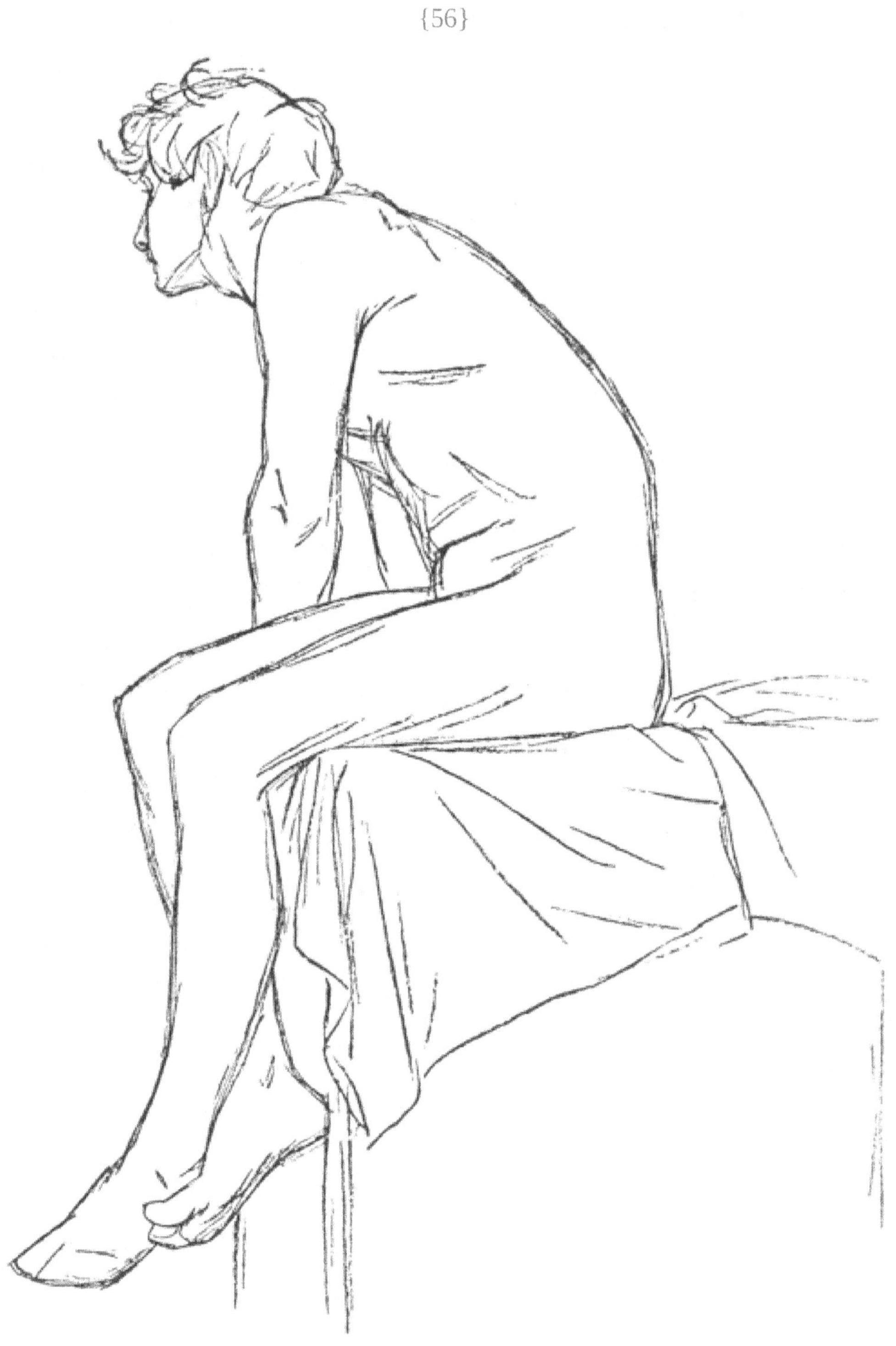

Example of French Art School studies from plates published under the direction of Bargue and Gérôme, showing the method of placing a figure before drawing the final outline or shading; also showing lines on the jaw, in the trunk and leg that are not contour lines.

CHAPTER VI.

VALUE OF A LINE — WHAT THE ARTIST SEES — LINES, NOT CONTOUR LINES, USED TO REPRESENT ORGANIC PARTS — "PLACING" ELEMENTS A MENTAL TRAINING — MORE IMPORTANT TO THE PRINTER-DRAFTSMAN THAN INTRICATE DETAIL — PLACING-LINES TO BE MADE CAREFULLY — SYNTHESIS OF THE HUMAN ARM REPRESENTED WITH A FEW LINES — THE DELIGHT OF AN ARTIST IN SYNTHETIC STUDIES — JAPANESE MASTERS OF SYNTHETIC DRAWING — GRASSET'S SILHOUETTE — THINK OF YOUR OBJECTS, WHEN PLACING THEM, AS SILHOUETTES — REDUCING CONTOUR LINES TO GEOMETRIC FIGURES — HERKOMER'S PINE TREES MAPPED OUT INTO POLYGONS — THIS METHOD NOT TO BE CARRIED TO EXCESS — CHARACTERISTICS OF OBJECTS TO BE LOOKED FOR — NATURE'S FORMS SOON RECOGNIZED IN SIMPLE POLYGONS.

IT Is difficult for the amateur to realize the value of a line as fully as the art student realizes it. We give an illustration of the first laying in or placing of a figure, as done in the Parisian art schools. The student who works for months and months in this manner sees a meaning in an artist's lines that the casual observer misses. Here, for example, all the lines on the arm represent swellings which are not merely temporary but are organic, belonging to every arm. So also with the cross lines on the abdomen; they are not as one might expect, chance lines, but divide the trunk into organic parts. Any model taking this pose would show some such lines, or rather the body would divide itself into {58} some such parts which would produce the wrinkles which these lines represent; no matter whether he were older or younger, stouter or thinner, the markings would be in about the same place. When we come to the analyzation of the human face this fact of representing parts of the body by lines that are not outlines—i. e., not contour lines—will be still clearer to you. Now, the point we want to make is that the method of "placing" objects, recommended in the last chapter, is not a mere process of procedure in drawing, but is quite as important a mental training as the making of the most intricate outline—in fact, for the printer-draftsman it is more important than the latter. If you wish to make a poster design, it is better that you should know how to place "the elements" of a branch of oak or ivy than that you should draw the venation of the leaves or the delicate modeling of the stems, because if printed in flat tones it is the big characteristics—showing the difference between an ivy leaf and an oak leaf—that you need to secure. Therefore, in all your preliminary sketching do not work carelessly just because you are finally going to rub out your placing lines; but rather try to see how much likeness to the object you can get by the most economical means, in your very placing of the object. In the man's arm, for example, even the inexperienced draftsman, who might not see the correctness of the drawing in the man's trunk, can realize that we have here the swelling of the deltoid, the curve of the biceps, the extreme width at the elbow, and the inside lines which mark bones and muscles at the elbow; all of which represent the synthesis of *the* human arm, though perhaps not the similitude {59} of any *one* arm. Were you, with an artist companion, looking over a collection of drawings by the masters you would be surprised at his delight in many drawings that were carried little further than this study of an arm. The Japanese are celebrated for their synthetic drawing; they have the ability to make a spot of green that is not a lily leaf in all its intricate detail, but which has all the characteristics of a lily leaf which distinguish it from every other kind of leaf, stand for a perfect lily leaf.

If you will turn to the Grasset design on page <u>39</u> you will realize that his wisteria is by no means a complete floral drawing, but simply gives the characteristics of the wisteria in its silhouette. Here you see we revert to the subject of our second chapter, and recommend that in placing your objects you think of them as silhouettes. This wisteria design suggests another help for the beginner. The flower itself in its entirety takes the form in nature of a cone, which in silhouette is a triangle; the entire branch of the ornament on page <u>48</u> takes the form of a triangle; and since geometrical forms are more easily analyzed than natural forms, it might be well for you to train yourself to notice if an object takes the general form of a quadrangle or a rectangle, a triangle or a polygon. The branches of trees can frequently be mapped out into triangles or polygons with not more than five or six sides, that are very easy to recognize.

We have made a tracing of the pine trees by Mr. Herkomer, in which we have mapped out the branches into polygons, A, B and C (page 60). The lines D E and F G are added to suggest how the tree trunks are

{60}

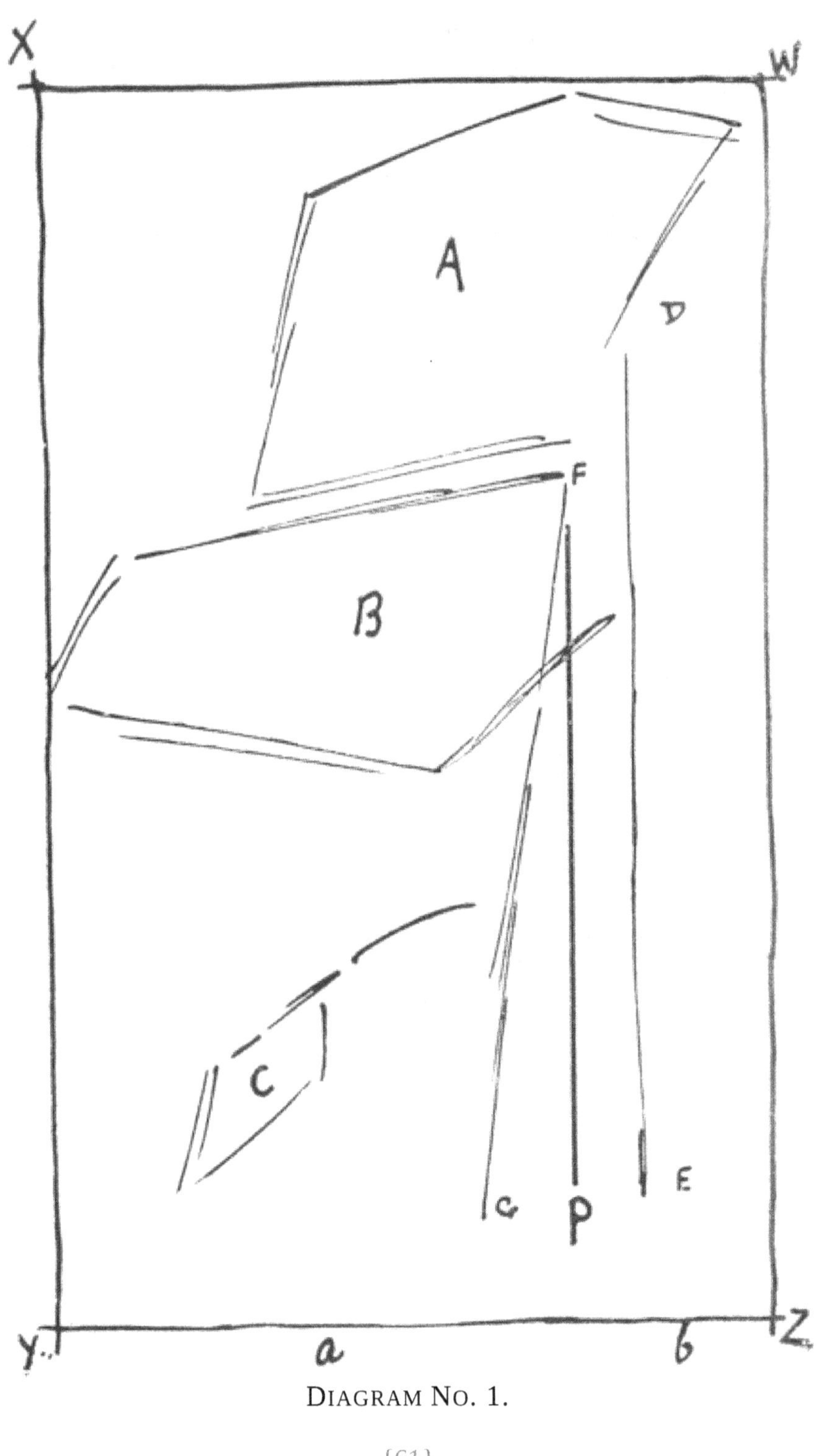

DIAGRAM NO. 1.

{61}

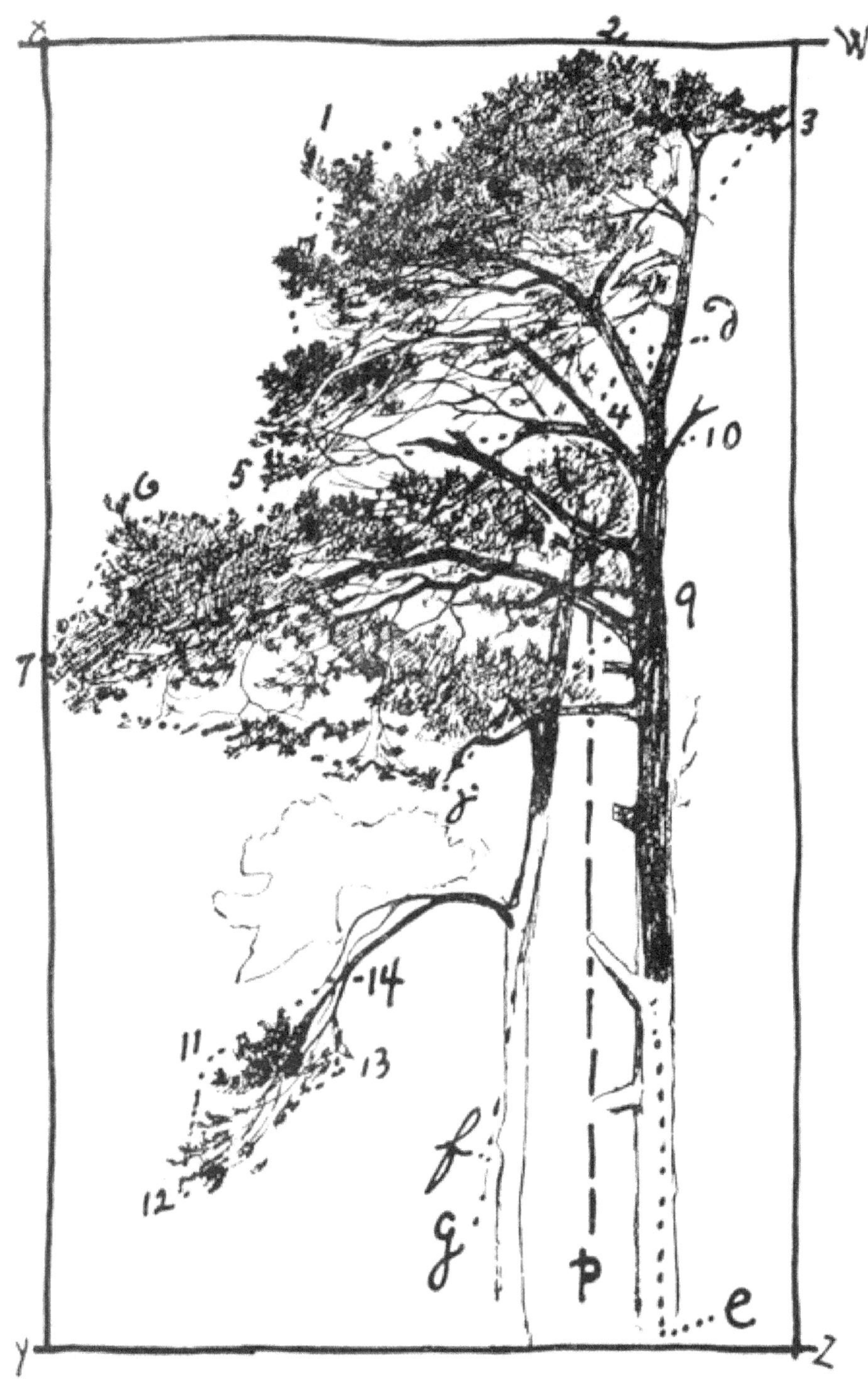

DIAGRAM NO. 2.

NO. 4—Study of Pine Tree, by Hubert Herkomer, with lines added showing rectangles *w x y z*, containing the whole group; polygons 1 to 14, containing branches, lines going through axes of trunk *e d*, and *f g*, and *p*, plumb-line to which *f g* is compared—that is, its angle obtained—as shown in diagram NO. 1.

{62} first put in as axes, F G being compared with the plumb-line P. W, X, Y and Z suggest a quadrangle, into which the whole tree could first be placed.

We wish to say, however, that we do not consider it advisable to reduce freehand drawings to geometrical forms to too great an extent. The art student in Paris does not think of his model as a combination of cubes and cylinders, but as a human figure; nor when he leaves the atelier does he consider a tree as a combination of cylinders and cones, but as an oak tree, or a maple or a pine; and whether his drawing is a moment's jotting in a sketch-book, or a week's study on canvas, he tries to get as much of the characteristics of the pine tree or the oak, in the moment or in the week, as his perception will allow.

You would be surprised, if you practiced this method for a few months, to see how much meaning these first polygons will have to you. If you will map out an elm tree, for example, and then turn to our diagram No. 2, you will instantly recognize that the forms A, B, C, could never be intended for an elm. This negative recognition would be followed by positive recognition, and you would guess at least, if you were not sure, that, in a sketch of a sea coast, certain polygons put more on one side of a line than on the other, which represented a tree trunk, were meant for the branches of a pine!

CHAPTER VII.

ORIGINAL "PLACING" AND FINISHED DRAWING COMPARED — SIZE OF THE FRAME DOES NOT AFFECT THE PROPORTIONS IF THE SAME DIMENSIONS ARE RETAINED — BLOCKING IN SHADOWS BY OUTLINE BEFORE SHADING — ALL PRACTICE IN DRAWING LINES WILL BE HELPFUL — LINES USED FOR CONTOUR BOTH OF OBJECTS AND OF SHADOWS — FINDING THE DIRECTION OF SHADOWS — WHY PLASTER CASTS ARE USED AS STUDIES — JAPANESE ART ENTIRELY WITHOUT LIGHT AND SHADE OF THE SORT MOST USUAL IN OCCIDENTAL MODELING — NOTING VALUES — MERE SHADING NOT THE END OF DRAWING.

IN ORDER that there may be no doubt about the method of placing elements, as suggested in the last chapter, we have made skeletons (2 and 4) of the Grasset and the Herkomer cuts, on which we have marked, so that there can be no misunderstanding, the lines given in our diagrams 2 and 3. In the Grasset diagram, No. 3, A B C D correspond to $a\ b\ c\ d$ in skeleton diagram No. 4, while the dotted forms, E and F, No. 3, correspond to e and f, No. 4.

In the Herkomer, No. 2, $w\ x\ y\ z$ is the rectangle W X Y Z of diagram No. 1; 1 2 3 4 5 correspond to A, 6 7 8 9 10 to B, 11 12 13 14 to C; while the $d\ e$ and $f\ g$ equal D E, F G; p is our plumb-line, P.

It must be distinctly understood that any number of objects may be contained in a rectangle; let a child scribble upon this page, anywhere, a dozen or more

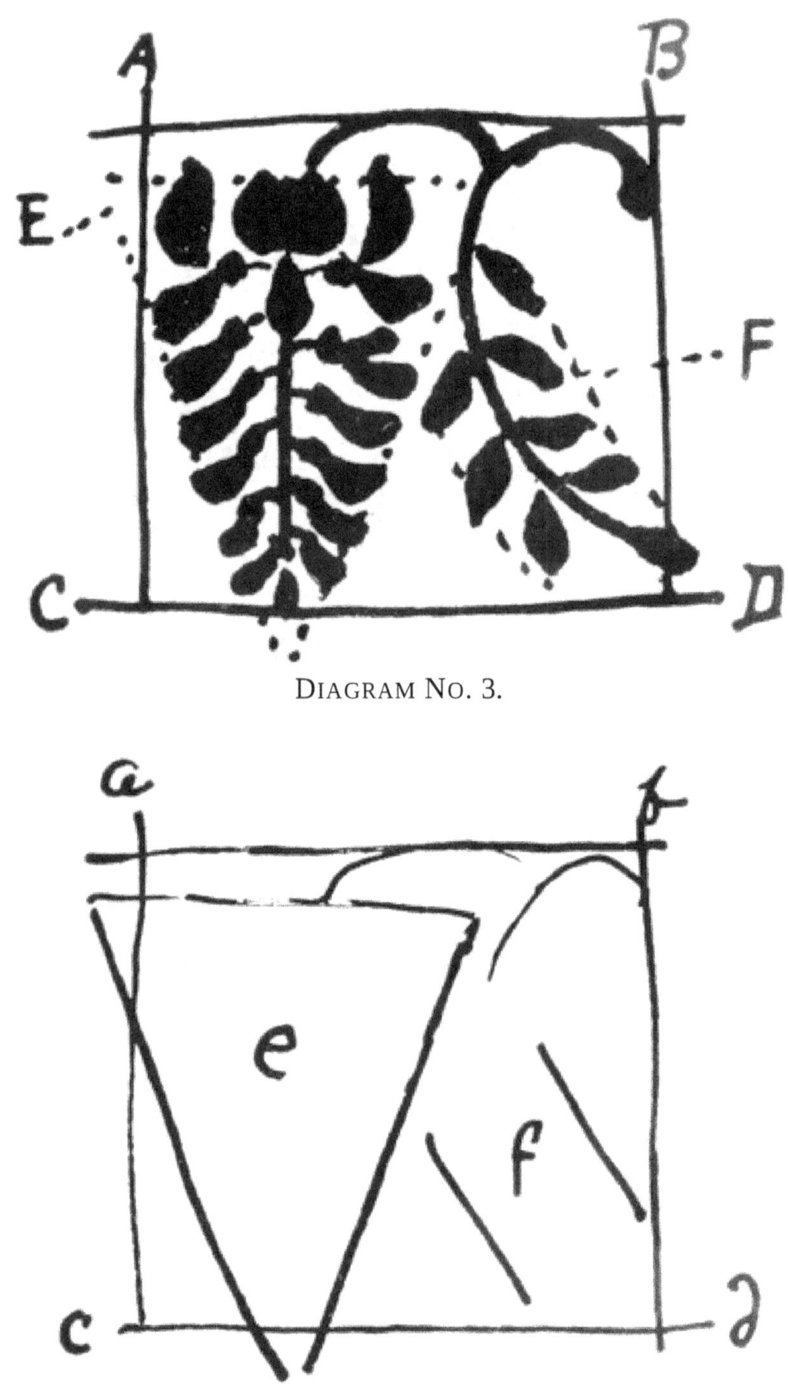

DIAGRAM NO. 3.

DIAGRAM NO. 4.

{65} forms, no matter how irregular, and a perpendicular through the extreme right-hand form, one through the left, and a horizontal through the top and the bottom form, and we have a rectangle which has given dimensions. It may be twice as high as wide, or three times as wide as high, no matter, let either of those *proportions* be preserved, and a rectangle *of the same proportions*, drawn upon a visiting card or covering the wall of a barn twenty feet high, will give you the right proportions for your group. And then, if you will find inside of the rectangle, one or a dozen polygons, like A, B, C, No. 1, and *f*, No. 4, you will be able to "place" the most irregular objects.

We give with this chapter also, two illustrations showing the manner in which shading is done in the art schools, but the main thing I wish you to note about the illustrations is, not the shaded drawing, but the drawing where the shadow is blocked in, Fig. A. Now, this is important to bear in mind: A line is used, not only for drawing the outside outline or *contour* of objects, but for drawing the outline of shadows *upon* and within them; therefore, every bit of practice you may have in drawing lines of any kind will be helpful to you when blocking in the shapes of shadows that bring out the form of an object. It is just as imperative, for example, that you compare the inside *margin of the shadows* upon the wrist (as indicated in Fig. A) with the plumb-line, so as to see their direction, as it is that you compare the trunk of the Herkomer tree with the plumb-line, that you may get its direction. (In obtaining the direction of small shadows the artist very frequently uses his pencil, held vertical, as a plumb-line.)

{67}

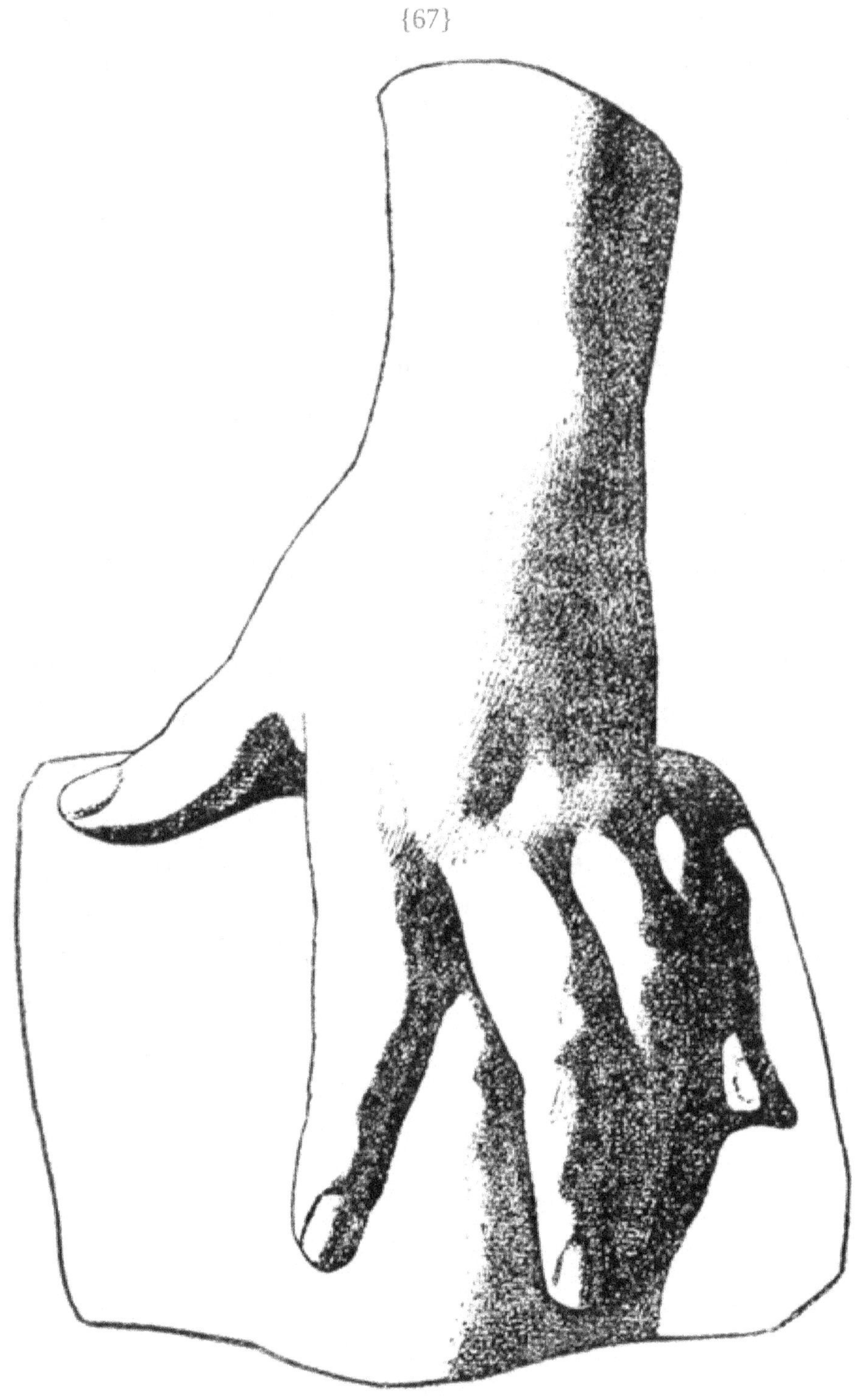

Fig. B.
Method of shading in simple tones, with very little reflected light or half-tones. (See Fig. A.)

{68}

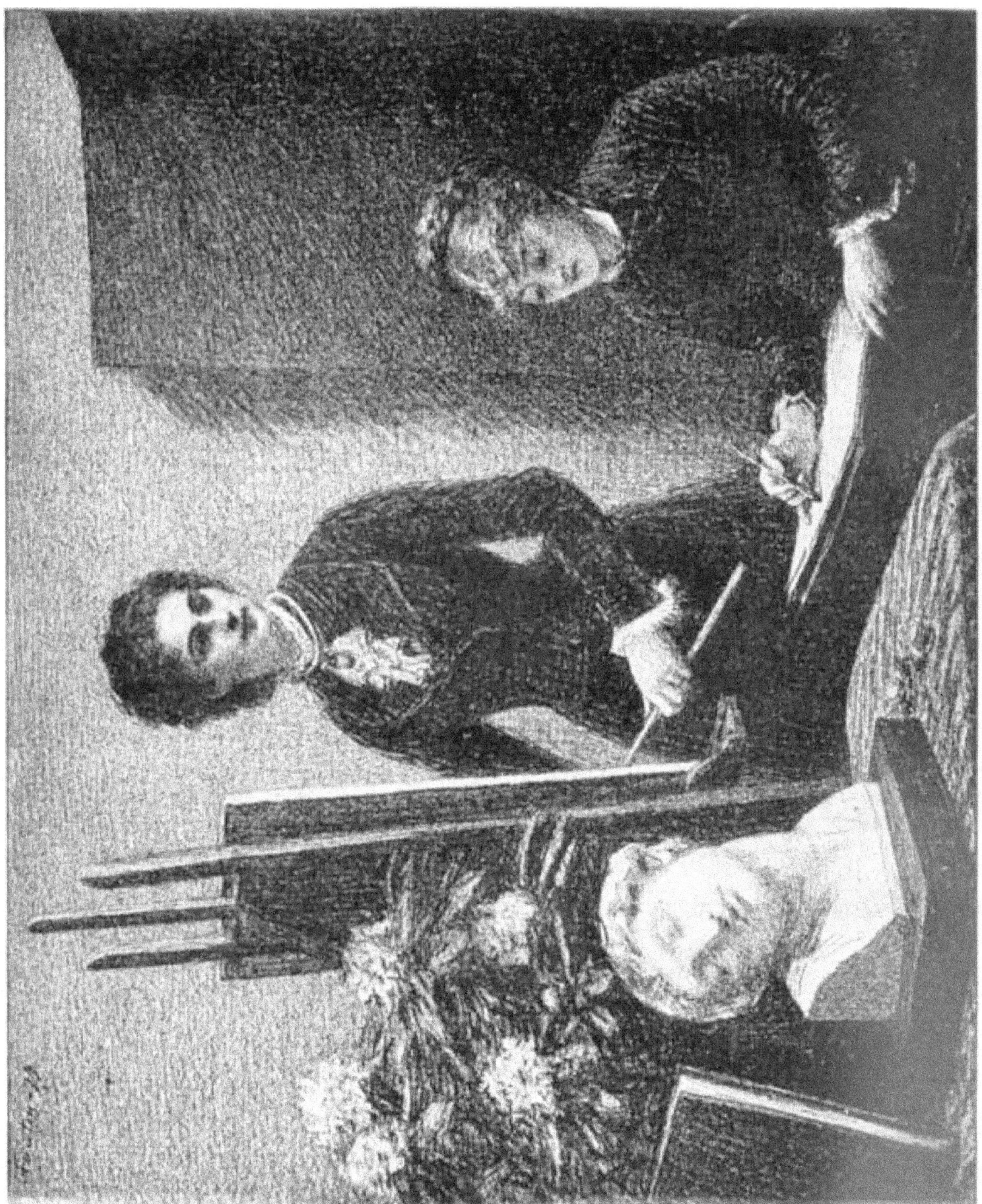

Portraits, drawn in crayon, by Fantin-La-Tour, from his painting in the Salon of 1879. An example of the rendering of "values" in black and white.

{69}

We give another illustration that we trust will interest you, the very beautiful drawing by Fantin-La-Tour. Our object in giving this is twofold:

first, to show you the drawing of the cast. We have said that the Bargue-Gérôme studies show how students learn to work in Paris. The truth is that nearly all over the world art students learn to draw from white plaster casts on which the shadows are very distinct. The eye is thus trained to see *form*, as we call it. And it will not be difficult for you to look from the cast drawing in the La-Tour to the head of the standing girl, and see how the form of her face is brought out by shading in the same manner as in the cast.

In publishing a drawing of this kind in a book for printers we do not recommend it as an example of drawing for the press (though it would be an excellent guide for lithography), but it is full of interest in that it exemplifies what artists consider artistic draftsmanship. It is evident that the author of it has studied in an art school and that he gets his effects, not by chance, but by deliberation. He is sensitive to the different degrees of darks upon the several objects. No matter how plainly he may see the shadow upon the cast, he knows that, in order to represent it as a light object, such shadows must *not* be black. So there is a vast difference between its dark tones and the dark tones of the block on which it stands. Also in drawing the human face he concentrates his darks about the eyes, nose and mouth; the rest of the face is shaded with great delicacy, for he knows that if he puts darks elsewhere he will get the undesirable effect of an old face. The printer is not expected to carry his art as far as this, but we must say {70} frankly that his degree of success depends entirely upon the extent of his knowledge of the truths herein stated. One need not go to an art school to see that a cast is white, and that its shadows are not as black as the shadows upon a bronze; but unless he trains his eye by observation to see this difference in other things, no tricks of pen-technic will help him when he comes to draw a white horse, or a white collar. He does not have to study portraiture in an art school in order to make a drawing in pen and ink, for his paper, from a photograph; but unless he will train himself to observe so that he realizes that in a young face the greatest darks are limited to the eyes, nose, and mouth, he will be likely to make his pen-portrait look more like an old person than a young person, even though in executing the same he imitates the most perfect pen-technic.

Now, as the placing of the shadows in the seated girl's face is not the same, it is a little difficult for you to realize that it contains the same kind of drawing as the blocked-in cast hand and head.

But the eye becomes trained from drawing casts to see the most delicate modeling of shadows, and the seated girl's face is really a complex style of drawing, of which the cast head and hand are simple specimens. I mean by "complex style of drawing" a method of getting effects by imitating the light and shade upon objects, as opposed to mere outline style or silhouette style.

Now, therefore, this illustration should indicate to you that it is well to draw from casts, as art students do, if you wish to make finished pictures in black and white.

In the foregoing statements I have been careful in {71} my language. I do not say students *all* over the world learn to draw in light and shade, for there is a great deal of wonderful Japanese art that is done entirely without knowledge of light and shade of the sort most usual in Occidental modeling. Nor do I say that you *must* draw from casts to learn to see light and shade, because during the middle ages many great artists learned to draw from life and not from casts. The cast is a comparatively modern art-school accessory.

Another reason for giving this La-Tour drawing is that it brings us a step farther into the consideration of values; we notice that in it the cast appears to be white, the girls' faces and hands lighter than their gowns, and one girl's hair lighter than the other's. Now, when an artist makes a difference between the degrees of the color of objects, we say he notes their values.

Bear this in mind, then, that mere shading is not the end of drawing. You can go a step farther and indicate the color value of a shadow, of which more hereafter.

{72}

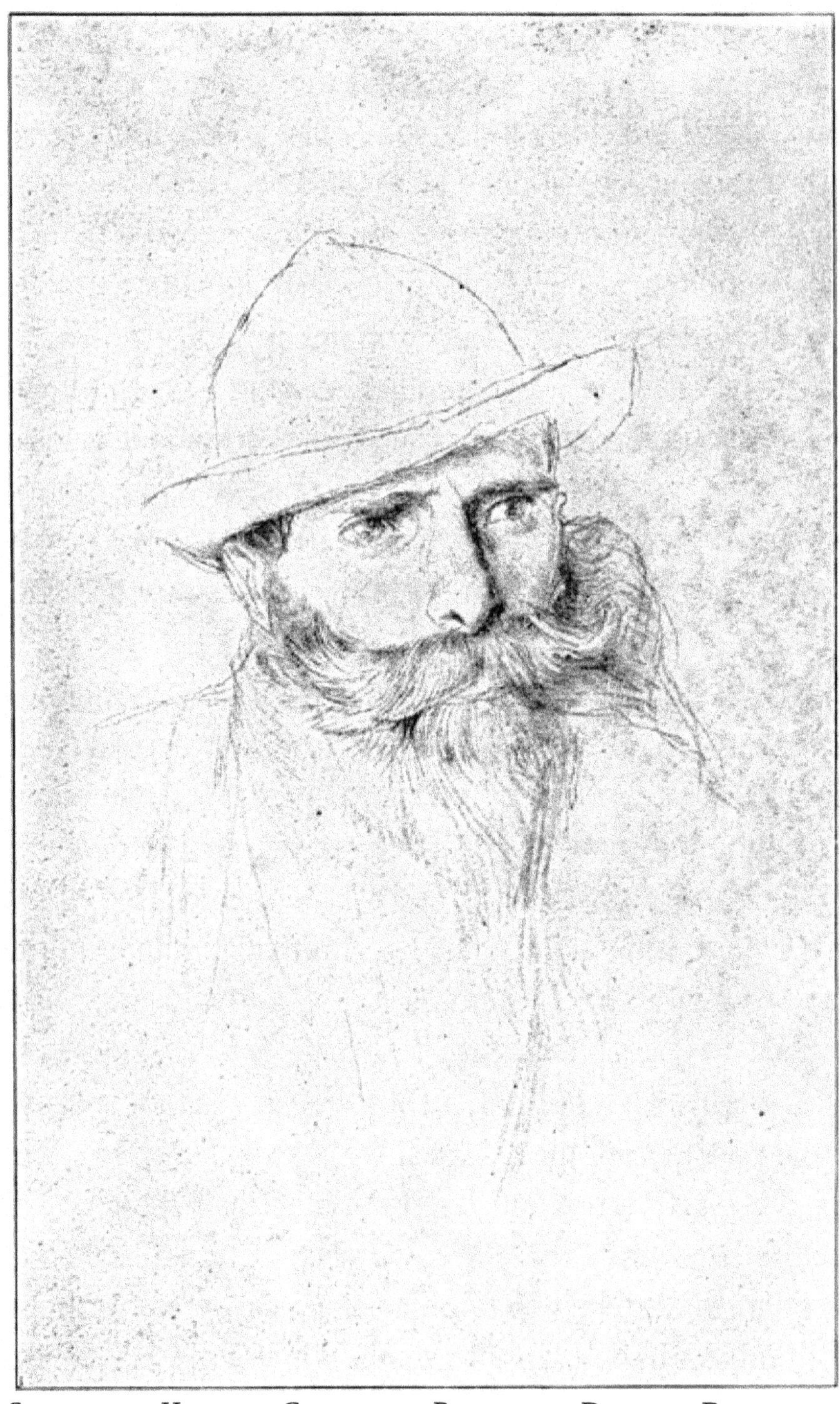

STUDY OF A HEAD, IN CRAYON OR PENCIL, BY DAGNAN-BOUVERET.
Showing method of sketching the outline of a hat.

CHAPTER VIII.

STUDY BY DAGNAN-BOUVERET — A HAT IN OUTLINE NOT MEANT FOR AN OUTLINE DRAWING — CONNECTING LINK BETWEEN OUTLINE AND SHADED DRAWING — MORE ABOUT ART-SCHOOL METHODS — METHOD OF DRAWING BASED UPON CAST DRAWING — THE BIG SHADOWS VERSUS MINOR SHADOWS — DO NOT DRAW INDIVIDUAL HAIRS — HAIR AND MUSTACHE TO BE CONSIDERED AS A MASS, NOT AS SEPARATE HAIRS — EFFECT TO BE OBTAINED BY MASSES OF SHADOWS — TRAIN THE EYE TO BECOME SENSITIVE TO GRADUATIONS OF LIGHT AND SHADE — LIGHT AND DARK IN THE HEAD INTENDED TO SHOW SHAPE OF THE SKULL, NOT TO INDICATE PARTI-COLORED HAIR — DRAWING FROM PASTEBOARD BOXES GOOD TRAINING IN LEARNING TO SEE LIGHT AND SHADE — CONTRASTING A FINISHED DRAWING (GAILLARD) WITH A ROUGH SKETCH — EQUAL ART IN EACH WHEN BOTH ARE WELL DONE — A NEWSPAPER CUT IN WHICH LIGHT AND SHADE ARE INDICATED BY VARIATION OF THICKNESS IN LINE — BROAD DRAWING RECOMMENDED TO PRINTERS — THE NASO-LABIAL LINE — RÉSUMÉ.

IN OUR illustration by Dagnan-Bouveret we find most interesting indications of how an artist works; and this head may serve as a connecting link between the chapter on outline and the one on shading. The hat is a beautiful piece of outline drawing, which, however, was not meant for an outline drawing. It is simply to serve as the placing of the hat, which would afterward be shaded as are the face and mustache. The eyes, {74} nose and mustache were first outlined in this way, and you will recognize, I think, that this is the same kind of drawing as that of which we treated in our first chapters, though, of course, the hat is not all in one plane.

But before you can thoroughly appreciate the drawing of the face it is necessary that I should explain a little further the study of drawing as it is taught in the art schools. This I will do with the help of the Lœwe-Marchand cut. In this, we see the method pursued in almost all art schools the world over: a method based upon cast drawing. It is found from experience that students learn to see form more prominently from a plaster cast, which is white, than from natural objects; and it is found that the best results are got if the students are taught to see the big shadows of an object rather than the multitude of minor shadows which may be seen upon close scrutiny. So the student is told not to look for these minor shadows, but to half close his eyes, and stand a good distance away from the object—say three times its height—and look for the form that he sees when the object becomes to his half-closed eyes nothing more than a mass with a light and a dark side. You can imagine that after a person has learned to get the effect of a hand and a foot, as in the illustration in Chapters VII and X, by merely noting the shape of the one big shadow, that it is not difficult for him to go farther and put in the minor shadows by opening his eyes and examining the object more closely; and that when he has learned to do this for several months, or perchance several years, in the antique class, and then for as long, or longer, in the life class, that he has become

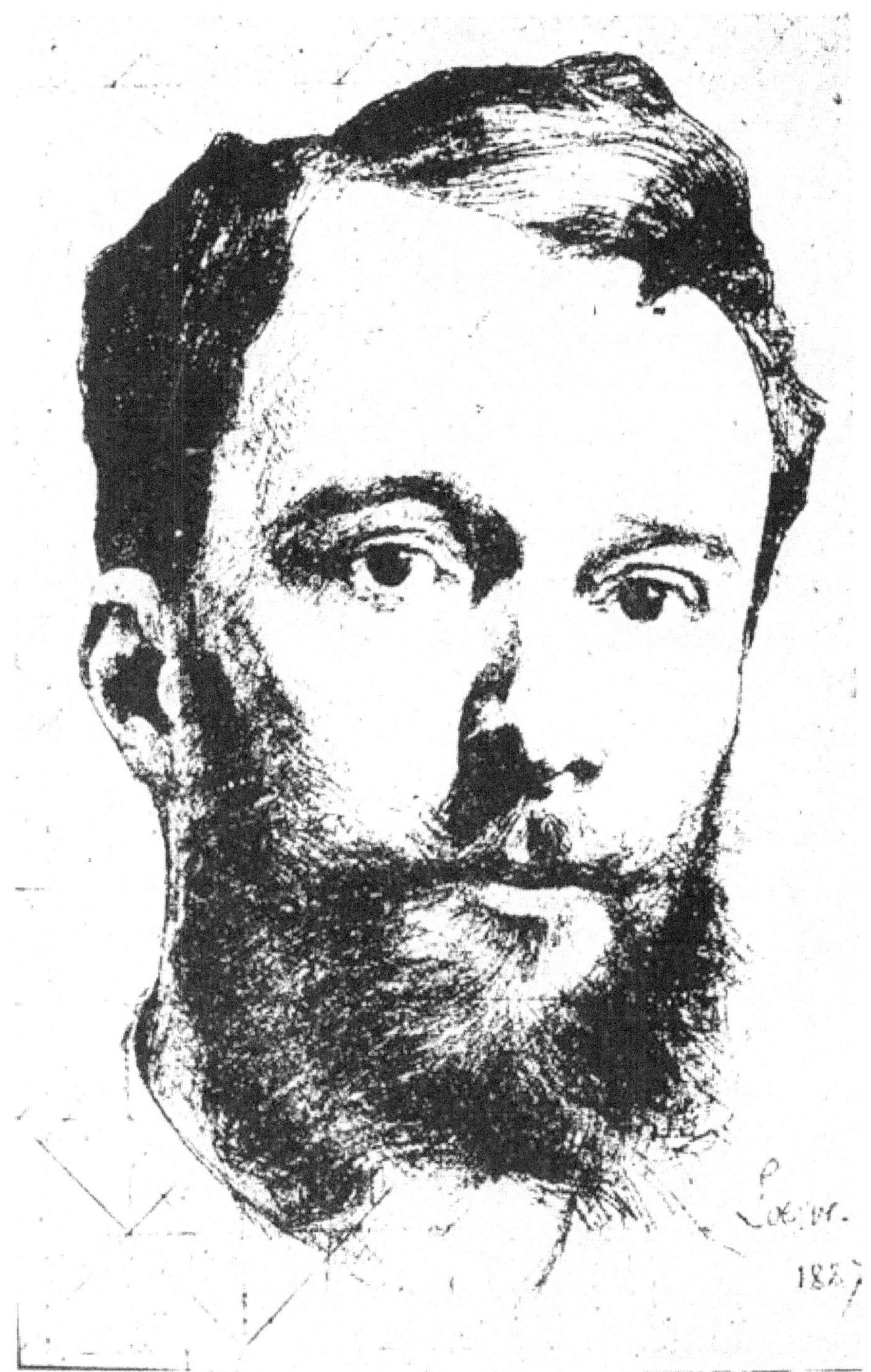

CHARCOAL DRAWING.
Portrait of M. X., by Lœwe-Marchand.

This drawing was doubtless made on a sheet of charcoal paper, possibly gray in color, and was then photographed for the direct process; and then, in order to indicate the gray paper, the photo-engraver tinted the zinc plate with a Ben Day film, which gives the stipple result. The cross lines in the corner indicate that after the artist made his study he wished to enlarge it upon a canvas preliminary to painting, which was done by covering the drawing with squares and adding a diagonal to the same. These squares and diagonals were repeated on a larger scale on the canvas and the drawing enlarged freehand by placing the different points of the original in the corresponding triangles on the canvas. This method of enlarging drawings has been used for five thousand years.

{76} so sensitive to seeing shadows that it is not difficult for him to discern them upon anything and everything. Now, that is the secret of the beautiful drawing of the mustache in the Dagnan-Bouveret drawing. The beginner draws the hairs of the mustache, and tries to get his effect in that way; but you cannot by drawing the pelt of a fox on a barn door get the effect of one with a real live body underneath it. The result in this drawing is due entirely to Dagnan-Bouveret's sensitiveness to light and shade. The lines, which the casual observer would take to be the hairs of the mustache, are really the shadows thrown by the groups of hairs as they part here and there. It is true that if he were etching this head or drawing it with a fine pen, he might in finishing it put in a few hairs, and even Albrecht Dürer would sometimes get a good effect by drawing the hairs of the mustache or the curls on a head. But in nearly all modern work, the hair, mustache or beard is considered as a mass receiving light and shade, and is so treated, there being no great difference between the golden hair of a child and the white hair of an old woman.

In the beautiful study by Gaillard we see the shape of the skull under the woman's hair, and there is a very great difference between the part that is in shadow around her ears and the part that is light on the top of her head. This does not mean that the hair was gray on top, and black around the ears, but it means that the light struck the hair on top, while it did not strike it on the sides.

Now, if you can give yourself the time to study from the cast, or even from simple pasteboard boxes, so that your eye will become sensitive to these graduations from

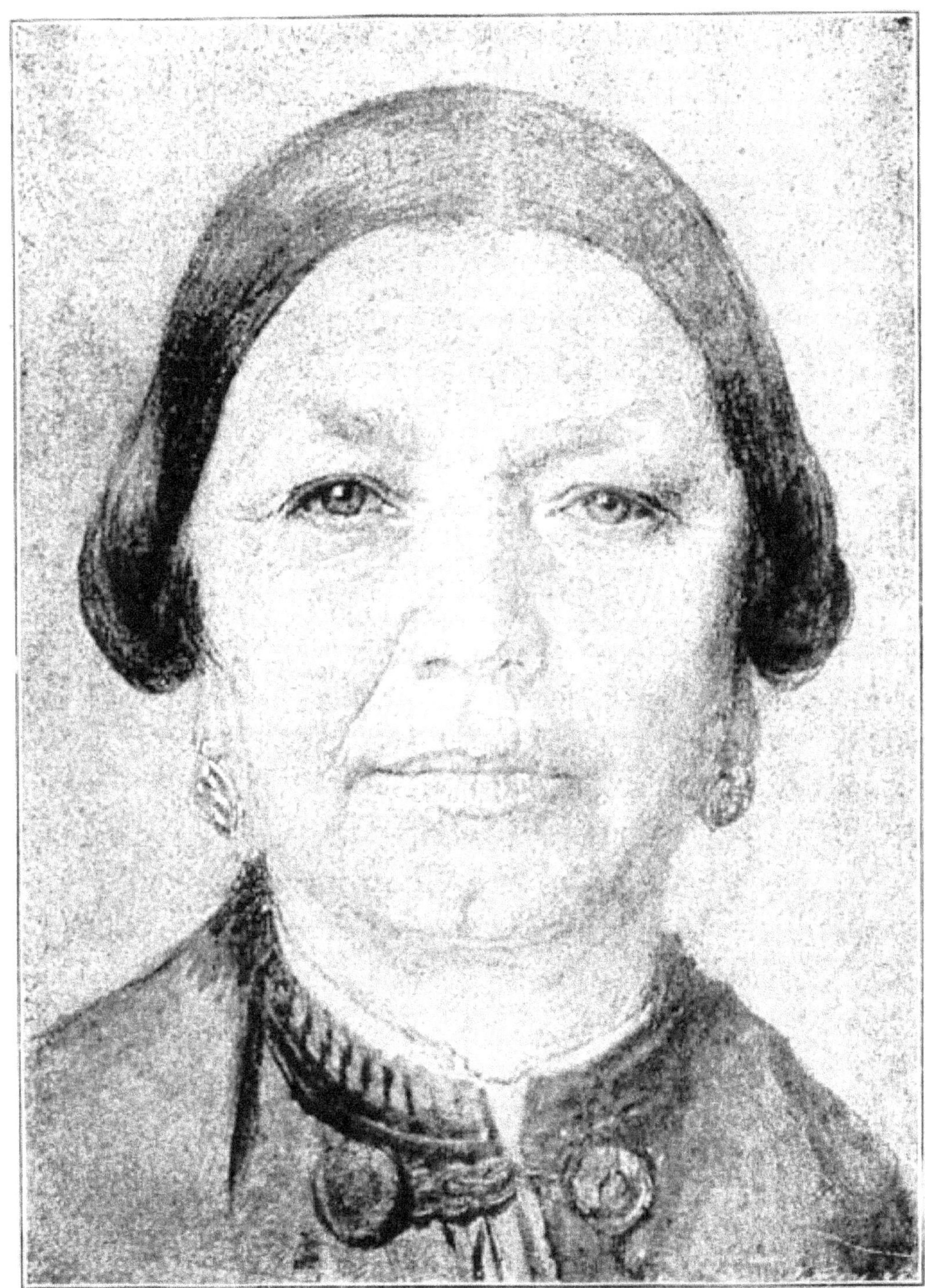

STUDY FOR THE PORTRAIT OF MME. R.
By C. F. Gaillard.

{78} light to dark, you will soon realize that, while in your drawing for printing you may never in a hundred years' practice draw anything so delicate as the Gaillard, yet in your simplest drawings you may put in practice the theory upon which it is made. For example, if you are drawing an old woman's head, even if you only use four or five lines to represent her hair, you will not press upon your pen when you are doing her hair on the top, but you will press upon it when you come within the region of the ears; and that pressure, though it will not represent hairs, nor the actual value of the shadow, will yet give *the difference* between the light on the top of the head and the shadow behind the ears, and this will suggest to the educated eye the roundness of the cranium.

Now we reproduce also the rough Watts drawing. Let us contrast these two drawings. The one is almost as finished as it can be, the other slight; yet I want you to realize why I recommend this slight drawing to printers and tell you that it is artistic. It is so because in the very heavy lines that you see in the ear, beard and coat there is knowledge of modeling. The artist knew his business just as Gaillard did, and every time he put down a blotty line it was meant to represent the presence of a shadow. This face is from a photograph; hundreds of delicate tones have been left out; and the white hair of the beard is modeled with nothing but thin and heavy lines while the shadows of the photograph were delicate gray tints! A clever penman drawing from a photograph uses darks which the uneducated eye will take to be arbitrary blackening of the drawing, but which an artist knows are the result of intelligent observation.

{79}

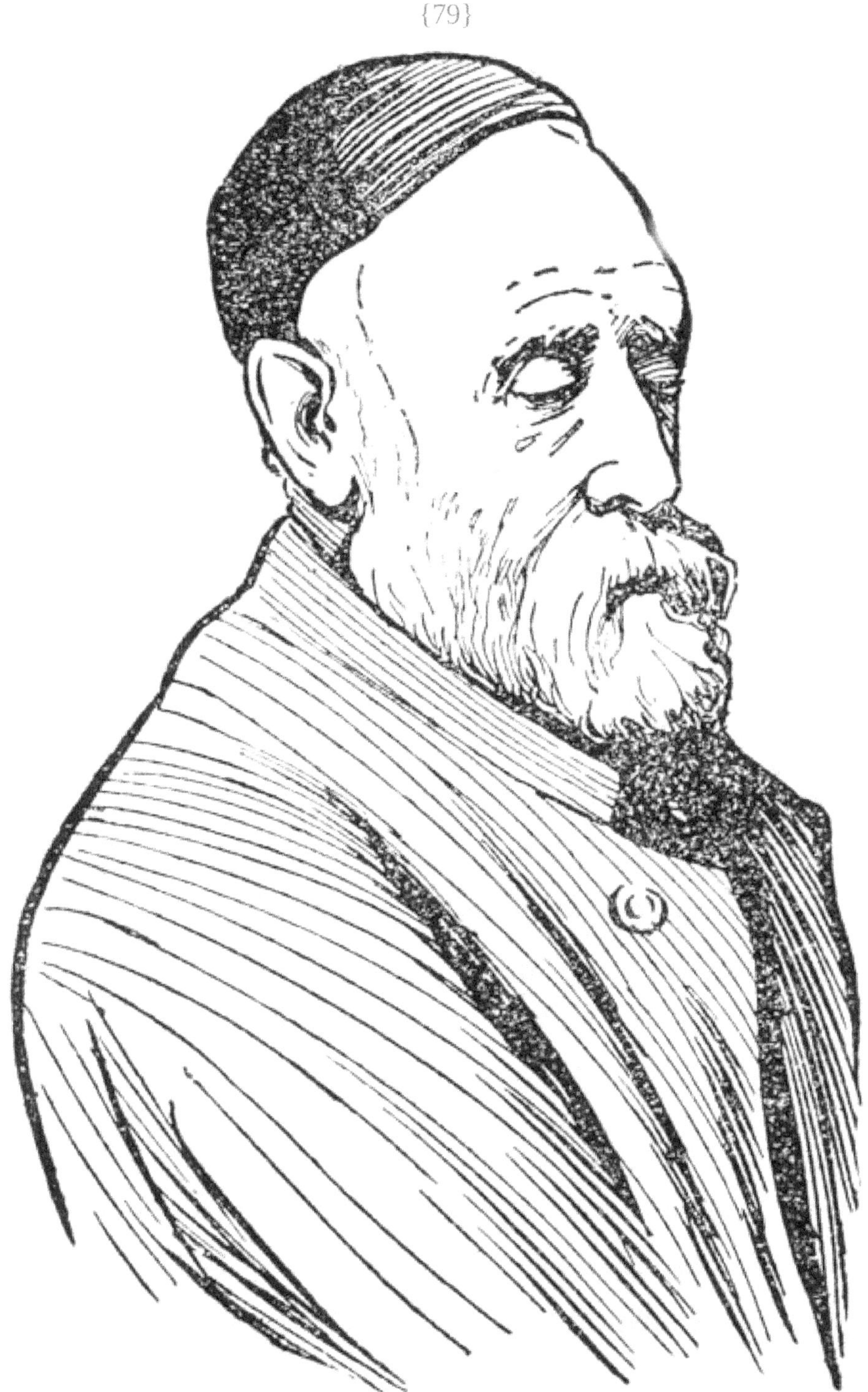

GEORGE FREDERICK WATTS, R. A.

An English newspaper cut from *Tid-Bits*, artist unknown. An excellent example of newspaper work. Note that the skull-cap is not represented partly gray and partly black because the artist meant to indicate a cap that was one color in front and another in the back, but he meant to show the rounding of the cranium, just as Gaillard did in varying the tones in the hair of the old woman.

{80}

Now, in the Gaillard drawing you see a very delicate line running diagonally from the wing of the nose almost to the corner of the lips. This is called the naso-labial line, and is found in every old face. I say again, that though you work for one hundred years as a printer you would probably never draw a delicate line like this. But if you should make studies in pencil and realize that this line is typical of old age, you would be able to put it in such a drawing as the Watts (the artist has used two lines to represent it), where, you will notice, it comes down about as far on the lower lip as in the Gaillard, and you would realize why it was left out in the Dagnan-Bouveret and Marchand younger subjects.

This chapter should be exceedingly interesting to you as indicating two things—one discouraging and the other encouraging. First, that when students of art have the opportunity to work so beautifully, as in the Bargue-Gérôme studies, and afterward from life, as in the Gaillard, they needs must see more than you do, and you must not expect to equal them if you, a busy printer, can only practice a few evenings a week. Therefore you should not attempt subtile renderings like the Gaillard, but should confine yourself to simple means. On the other hand, when I tell you that this is about all the study there is gone through with in an art school (I say about all, for besides blocking-in, students learn a good deal about values; this we shall treat of in a succeeding chapter), it should be interesting to you to realize that if you will simply train yourself to see light and shade like the plinth in the foot studies given in Chapter XII by drawing a pasteboard box, and then afterward draw from life, so as to see that hair is darker {81} in shaded portions than in light ones, and that in an old person the naso-labial line is marked and shows darker than the cheeks, you will, when copying a photograph for your paper, no matter how roughly you work, be able to indicate the shadows in the hair and the dark naso-labial line, as in the Watts portrait. This, I say, should encourage you, and it is the only way for you to learn to draw.

CHAPTER IX.

HEAD BY KNAUS ANALYZED — DRAWN IN THE MANNER OF THE DAGNAN-BOUVERET AND CONTAINING LINES LIKE THE WATTS — THE NASO-LABIAL LINE USED TO DELINEATE OLD AGE — THE SHADOW OF THE NOSTRIL — THE WING OF THE NOSE — THE NOSTRIL USUALLY THE DARKEST SHADOW LINE IN A FACE.

LET US RESUME the subject of Chapter VIII. We give a fine drawing of an old man's head by Knaus, and we will ask you to look at it and see if you cannot realize two things about it—first, that no matter how many lines there may be upon the hat, which make it look battered and different in texture from a new silk hat, it was first drawn as was the Dagnan-Bouveret given in the last chapter; secondly, do you notice the oblique naso-labial line, which we spoke of in connection with the Gaillard and Watts? and do you realize one of two things from this also, that, either this line in the original drawing ran up to the wing of the nose but was lost in the several engravings, or else the artist wished to indicate that his model was not a very old man, and he did not make the line very strong in that place? If so, you have learned some important principles that will help you in drawing, for you will be able to sketch any hat you wish to draw by the same process that the best artists employ. Again, you will be able to use proper judgment in introducing the lines into a face. If, for example, you were copying, in pen-and-ink, chalk-plate or wood engraving,

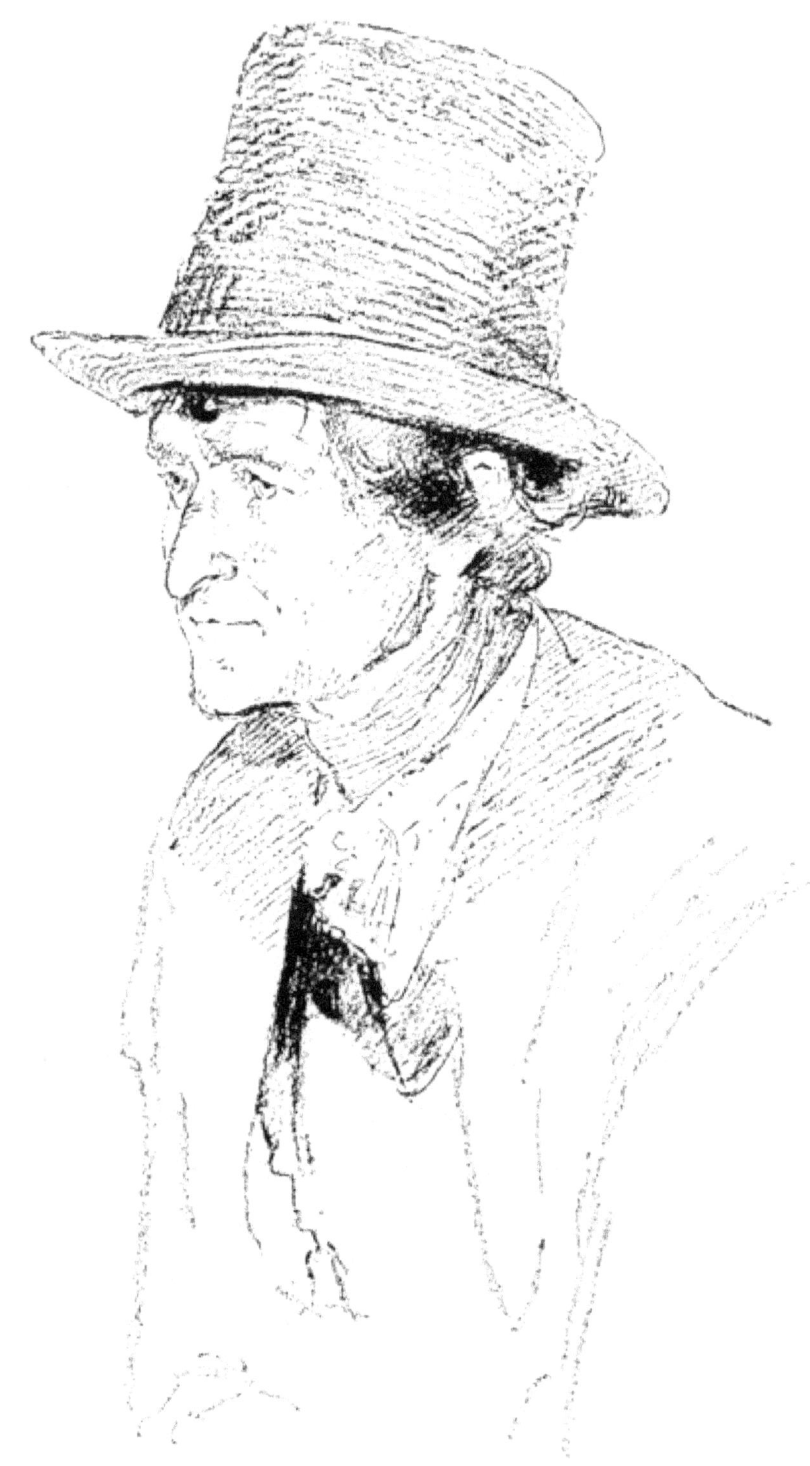

OLD MAN'S HEAD.
Crayon Drawing by Ludwig Knaus.

{84} from some half-obliterated etching or from some faded daguerreotype, an old man's head like the Knaus, you would have the knowledge back of you that would permit you to draw in the naso-labial with proper accentuation. If you knew the original was a centenarian you would most certainly continue the line up to the wing of the nose and draw it continuously without a break; or if he were but a sexagenarian of whom the biographical dictionaries said "he carried his years lightly," you might purposely break this line as in the Knaus.

So far, so good. And now for some other lines in the face. At the base of the nose we have the shadow of the nostril, and the curved portion of the nose around it called the wing of the nose; these are nearly always introduced into drawings. In the Knaus they are very happily drawn. Revert to the illustrations of the last chapter, and see if you can find them. In the Marchand and Gaillard they are represented by modeling rather than lines, but they are outlined in the Dagnan-Bouveret and the Watts, the former being in pencil. We notice that one of these objects is grayer than the other; which is it? It is the naso-labial line, and the shadow of the nostril is much the darker. The same effect is got in the Watts by using a fine line for the naso-labial line and a thicker line, or a blot, for the nostril. If, therefore, you were drawing the Gaillard in line, can you not realize that you would approximate the effect of our half-tone by making the outline of the wing of the nose the lightest of your lines, the naso-labial line darker, and the shadow of the nostril the darkest of the three? This order can {85} usually be followed in drawing an old person, and in almost every case (young or old) the nostril shadow is the darker of the three lines mentioned. In regard to the nostril being sometimes a line and sometimes a blot, the difference lies in the character of the original; with some persons the nostril is very straight and little of the inside of the nose shows. This was evidently the case in the Knaus original, so the artist uses a line and nothing more for the nostril (you will, however, not fail to note the subtlety of the artist's touch, which gives us a strongly marked line for the nostril, but a more delicate line for the wing of the nose). In the Dagnan-Bouveret, however, the nostril goes up at quite an angle, exposing much more of the inside of the nose than in the Knaus; therefore, were you rendering this drawing in pen-and-ink, you could use a blot in the nostril similar in heaviness to that in the Watts portrait on page 79.

We should advise you, by the way, in following these chapters, to make tracings of all our half-tone cuts and render them in pen-line like the Watts; this will help you immensely to understand an analyzation of them.

CHAPTER X.

THE ANALYZATION OF THE NASO-LABIAL LINE INDICATES THE FOUNDATION OF ART STUDY — WHEN THE LINE IS PROPERLY SEEN IT MAY BE DRAWN WITH ANY MEDIUM — CHOUDIEU HEAD BY BONNARD — ITS SIMILARITY TO THE WATTS — STRONG MARKING OF THE NASO-LABIAL LINE IN IT — A SIMILAR ANALYZATION TO THAT GIVEN THE WATTS DRAWING — PORTRAIT BY TOUSSAINT — HOW IT MIGHT BE RENDERED IN SIMPLE PEN LINES LIKE THE WATTS — DRAWING BY BONNARD — ITS HEAVY OUTLINE APPROPRIATE TO PRINTING — THE MEANING OF BLACKS IN A DRAWING — DRAWING BY BONNAT — EXAMPLE OF DRAWING BY LIGHT AND DARK MASSES — THE EMPLOYMENT OF WHITES IN SCRATCH-BOARD AND IN WOOD ENGRAVING — BONNARD'S DRAWING OF CURTAIN — BRUN DRAWING CORRECT IN COLOR VALUES — DIGRESSION IN REGARD TO FRENCH NAMES — DRAWING OF A FOOT SHOWING ART SCHOOL METHODS.

SOME of the most valuable hints we have given our readers are those of Chapters VIII and IX, in connection with the naso-labial line. In these you will find the foundation of our teaching—that is, we do not say that a human face must be made by putting in a black line running obliquely from the nose to the lip, made with such or such a pen, such or such a crayon, ink, or charcoal, but we point out the line in *nature*, and say that because it is found in nature, artists put it in their drawings. When not found in a face, as that of a young person, then it is left out in a good artist's drawing of a young face. Whether he uses pen, wash, {87} or crayon, has very little to do with the case. There are some methods of using the pen, wash, or crayon, that are better than others; but, if you are taught to see the naso-labial line in nature, it is very easy to learn to draw it in one of those mediums, and having drawn it in one, it is easier to learn to draw it in other mediums.

We give, with this chapter, the head of Choudieu, in which this line is marked as conspicuously as in the

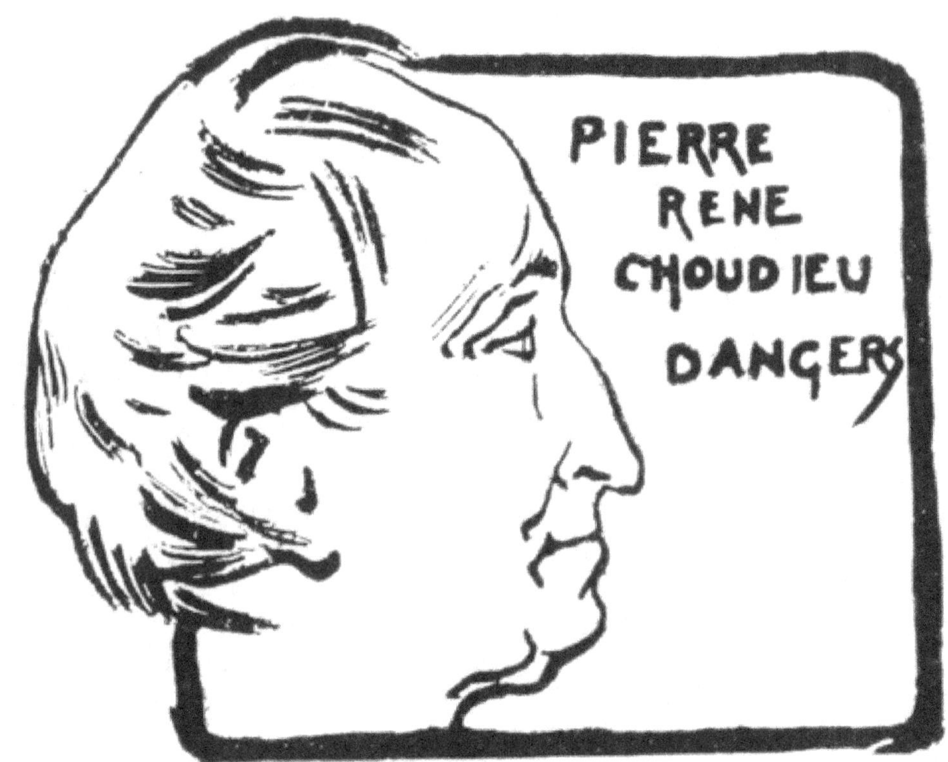

HEAD OF PIERRE RENE CHOUDIEU.
Drawn by Pierre Bonnard (probably from a medallion, and possibly with a quill pen), for *La Revue Blanche*.

Watts. This drawing might have been made with an ordinary pen, somewhat worn, or (as was probably the case) with a quill pen, or with a camel's-hair brush, or with a Japanese brush (which, like the quill pen, is a delightful instrument with which to draw heavy lines); but are we not right in surmising that you are better prepared to draw such a head because we pointed out in {88} the last chapter that the naso-labial line was a characteristic mark of an old man's face than if we had given you directions for using the quill pen or the brush and said nothing about this line? Of course, we do not mean to suggest that, were you making a copy from *this* line drawing, you would be so careless as to leave out the naso-labial line, but if you were drawing an old man's face from a photograph, might you not easily overlook this line if it had never been pointed out to you? If you agree with this proposition you will be in thorough sympathy with the spirit in which this work is written, and when our chapter on expression comes you will not at all regret that it is not a technical chapter on the use of a drawing instrument.

Now, let us consider the Choudieu drawing a little more fully, and in doing so we shall ask you to notice that the words follow almost verbatim the part of Chapter VIII referring to the Watts head. This does not mean that we are at a loss for a vocabulary, but it is done purposely so that we may thus call attention to it, and that you may realize that we have called your attention to a vital principle; moreover, that principle may be referred to again and again in almost every case where an old person's head is under consideration. We publish also the Duc d'Aumale drawing, in which you will see the line is again marked. Now, we publish this drawing mainly in connection with the highly finished drawings illustrating Chapter VIII, by Dagnan-Bouveret, Lœwe-Marchand and Gaillard, but you may profitably note also that were you tracing it, intending to make a line drawing of it in pen and ink, you would

{89}

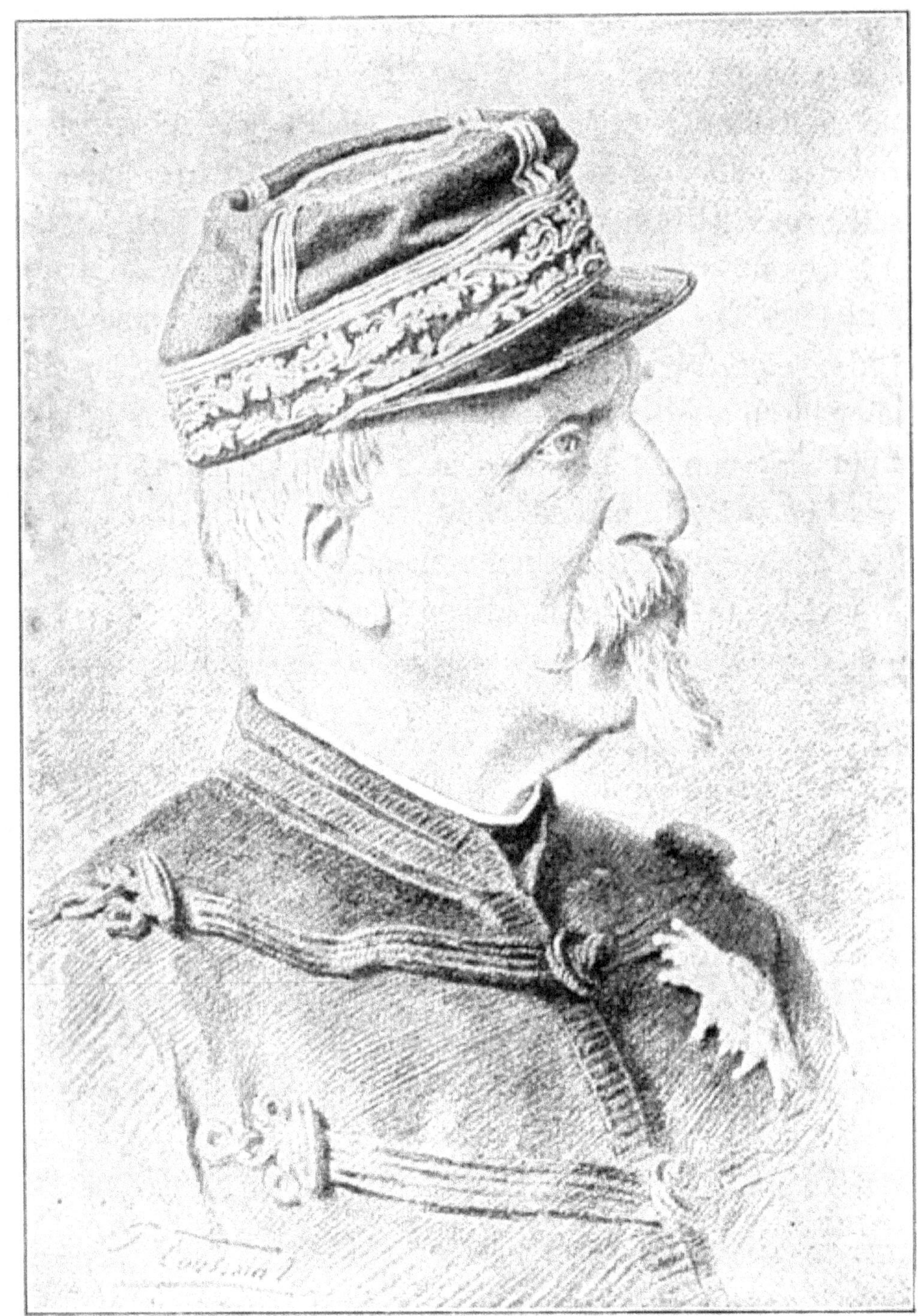

THE LATE DUC D'AUMALE.
Drawn in crayon, by T. Toussaint, and engraved by half-tone.

{90} represent this muscular indentation with a strong line, as in the Watts portrait. You will not fail to notice also the line in the throat corresponding to the one in Bonnard's Choudieu, now presented for consideration.

This Bonnard is a slight drawing, but it is recommended to printers because it is both artistic in treatment and easily printed. It is artistic because in the heavy lines that you see in the ear and hair there is a knowledge of modeling. The artist knew his business just as Gaillard did, and every time he put down a blotty line it was meant to represent the presence of a shadow. We have no means of determining whether this was from an actual plaster or bronze medallion, or whether the artist worked from a photograph and from his imagination rendered the effect of a modeled relief; but in either case, in the photograph or in nature, there were thousands of little tones that have been left out. A clever pen draftsman works in the same manner, using darks which the uneducated eye will take to be arbitrary blackening of the drawing, but which an artist knows is the result of the intelligent observation of the shapes of shadows, and of the most important shadows of a face. Now, one of the most conspicuous lines in this drawing is the one running diagonally from the wing of the nose almost to the corner of the lips. This is called the naso-labial line, and is found in every old face. I say again, that though you work for one hundred years as a printer, you would probably never draw as correct a line as this. But if you should make studies in pencil and realize that this line is typical of old age, you would be able to put it in such a drawing

{91}

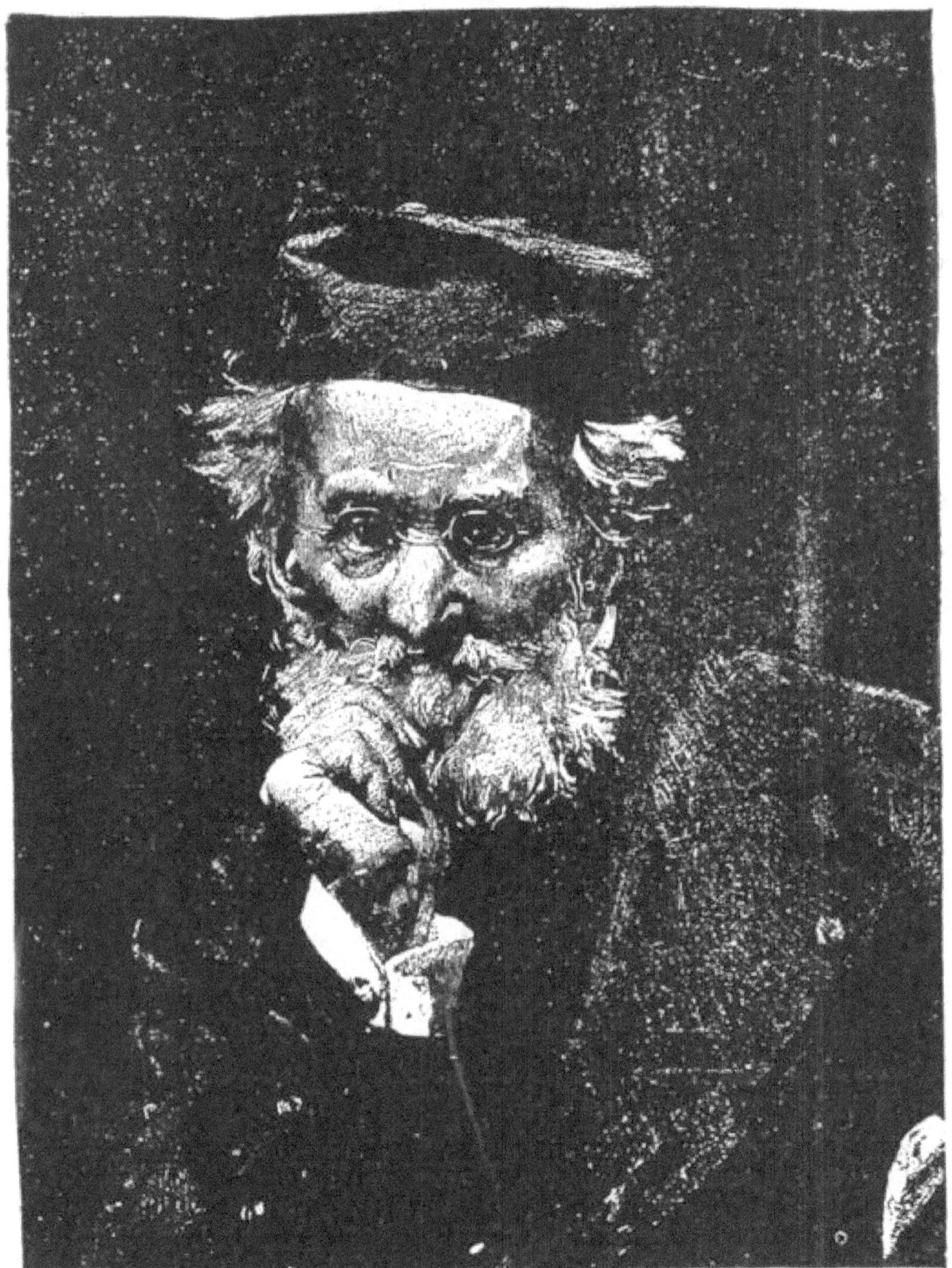

PORTRAIT OF LEON COGNIET.
After the painting by L. Bonnat, drawn, probably, by the painter himself, upon grained scratch-board with lithographic crayon (?), the lights scratched out with a penknife.

{92} as the Bonnard where, you will notice, it comes down about as far as the lower lip, as in the Gaillard, and you would realize why it was left out in the Dagnan-Bouveret and Marchand drawings.

The Bonnat portrait of Cogniet becomes particularly interesting from this view point, e. g., practice for the sake of observation. It is executed by a process of no value to the printer of the country newspaper, but there is food for thought in the way the form is brought out by the juxtaposition of masses of light and dark that are not lines. Ordinarily we do not recommend to the printer to experiment with such effects, but rather to confine himself to outline or silhouette, but the value of the white-line will be considered in connection with wood engraving, and any practice in drawing from nature in light masses will help you appreciate the judicious use of white-line in wood engraving, or strong contrasts of white and black in any medium. We publish, for example, two very different kinds of drawing as companions to the Bonnat. One in which Verdyen has obtained an effect of the brilliancy of fireworks by scratching out whites from a very black drawing. Similar effects may be got with great ease in wood engraving.

A still more clear effect of light is got in the Bonnard tailpiece, where, by simply breaking the window sash with the light fold of a curtain, he makes us feel the color of the curtain from the top to the bottom of the picture. We should advise you to practice in any medium, endeavoring to get similar effects, as they are most valuable in saving a drawing from monotony. In the Brun drawing, for example, no casual observer

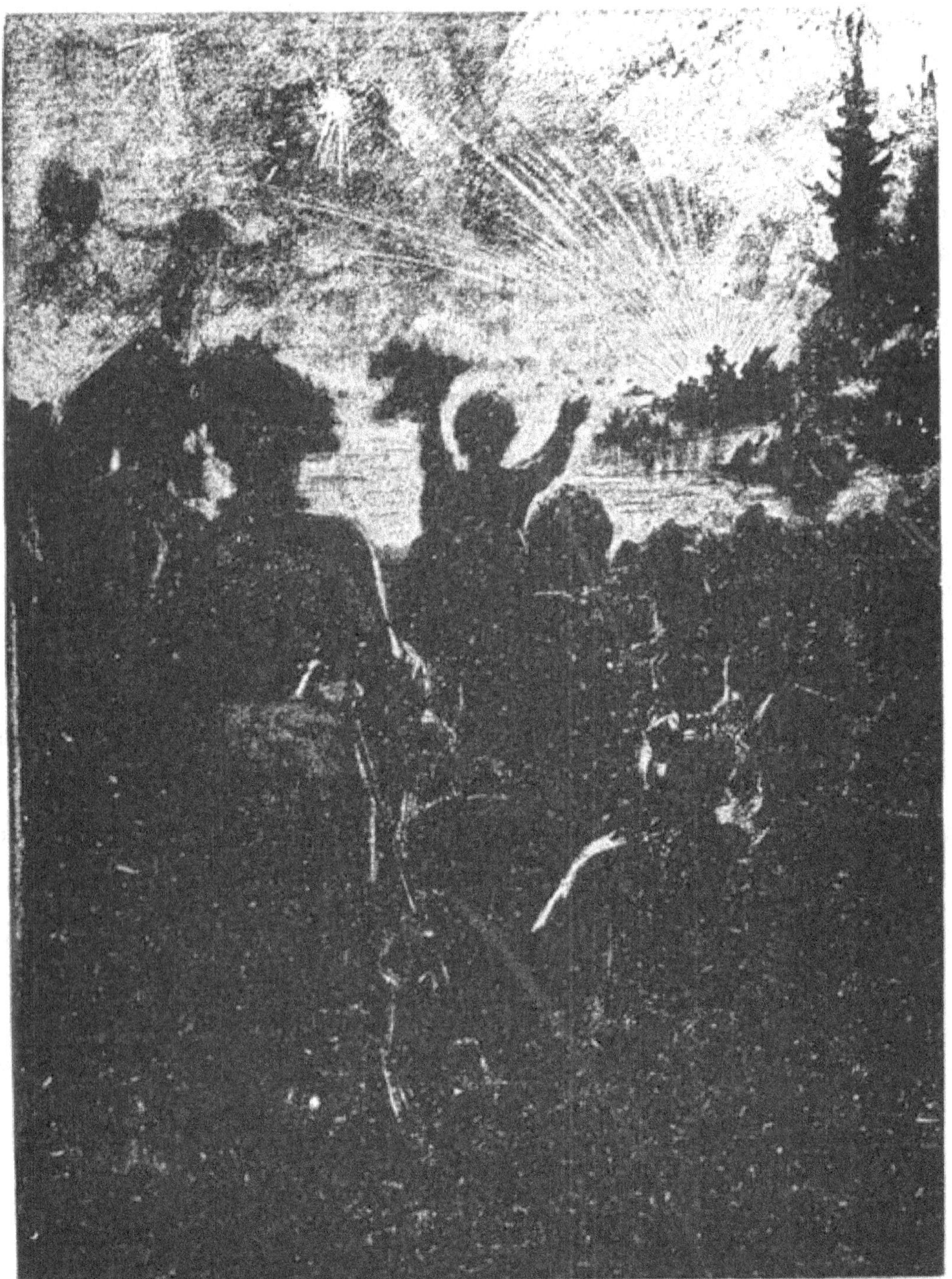

A FETE AT BRUSSELS.

Drawn by Verdyen, probably on ruled scratch-board (see tones in the sky), with crayon, in sky, and with brush, in figures; the plate very much retouched by hand.

{94} would appreciate the white pillars, and an untrained draftsman would be likely to cover them with tones, but as a matter of fact they help immensely to give variety to the drawing. In an architectural exhibition we are frequently tired by the monotony of similar drawings where the draftsmen, in their desire to render texture and local color, cover such surfaces with lines meant to represent stone, brick or mortar.

We would remark also that just as our own repetition of the Watts analysis apropos of the Bonnard's Choudieu portrait was intentional, so the apparent conglomeration of portrait studies, landscapes and buildings is not the result of careless arrangement on our part, but is intentional, that it may be shown that a certain principle in drawing, studied from one object, may be applied to any other. If you draw a friend's face by lamplight and pick out the lights upon it and his cuff, as in the Bonnat Cogniet, you will be prepared to pick out similar lights on portions of buildings as in the pillars in the Brun drawing; or on window curtain folds as in Bonnard's tailpiece.

It may be interesting to printers for us to narrate the difficulty of preparing a proper legend for the Choudieu. It was a tailpiece to an article in a French magazine, and bore no legend. To all appearances it was the portrait of one Mr. Dangers, but knowing how liberal the French are in their use of cognomens, we took the precaution to investigate. A Frenchman may be born Smith, but in manhood is known to the public by one or a dozen other names. He may marry Miss Brown, and, therefore, parade as Mr. Brown; his Uncle Jones

{95}

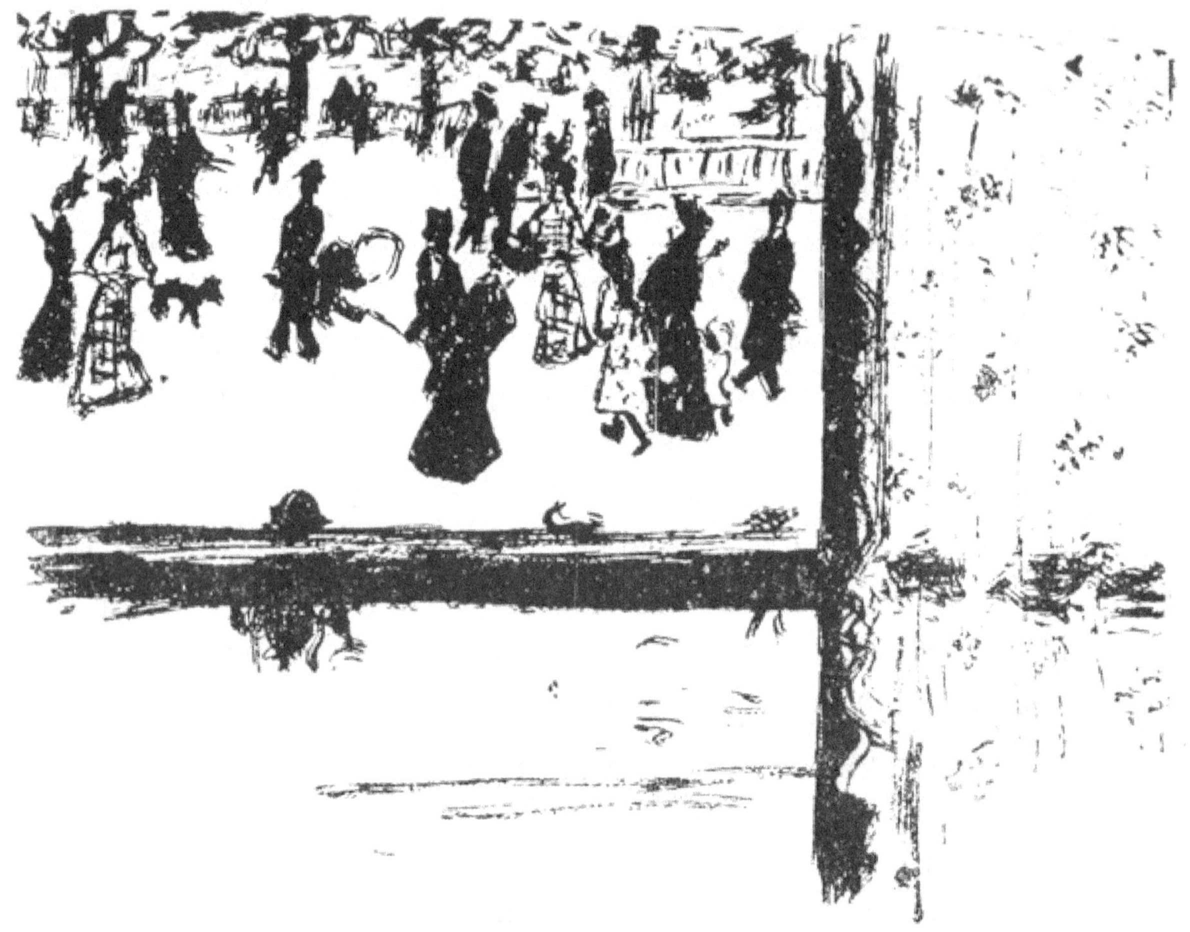

TAILPIECE, BY PIERRE BONNARD.

{96} may leave him money, so he publishes his articles under the name of Jones; he was born in the city of Boston, so he signs himself *de* Boston, meaning *of*, or *from*, Boston. Under this name he paints his first picture, but the town council does not buy his works as he hoped it would, and the council of Albany does, so he discards "de Boston" and, in his gratitude, he afterward signs his canvases d'Albany (abbreviation of *de* Albany). But now as to Christian names. Our friend Smith was, perhaps, named by his father Henry, but at his baptism there were added the names of Lewis and Charles and his mother's name, Black. Then, when at the age of fifteen he comes to be confirmed, he takes the name of Matthew, Mark, Luke, John, plus Mary. And with any of his surnyms he may at any time combine any two or half a dozen of these pronyms. So that a French biographical dictionary is one-half biography and one-half cross-reference. Thus— *Brown*, see *Jones*; *Black*, see *White*.

Knowing this, we referred to the periodical from which this was cut, and found it was a tailpiece to an article signed Pierre Réné Choudieu. Ah! this gave us a clue; but, who then was Dangers? Was Choudieu a sculptor as well as a writer, and was this a medallion portrait by him of Dangers? Or was it a portrait of Choudieu by a draftsman named Dangers? The artists were not mentioned in the index nor on any page in the body of the magazine, but on the title-page we found "Dessins de Pierre Bonnard," meaning that the drawings in the magazine were by one artist—Pierre Bonnard. Therefore, D'Angers could not have been the artist, so

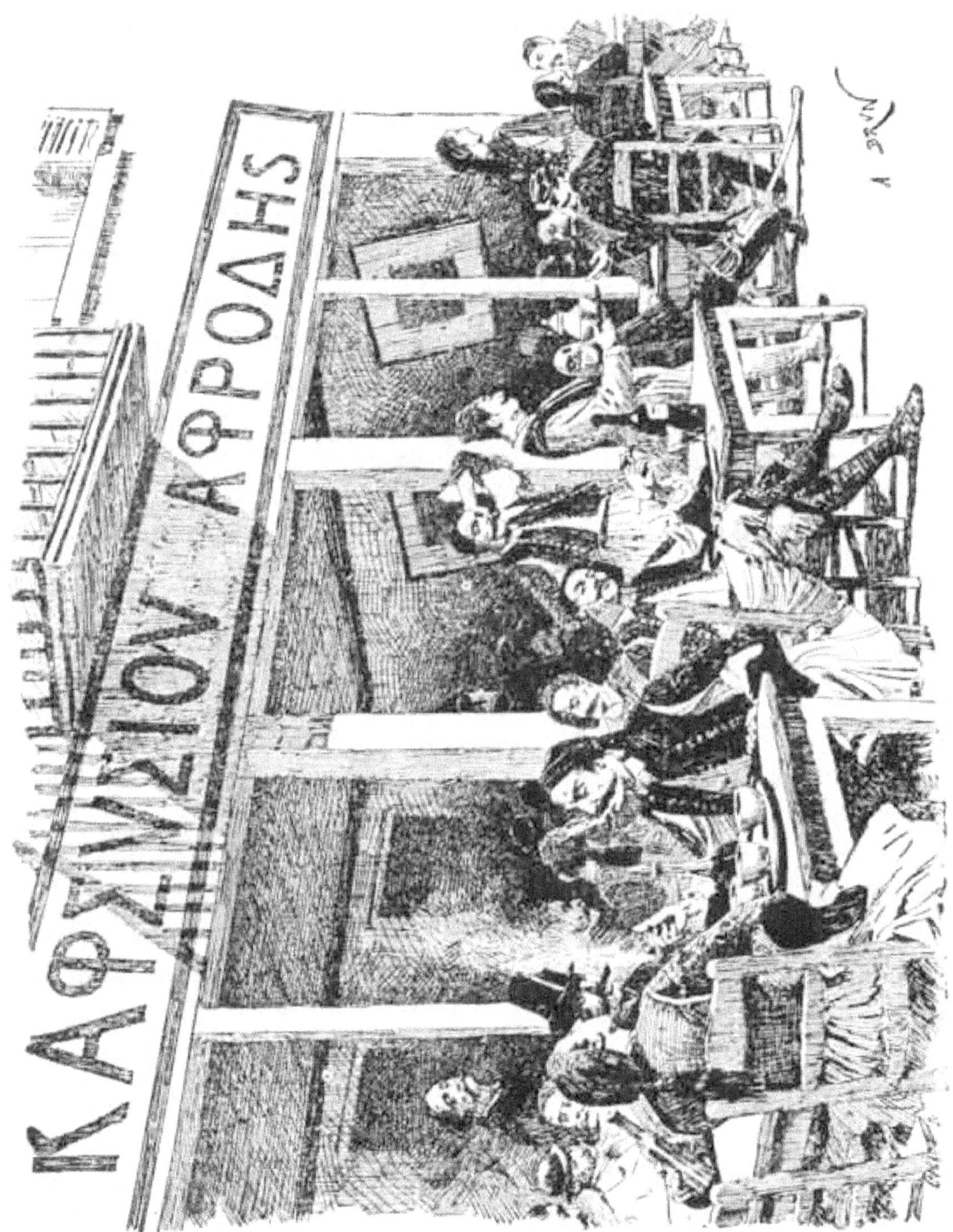

AT THE CAFÉ APHRODITE.
Pen Drawing by A. Brun.

{98}

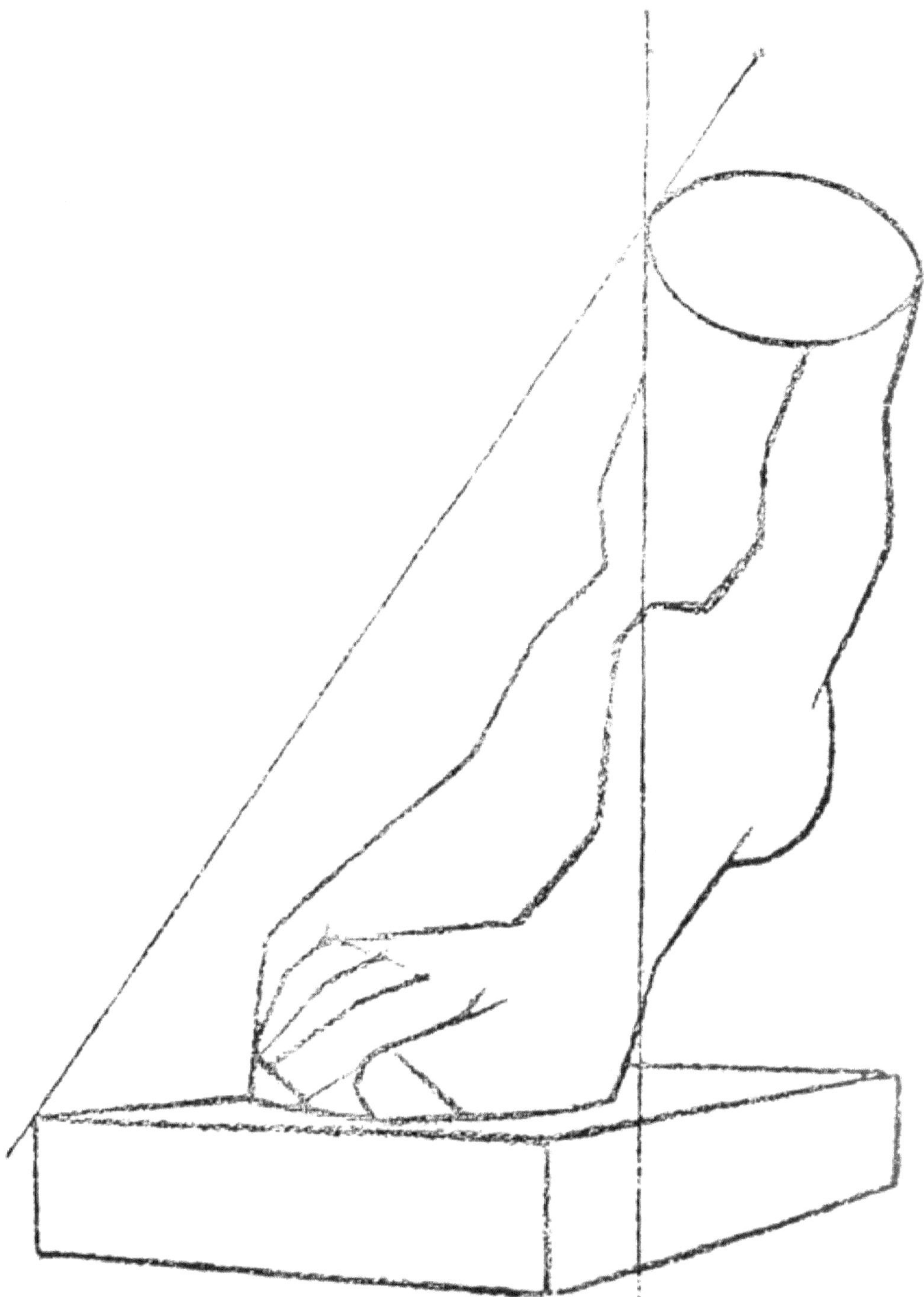

Example of French Art School studies, from plates published under the direction of Bargue and Gérôme, showing method of blocking in a cast, both outline and shadows.

{99}

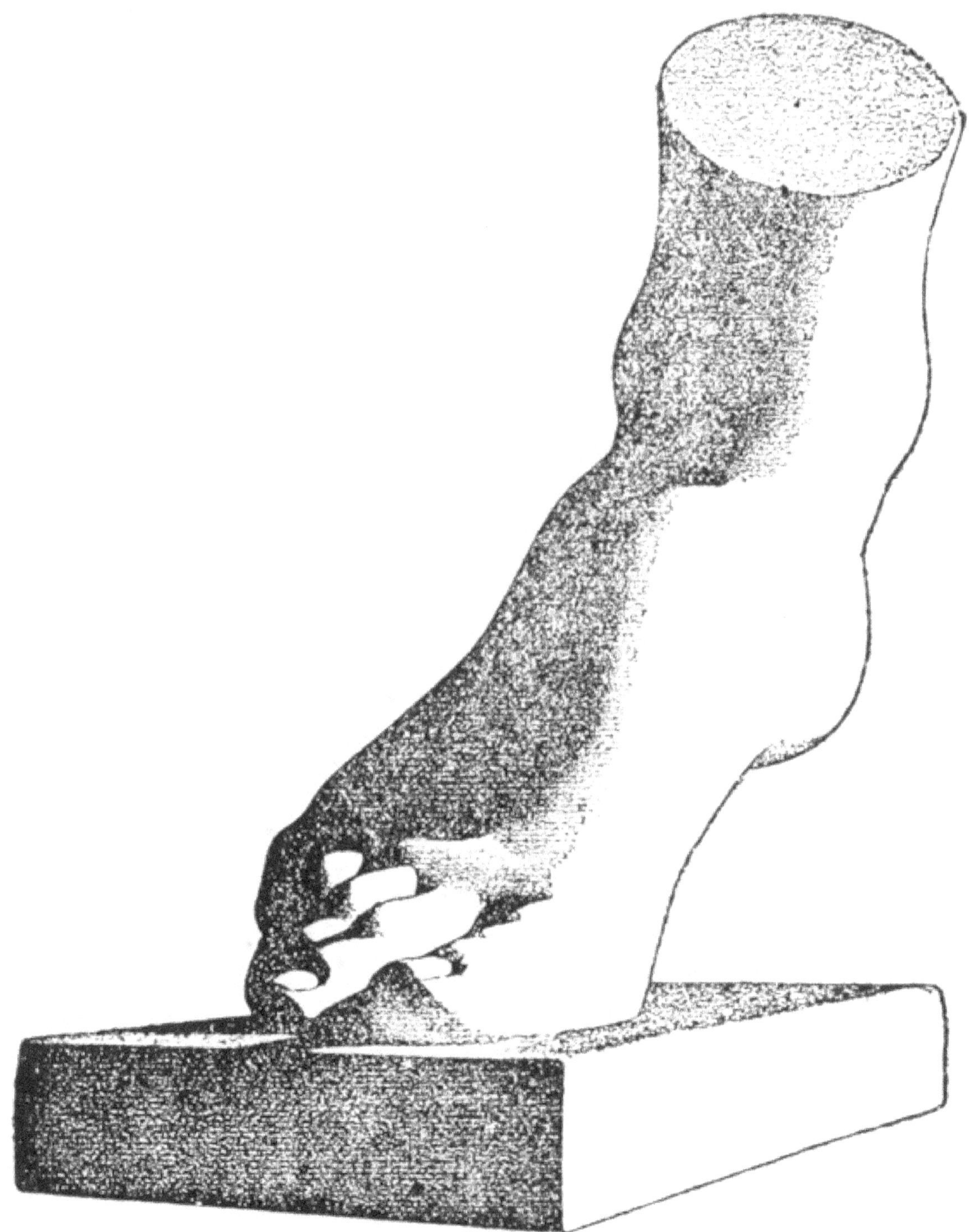

Example of French Art School studies, from plates published under the direction of Bargue and Gérôme, showing method of shading in simple tones without much reflected light or half-tones.

{100} we must search further; this we did, and luckily, in the back of the magazine, found the advertisement of a series of articles by Pierre Choudieu, and one of the paragraphs in it read, "Pierre Réné Choudieu, naquit a Angers," etc. This translated meant that he, Choudieu, was *born at Angers*, so that we fathomed our problem at last, and give the result under the cut.

The foot plates are identical in treatment with the plates of hands given on pages 66 and 67. The reader should compare these plates, that he may understand that a method may be learned from the drawing of one object and applied to the drawing of a thousand other objects. You must not expect that in a brief treatise of this kind we can give specimens of every object that the printer may have occasion to draw—we should have to publish an encyclopædia for that—but we do purpose to give *methods* which will enable him to draw every kind of tangible object with light and shade upon it. These hands and feet studies may be used as guides to show how any such object may be "modeled," i. e., shaded so that the object seems to be solid.

CHAPTER XI.

MORE ABOUT THE NASO-LABIAL LINE — IT SUGGESTS OLD AGE — ABSENT IN YOUTH — DRAWING NOT ARBITRARY — LINES INTRODUCED BECAUSE THEY ARE IN NATURE — LINES MADE BY THE ORBICULAR MUSCLE AND THE CROW'S FEET (THESE SUGGESTIVE OF OLD AGE) — LINE AT THE CORNER OF THE MOUTH — LINES MADE BY THE FRONTAL MUSCLE — SUGGESTIVE OF OLD AGE OR OF PASSION — MUCH USED BY THE ACTOR.

LET us harp a little longer upon the naso-labial line. We reproduce two very beautiful drawings by Grellet, the one of a young girl, the other of an old man. How suggestive is the old man's head because of the strong marking of the naso-labial line. Do you not realize how easily you could draw this line, and the whole head for that matter, in the manner of the Bonnard Choudieu? But valuable as it is by itself, how much more suggestive in connection with the young girl's head, where the naso-labial line is hardly perceptible. This is a lesson in negation, at the value of which we have hinted so often. It is your business to learn when to put in a line, but equally your business to learn when to leave it out. Therefore we give with this chapter some heads of younger persons, that you may learn this very lesson. Take the Fred Walker head. How like the Watts drawing, so far as its treatment goes; but the naso-labial line is missing. What is the result?

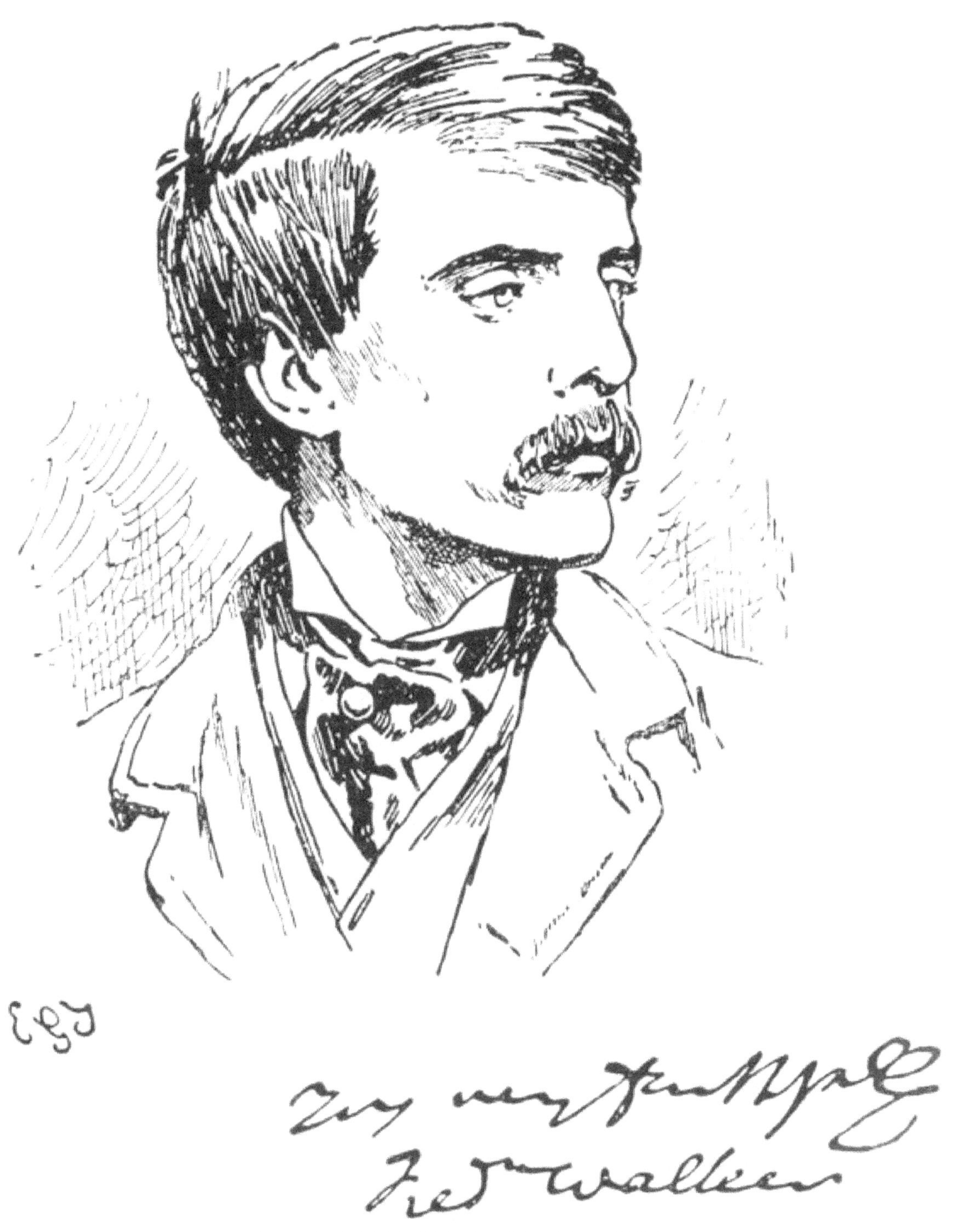

PORTRAIT OF FRED WALKER.
Pen drawing by E. G. T.
Note entire absence of naso-labial line, and of line about orbicular muscles. Absence of these lines indicate youth. Contrast with the Watts and Choudieu heads, where strong markings are prominent because of advanced age of the subjects.

{103} Why, we have the characteristics of a younger man. In this little comparison you have the foundation of all art study. Drawing is not arbitrary; we do not introduce lines into a face simply because this artist or that artist did so; we introduce them because their counterpart is found in nature. It is not in the province of these papers, as we have said, to tell the printer how he should draw every object he may attempt to delineate—a waste-paper basket, the head of a cow, a printing press, or a hat. But we can give him hints which will help him to observe for himself the characteristics of any object under the sun which he may wish to draw. If he finds around the mouth of a cow more pronounced lines than in a calf, he must put them in. If in one trash basket the wickerwork runs upward with each line parallel, he must draw it by perpendicular parallel lines, while in another one the wickerwork is interwoven diagonally and he must represent it by diagonal lines. In a coat sleeve, the arm hanging down, there are but few cross-folds, so he introduces few cross-lines into a sketch of such a sleeve, but when the arm is bent many more folds occur at the elbow and he therefore introduces more cross-lines in his drawing of the sleeve. This is about all there is to the science of drawing.

Now let us proceed a little further. In the Watts we notice two or three lines below the lower eyelid; these we find also in the Gaillard, but they are absent in the Donatello Young Girl's Head by Grellet; they are very perceptible in the Brontolone. Here we have to do with another muscle. In the human head the eye is

{104}

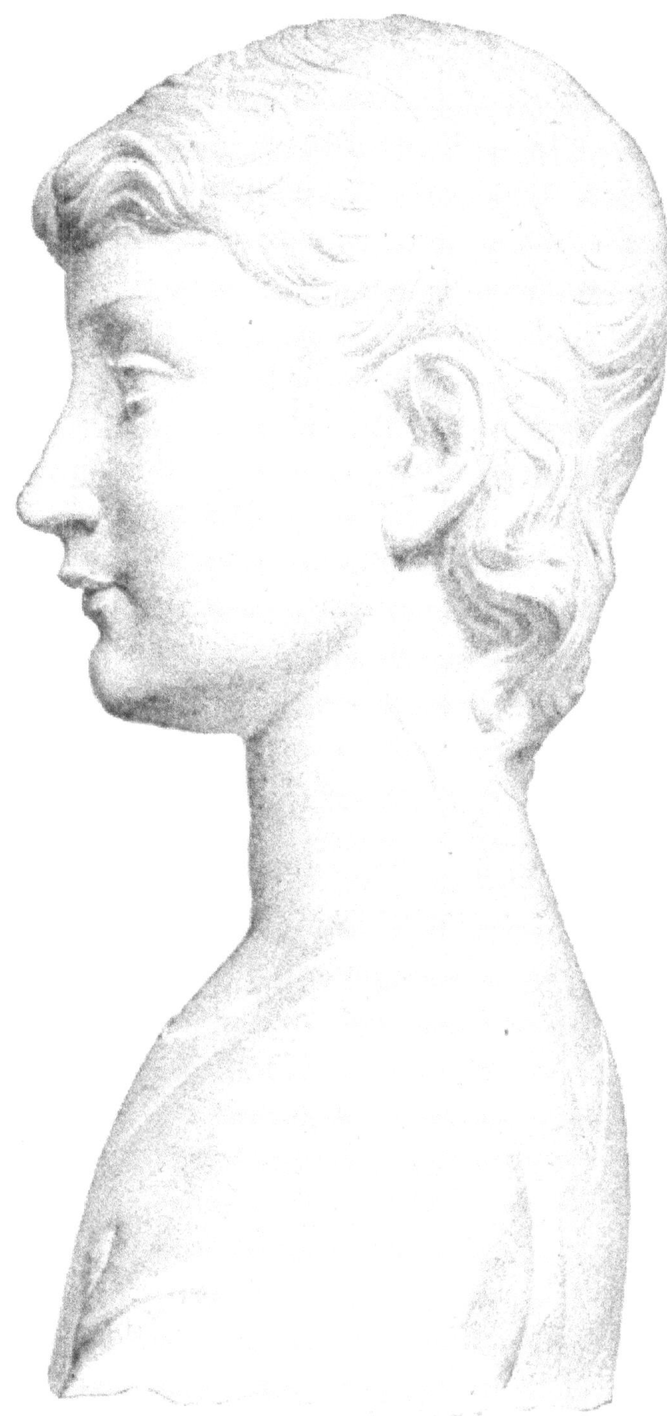

LITHOGRAPH CRAYON DRAWING.
From bust of a young girl by Donatello, by F. Grellet.
Note absence of strong marking of naso-labial line, the absence of line at the angle of the lips, and of orbicular muscles. The absence of these markings indicates youth. To be compared with the Lefebvre drawing.

{105} set in a cavity in the skull called the orbital orifice, and in a very old person the lower edge of this cavity is sometimes perceptible under the flesh, and occasions a line in an artist's drawing. But the main cause for the lines around the edge of an eye is that the eye is surrounded by a soft muscle, which is called the orbicular muscle. The part of this muscle which forms the eyelid is called the palpebral part; the part above the eyelid, the superior orbital orbicular; and the part below the lower eyelid, the inferior orbital orbicular. At the outer corner of the eye, as the two parts come together, they show in an old person's face habitually, and in a child's face laughter creates radiating lines called crow's-feet. These lines called the crow's-feet, and still more the folds in the muscles below the eye between the lower eyelid and the base of the orbital orifice are, like the naso-labial line, very conspicuous in old age and almost entirely absent in childhood. If you understand this you will turn to the beautiful drawing by Lefebvre, and realize why, although there is a great deal of shading on the hair, ear and jaw, and quite a perceptible piece of shading on the wing of the nose, there are no lines down the cheek between the eye and the lips. Indeed, in the original drawing, the white paper was there left entirely uncovered. Of course, the artist might have filled the entire space with shading, but in that case it would have been a graduated tint suggesting the roundness of the cheek, as in the Grellet Young Girl, but there would have been no suggestion of lines; the moment lines are introduced the characteristics of old age are {106} suggested. At the corner of the mouth is a line which runs in about the same direction as the naso-labial line. In youth the cheek is slightly rounded out from the lip, and in a side view it is usually the outline of the cheek which makes the little line at the corner of the lips in the Lefebvre and the Grellet Young Girl, and always in the side view of a baby's head; but as the head becomes less babyish it is the muscles of the lips which cause this line. The muscles of the lips are exactly like those of the eye; they run entirely around the lips, but at the corner of the mouth, instead of having the radiating line like the crow's-feet, the threads of the muscle have a more perpendicular trend and create a line running in the same direction as the naso-labial line; while below this, but attached to it, is

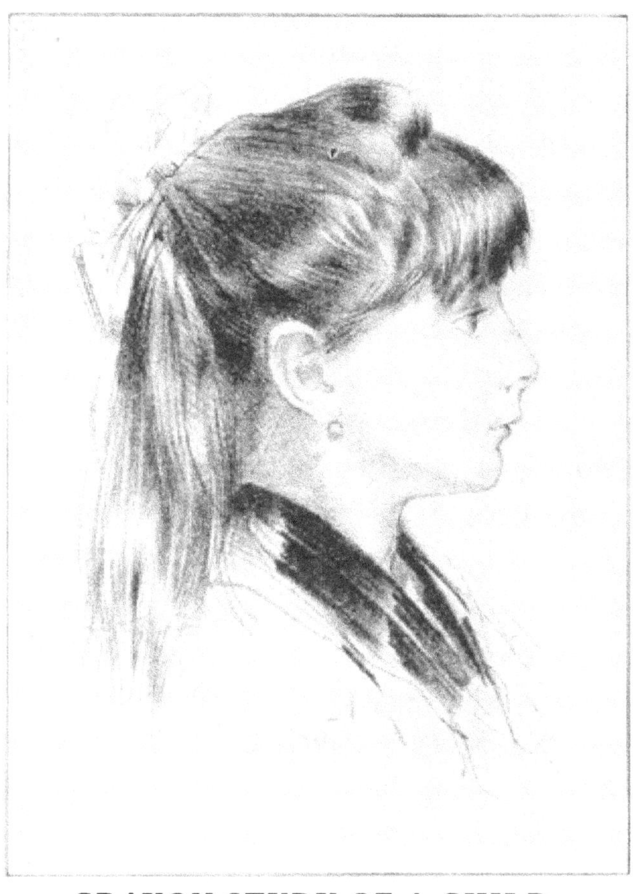

CRAYON STUDY OF A CHILD.
By J. Lefebvre.
Half-tone from a lithographic
reproduction by F. Grellet.

the triangular muscle of the lips, or the {107} depressor of the angle of the lips; this, in the ordinary old person, creates a long line, starting at the corner of the lip, running down considerably. This line is very conspicuous in the Brontolone, but absent in the Young Girl and the Lefebvre. It is seen plainly in the Choudieu, and we do not see how you can ask for a better lesson in drawing than the comparing of the highly finished Brontolone with the very simple Choudieu!

Once more, above the eyes the forehead is covered with the frontal muscle. The fibers run perpendicularly, but when they contract, as when a person frowns, the folds in the flesh run horizontally; these folds are particularly perceptible in old age. Though every mother will remember their alarming occurence in babyhood, we do not associate them with youth; and so in the Grellet Young Girl we find no lines in the forehead, nor are they in the Lœwe-Marchand, hence a placid temperament is suggested in that portrait. Many men no older than Monsieur X. have constant lines in their forehead, and the actor uses these muscles continually for expression. We write the plural because the muscle is frequently divided into right and left portions which follow the direction of the eyebrows, so that when the muscle is contracted the eyebrow's are no longer horizontal but have an M shape across the forehead. In the Watts there is a very perceptible line which curves over the right eye, taking the direction of the eyebrow; this is part of the frontalis muscle. If the line on the other side were completed it would take a similar direction over the left eye.

{108}

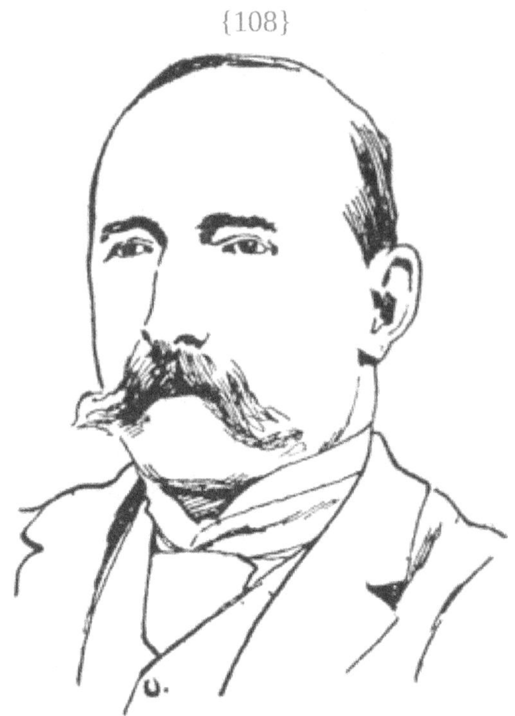

MR. COLQUHOUN.

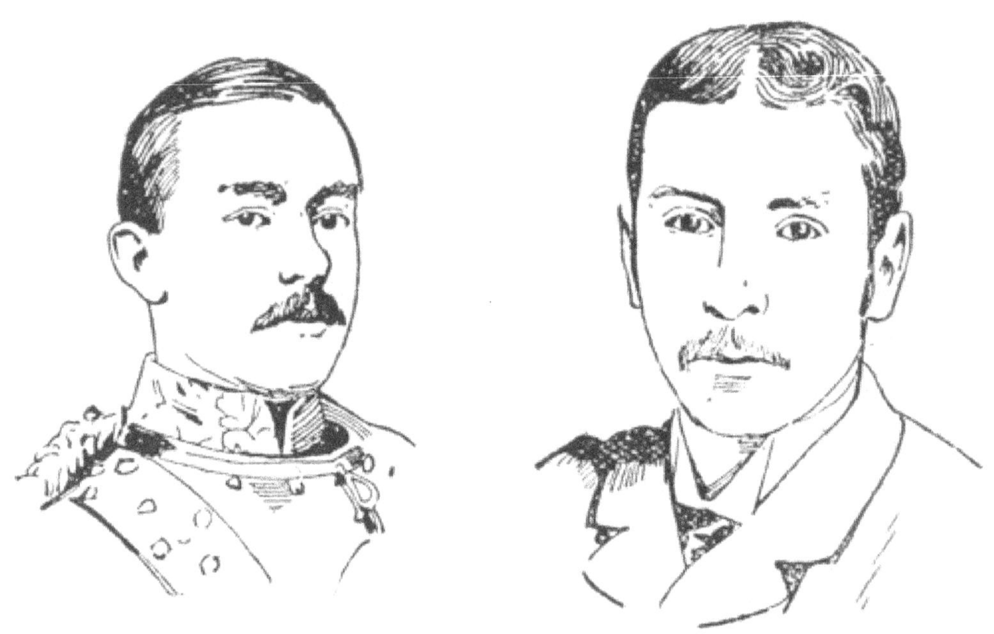

SIR JOHN WILLOUGHBY.   MR. H. H. CHAMPION.

ENGLISH NEWSPAPER PORTRAITS.

A Practical Treatise Of Designing And Illustration

Sir John Willoughby, Mr. Colquhoun, and Mr. H. H. Champion, from the *Pall Mall Gazette*. Undoubtedly traced from photographs. Executed in a simple manner, suitable for quick printing on a cylinder press. Note absence of naso-labial line, except perhaps in the case of the right-hand side of Mr. Colquhoun's head. This is either a slip of the pen, meant to come lower down to represent the mustache, or it is the naso-labial line, and its companion was lost in the engraving process. (This line could very well have remained in Mr. Colquhoun's face, as he is evidently much older than Mr. Champion and Sir John Willoughby.) Also note absence of strong marking about the orbicular muscles, and absence of lines in the frontalis. The absence of these lines indicates youth. Compare with the Choudieu and Watts, where the introduction of these lines represents old age.

{109}

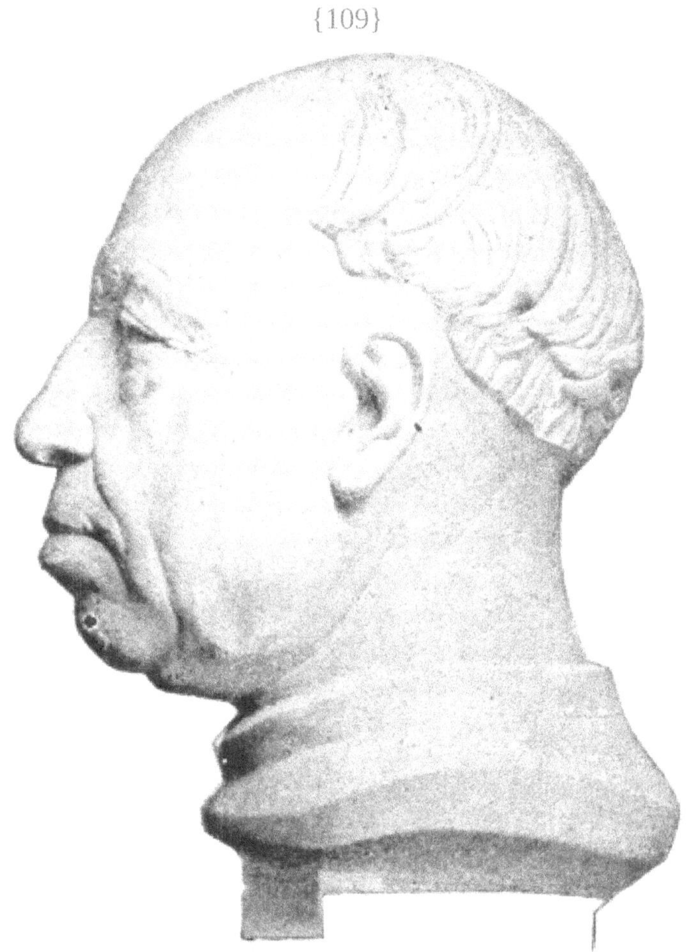

LITHOGRAPH CRAYON DRAWING.
From Bust of Brontolone by Luca della Robbia, by F. Grellet.
Reproduced by half-tone. The original was 12 by 9 inches. Strong marking of the naso-labial line, line at the corner of the lips, crow's-feet, and orbicular muscle, typical of old age. To be compared with the Bonnard Choudieu.

We have thus covered the muscles of the face which have most to do with expression, and so you see that, besides drawing the eyebrows, eyelashes, eyeballs, the bridge of the nose, the nostril, the lips, and the chin, the artist has to do with a great many muscles, and the novice must not only be warned about them, that he may know when to introduce them, but he must remember that they have principally to do with old age or {110} abnormal expression (laughter, grief, hate, etc.), and they must be used to express such attributes only. Hence the three English drawings represent very admirably the normal, placid expression of middle-aged men. If with the foregoing hints you attempt to draw a portrait for your newspaper, we fancy that, if you follow our advice faithfully, you will meet with more success than you imagine.

CHAPTER XII.

THE SCIENCE OF PEN DRAWING — PEN DRAWING MAY BE ANY SIZE — THE WATTS IN TWO SIZES — DRAWING MAY BE ENLARGED OR REDUCED — FROM THE PRINTER'S VIEWPOINT PEN TECHNIC LESS IMPORTANT AS REGARDS ITS ADAPTABILITY TO REDUCTION THAN AS REGARDS THE PRINTABILITY OF THE CUT MADE FROM IT — THE PRINTER'S OWN EXPERIENCE A GUIDE IN THIS MATTER — THREE KINDS OF PRINTING CONSIDERED, FOR CONVENIENCE CHARACTERIZED AS I. "MAGAZINE," II. "CITY NEWSPAPER," III. "COUNTRY NEWSPAPER" PRINTING — CROSS-HATCHED LINES SUPPOSED TO FILL UP MORE RAPIDLY THAN SINGLE LINES — PORTRAIT OF STEVENSON BY WYATT EATON THE NE PLUS ULTRA OF NEWSPAPER PORTRAITURE — THE NASO-LABIAL LINE IN THIS DRAWING SUGGESTED BY SHADING, NOT BY A SINGLE LINE — A DRAWING BY SICKERT — ANY PEN MAY BE USED FOR THESE DRAWINGS, BUT THE LINES MAINLY TO BE CONSIDERED AS THICK OR THIN, SINCE THEY MAY BE PUT UPON CHALK PLATE, AND NOT DRAWN IN PEN-AND-INK AT ALL.

IN our last chapter we said that we believed that if you would attempt to draw a portrait for your newspaper, following our advice faithfully, you would meet with more success than you would imagine. But you say, perhaps, that you are not prepared to attempt a portrait because we have given you no directions for pen drawing. Well, here you are partly right and partly wrong. There *is* a science of pen drawing that

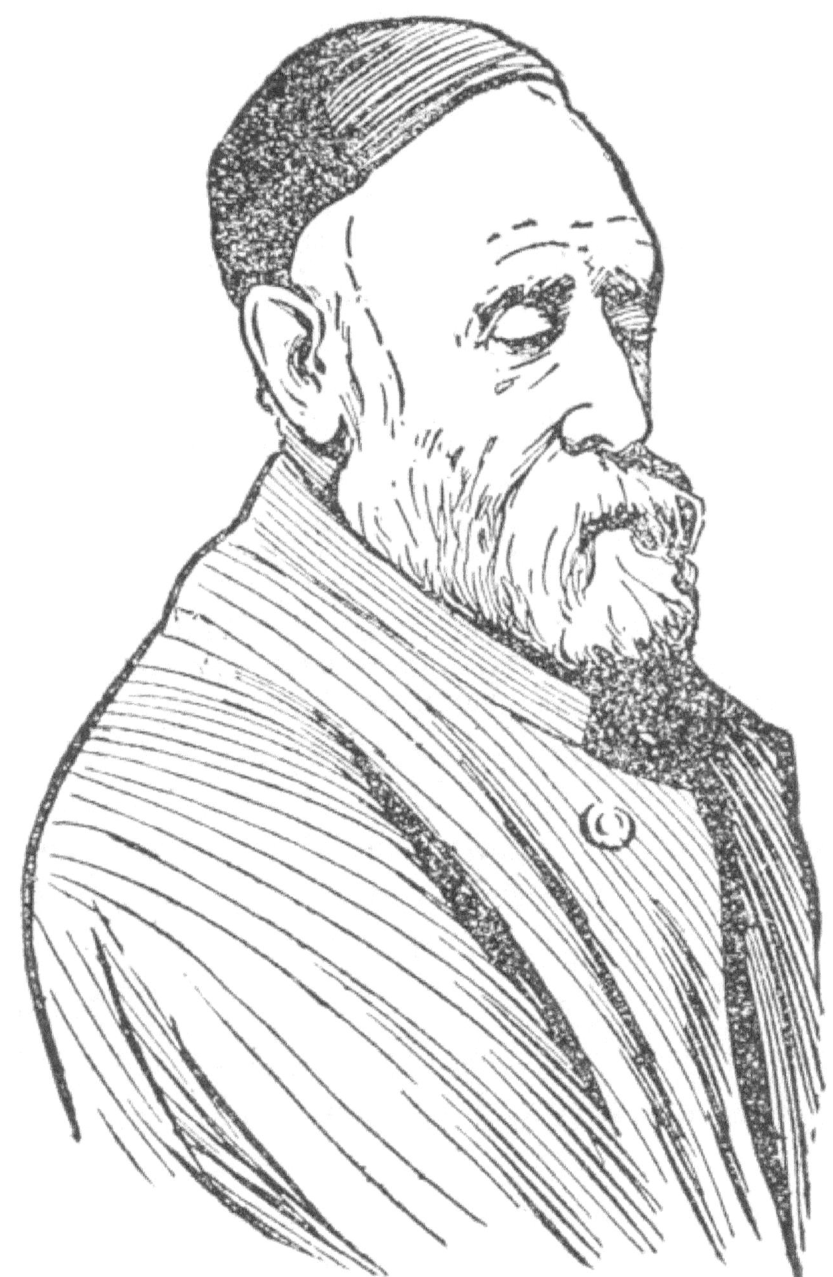

GEORGE FREDERICK WATTS, R.A.

An English newspaper cut—from *Tit-Bits*, artist unknown. An excellent example of newspaper work. Note that the skull-cap is not represented partly gray and partly black because the artist meant to indicate a cap that was one color in front and another in the back, but he meant to show the rounding of the cranium, just as Gaillard did in varying the tones in the hair of the old woman.

An enlargement of this cut was given in Chapter VIII. If a drawing is made the size of that enlargement, it can satisfactorily be reduced to the size of the cut above. Of course it may reduce to smaller dimensions; the greater the reduction the nearer the lines come together, and their closeness makes them more difficult to print.

{113} you may study with profit, but in order to draw a simple portrait for your newspaper it is not necessary for you to have any further instruction than we have given you. If it is going to pay you to follow drawing at all, you should be able at this stage of progress to make a tolerably good drawing for a newspaper portrait. But, you say, "What size should I make the drawing?" We reply, "Almost any size, though usually not smaller than the cut is to appear." But that it may be smaller is seen by our two Watts cuts. Here is a cut the exact size of the original Watts, as it went to the engraver, who by mistake enlarged it to the size it appeared in Chapter VIII. I accepted this enlargement gladly, so as to show you that a drawing may be enlarged or reduced, but more especially with the idea of showing you the usual size that a drawing is made for reduction; for you will always be safe in making your portrait the size of the Watts in Chapter VIII if you wish it to appear the size of the present cut. I cannot over-emphasize the importance of your realizing that you have been told sufficient about pen drawing for you to go ahead and make drawings for your paper. If there is anything more to be learned I am candid in saying that you are better able to find out what it is than I am, for it is almost entirely a matter of printing, and not of engraving. Photo-engravers can nowadays reproduce almost any kind of a drawing, but a cut which might print well in a magazine might not print at all in your country newspaper. You know better than I do the trouble of "bringing up" a fine cut on poor

{114}

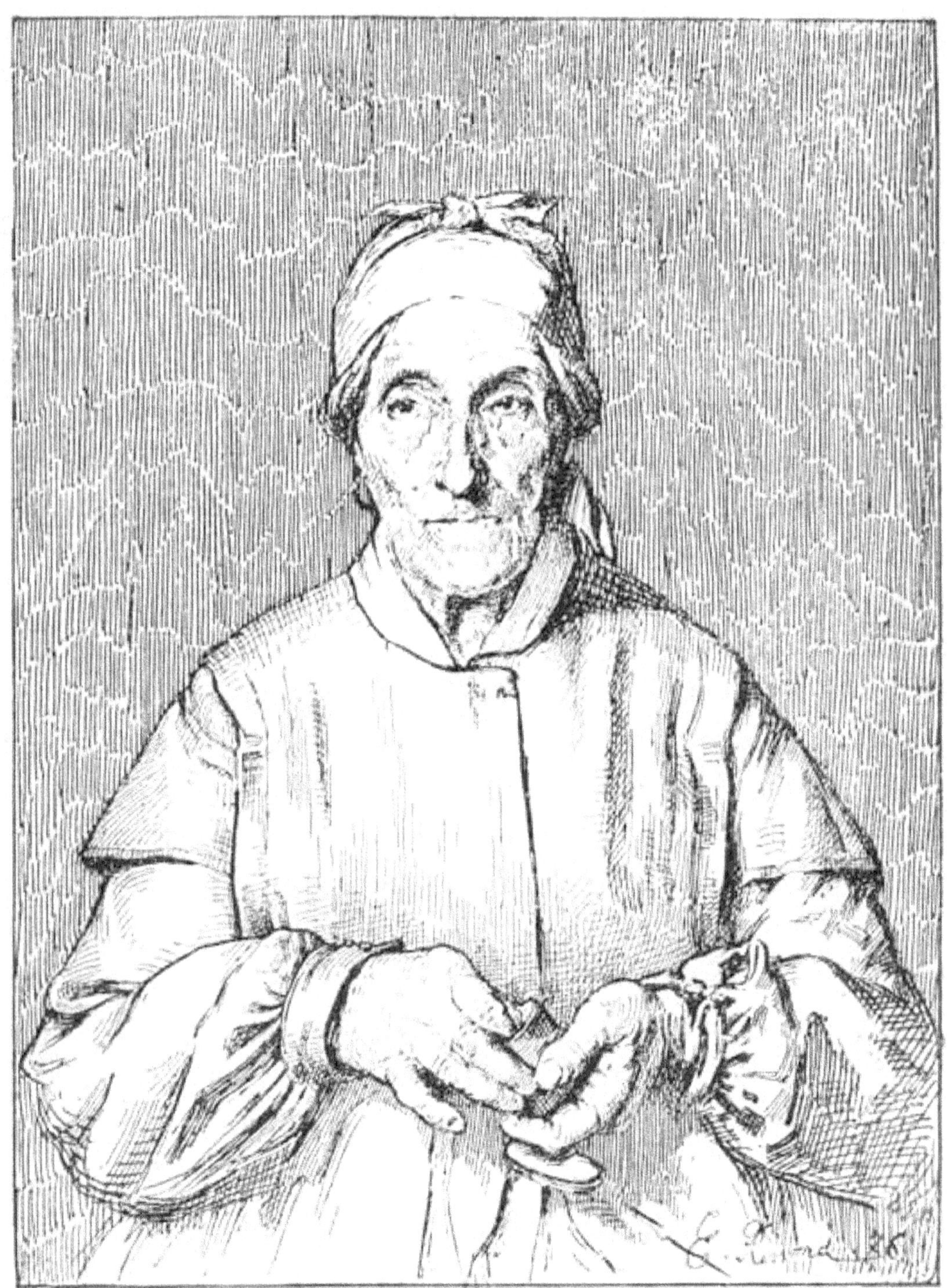

THE GRANDMOTHER.
Pen Drawing, by E. Renard, from a French Catalogue.

The parallel lines in the background represent a tint, and herein is the foundation of pen drawing, as distinguished from wash drawing: parallel lines are used to represent a tint; if they are farther apart they represent a lighter tint, if nearer together a darker tint; or again, if the artist presses on his pen more heavily on one set of lines than another, he can also get a darker tone without putting the lines any closer together. For newspaper work such a method is preferable to placing the lines near together; the Wyatt Eaton shows the pressing on the pen method perfectly.

{115} paper, on a cylinder press, and when you are making your drawing it is for you to keep in mind the kind of paper it is to be printed on, and to keep your lines sufficiently open accordingly. Ordinary intelligence should be your guide. Let us take the Renard Grandmother for an example; in the background is a series of the simplest lines imaginable. If you should make your drawing the same size as our cut, and the lines the same distance apart, it could be easily reduced to an inch wide, and print in a magazine, but it would not then print in a country newspaper; the lines would be so near together that they would fill up. The cut might print in a city newspaper, but it is not likely. The truth is that a printer can tell better about this than I can. All I can say is that as a general thing a set of parallel lines print better than cross-hatched lines.

(In using the expressions, "a magazine," "a city newspaper" and "a country newspaper," to represent first, second and third class printing, I am well aware that the distinction is an arbitrary and not a real one; that sometimes by using good ink, good stock and by printing *slowly*, the country printer can run a cut in his newspaper with better results than can a city paper using poorer stock and ink for the sake of economy, and printing at lightning speed. But the reader will kindly let the expressions stand for (1) perfect press, good stock and ink, and expert overlaying; (2) perfect press, ordinary "news" stock, poor ink, and little overlaying; (3) poorest stock, ink, cheap press, and not expert overlaying.)

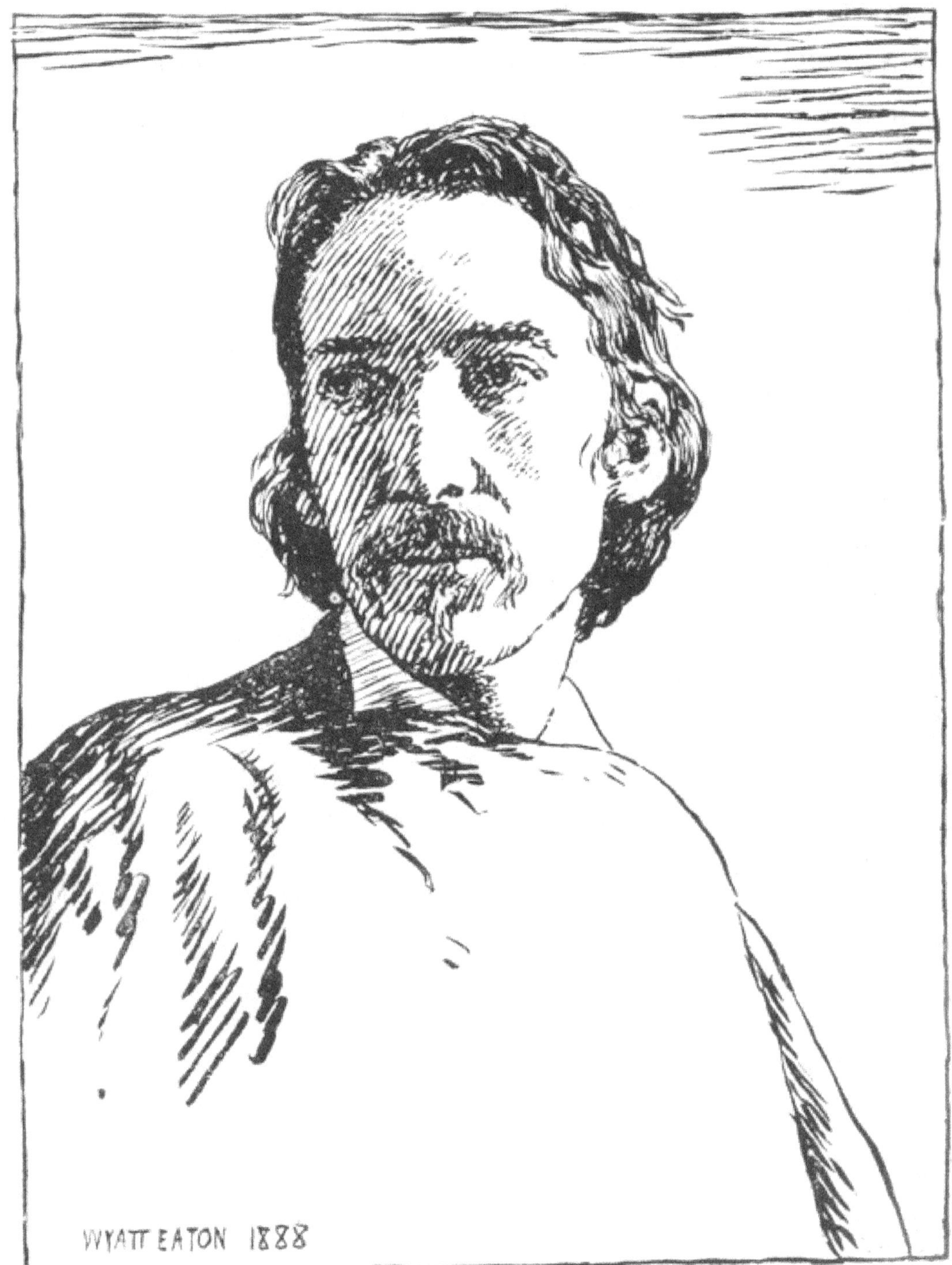

PORTRAIT OF ROBERT LOUIS STEVENSON.

Drawn, probably with a quill pen, by Wyatt Eaton, in 1888, the original 8 by 10 inches. The drawing was made in an open manner so that it would print on the poorest kind of paper, as it was used as a placard to announce a story by Stevenson, in the New York *Sun*. Reproduced by kind permission of the S. S. McClure Co., by whom it is copyrighted. A reduction of this drawing, greater than the above, adorned the cover of the March, 1897, *McClure's Magazine*.

{117}

Next to the preference of one set of lines to cross-hatched lines, it is to be said that a dark is better obtained by pressing on the pen than by putting the lines near together. We publish a superb example of pen drawing for newspaper work—the Stevenson, by Wyatt Eaton. We believe that this is the *ne plus ultra* of newspaper portraiture, for the lines are strong and vigorous, there being no possibility of their running together in printing. I should advise you to look at this portrait under a magnifying glass that you may realize how very simple the treatment is.

McClure's "Human Documents" contains a baker's dozen of half-tones of Stevenson, from photographs. You might procure this pamphlet and copy the half-tones in pen, using the Wyatt Eaton as a guide.

(And in parentheses I would say you will notice that the naso-labial lines on both sides of the face are strongly marked, and yet instead of there being one line going in the direction of the muscle, as in Bonnard's "Choudieu," we have on the light side of the face eight perpendicular lines, and on the shaded side six blots with almost horizonal, but slightly oblique, direction! Do you not, therefore, see that it is not the kind of line you use, not a matter of "what way the lines go," but where you put your tones, that counts in drawing? If Wyatt Eaton had not seen the strongly marked naso-labial line on Stevenson's face, he would not have put these two triangular forms radiating from the nostril. Moreover, Eaton could have represented these lines in another way just as well. Also, it would {118} take too long to explain other subtle features of this drawing, but we would add that you will rarely see so much tone on the light cheek as in this drawing. Stevenson was an invalid, and this tone represents the sunken cheek of ill-health.)

Now, if you will examine the Sickert portrait of Wilson, you will find an equally artistic drawing, but one not quite so adaptable to newspaper printing; for the darks are partly obtained by putting the lines near together rather than by great pressure, and in our reproduction they have frequently run together where in the original print, which was 6 by 9 inches, they were separated. And so also in printing on poor paper; there is a chance that the interstices will fill up, while they would not in the Eaton.

As, however, this drawing was made for printing on a thin manila paper, not on coated paper, and there is great deal of pressure on the pen (note especially the side of the nose), which was put on knowingly by the artist, it contains much that should be imitated in newspaper work.

In regard to the way to make such heavy lines, we would say that it is a mere matter of practice; the selection of pen has little to do with it. Excellent results may be got by using a brush instead of the pen, and we dare say that Mr. Eaton used a quill pen. But as a matter of fact, the artist usually prefers to use a very fine pen such as a crow quill, or mapping pen, which is flexible, it thus being that a dark line is got, not by a blunt-pointed pen, but by allowing the nibs of

{119}

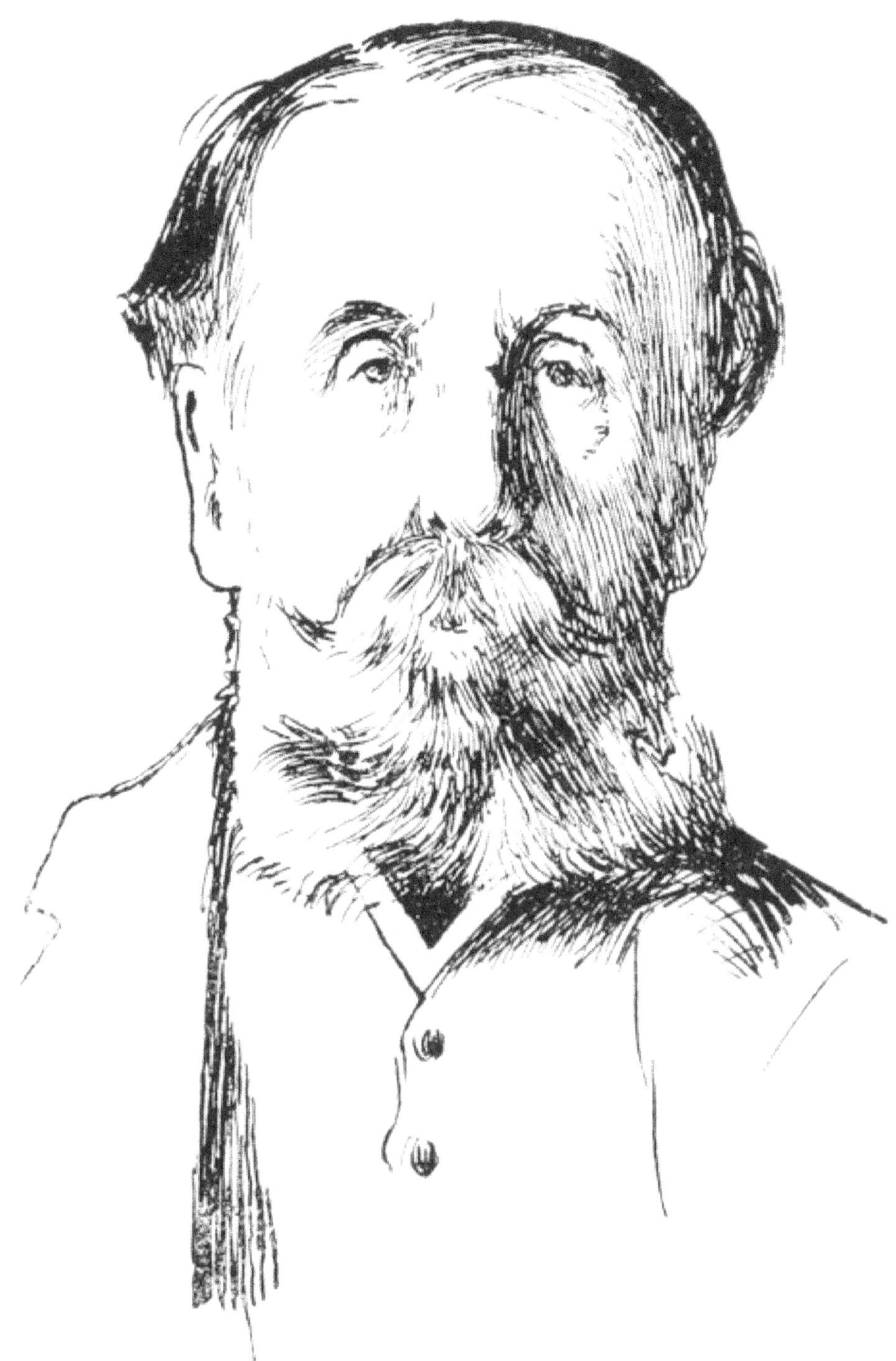

PORTRAIT OF C. RIVERS WILSON.
Pen drawing by Walter Sickert. From the London *Whirlwind*, 1890. An example of artistic portrait-drawing suitable for newspapers, showing darks obtained both by placing fine lines near together (see just above mustache on shaded side), and darks obtained by pressing on the pen (see heavy lines on shaded side of nose).

{120} a flexible pen to spread so that the ink flows very freely from it. For ordinary purposes a Gillot 303 or 170 is frequently used by the artists. But it is a matter of practice mainly, and the pen you usually write with is apt to be the best medium for practice at first. In fact, we are particularly anxious to have our reader not worry about pen technic. Let him realize that he might wish to put his drawing upon the chalk plate, in which case he would make a tracing of a photograph, and, placing it upon the chalk, press upon it with a hard-pointed pencil, and thus transfer his outline into an indentation on the chalk. He would then take the scraping tool and clear away the chalk wherever he wishes a line. The fact being that he would introduce lines only where he knew there should be lines in nature, as in the case of the naso-labial line, the eyelids, etc.; and he would broaden his lines only where he knew the tones should be darker in nature than where he had used a set of fine lines. There would be no use of pen at all!

So you see we have come right to the milk in the cocoanut—right to the matter this series was to teach. Many readers no doubt were disgusted when they did not find in our first chapters directions for the use of the pen and a list of materials for pen drawing, but those who may have occasion to do their portraits in chalk plate will thank us for our hints on the study of nature and the study of lines, no matter how made.

CHAPTER XIII.

STUDY OF PEN TECHNIC CONTINUED — THE PRINTER MUST NOT EXPECT THE KNOWLEDGE OF PEN TECHNIC TO TAKE THE PLACE OF KNOWLEDGE OF DRAWING — EXAMPLES CONSIDERED — THE GRANDMOTHER BY RENARD — THE MARCHETTI, THE VIERGE, THE ST. ELME, ARE GOOD EXAMPLES OF PEN DRAWING — THE GUILLAUME AN AMUSING EXAMPLE OF USE OF PARALLEL LINES — THE FORAIN A GOOD EXAMPLE OF NEWSPAPER CARTOON STYLE; THE VALLET, OF NEWSPAPER NEWS STYLE — THE MOULLIER AN EXAMPLE OF ECCENTRIC USE OF DOTS — METHOD OF PEN PRACTICE SUGGESTED.

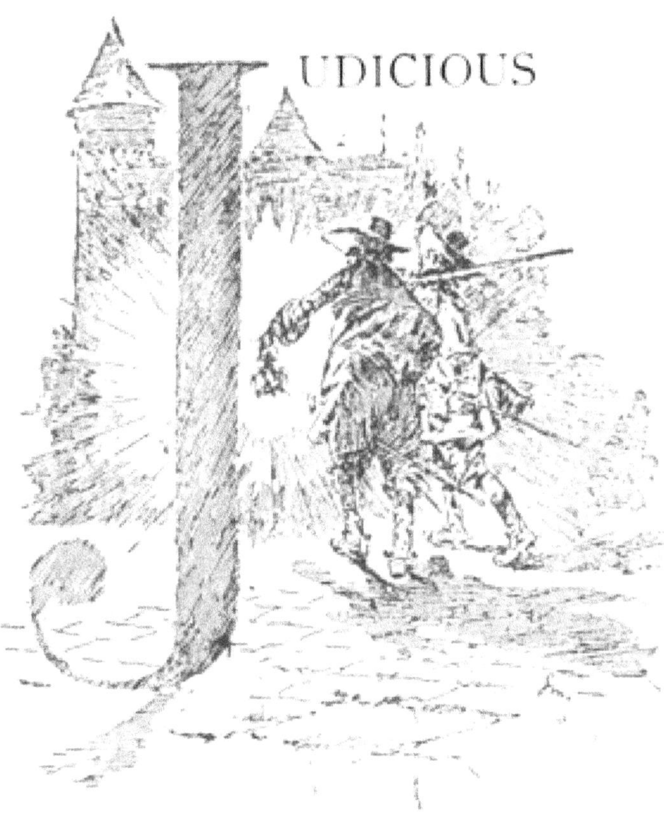

INITIAL LETTER BY MARCHETTI.
Pen drawing from *Paris Illustré*.

study of pen technic is helpful to the printer-designer. I use the adjective "judicious" because I need a word beginning with J for our initial letter. What I mean is, that just so far as the printer studies drawing, he may study pen technic, but he must not expect to progress further in the latter than he has progressed in the former; so while this chapter will be exceedingly helpful to the reader who has followed the previous ones, it will only lead to failure

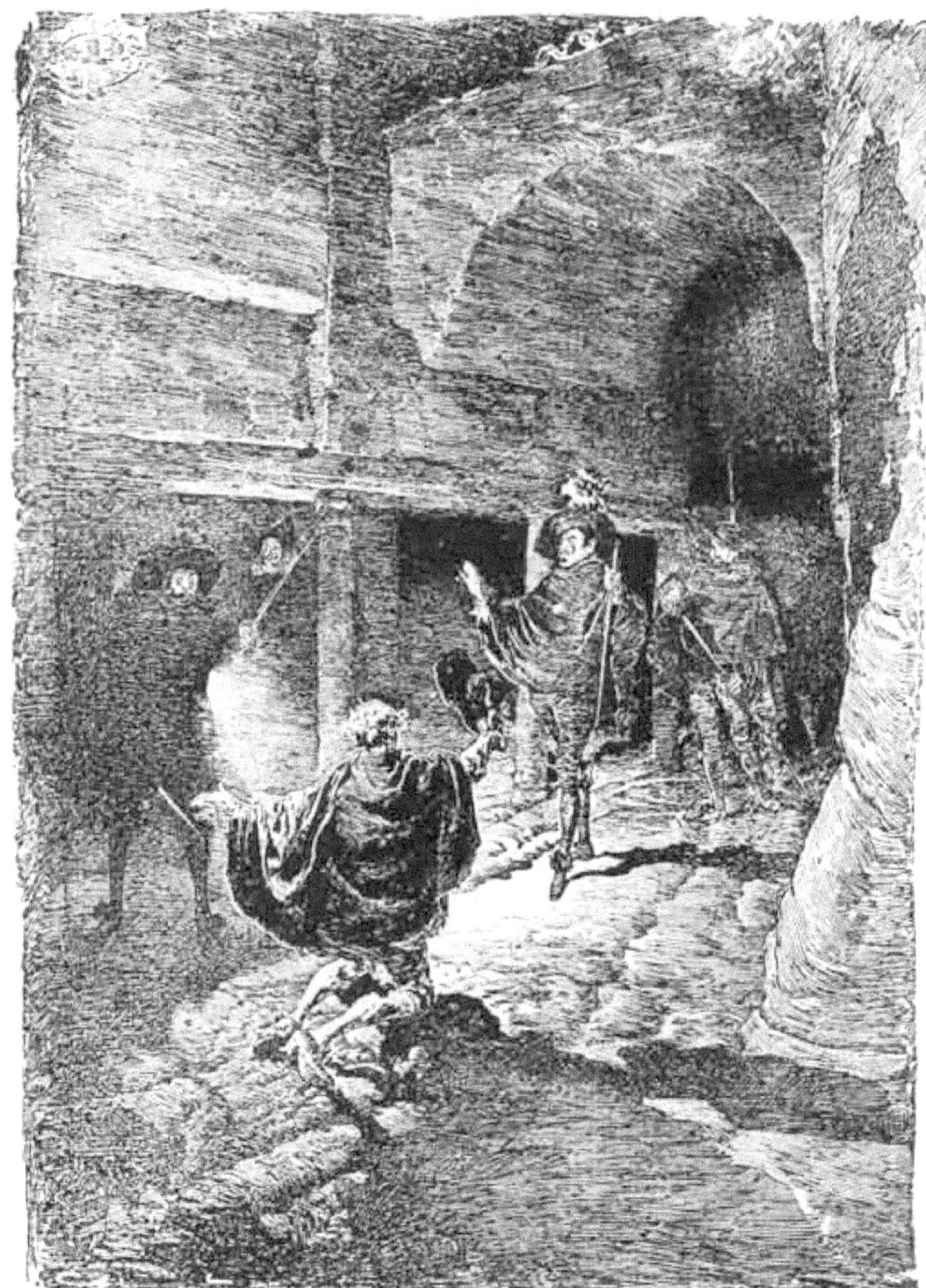

ILLUSTRATION TO PABLO DE SEGOVIE.

Pen drawing by Daniel Vierge, one of the most celebrated of modern pen-draftsmen. If you will scrutinize this drawing under a magnifying glass you can examine this technic with more ease than with the naked eye.

{123} if the reader does not follow our advice in regard to training the eyes to see as well as in regard to pen technic.

We said in our last chapter that the parallel lines in the background of "The Grandmother," by Renard, showed the foundation of pen drawing. The same is true of our initial letter, in which we find a set of parallel lines which, contrasted with the white of the illumination thrown by the lantern, gives us an effect of gray. This is found again in the other drawing by Marchetti; and if you will study these two drawings, and then turn to the Vierge, you will find that nine-tenths of it is drawn in the same way. Here and there to get a certain vibration of tone, Vierge uses crosshatch, but you will notice that the lightest gray and the intensest dark are got without crosshatching.

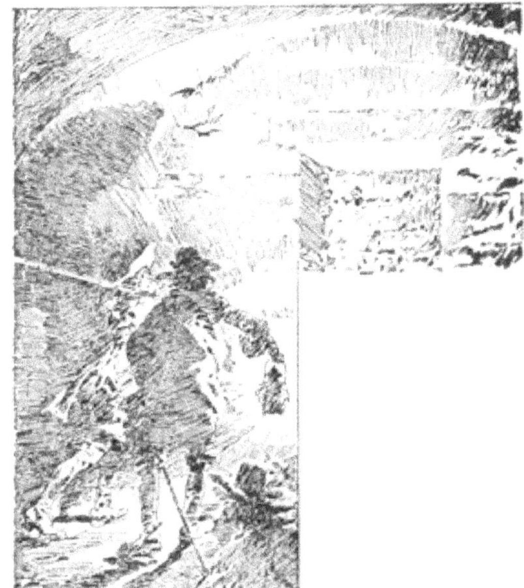

Illustration (pen drawing); chapter heading, but without initial letter, by Marchetti. From *Paris Illustré*.

In the St. Elme you may also distinguish very clever use of parallel lines, without much crosshatching. We have purposely reproduced this, together with the page it decorated, so that you may see the artist had a good reason for not crosshatching; he wished his drawing to form a decoration about the page, and he did not want it to be too heavy, so he abstained from crosshatching.

{124}

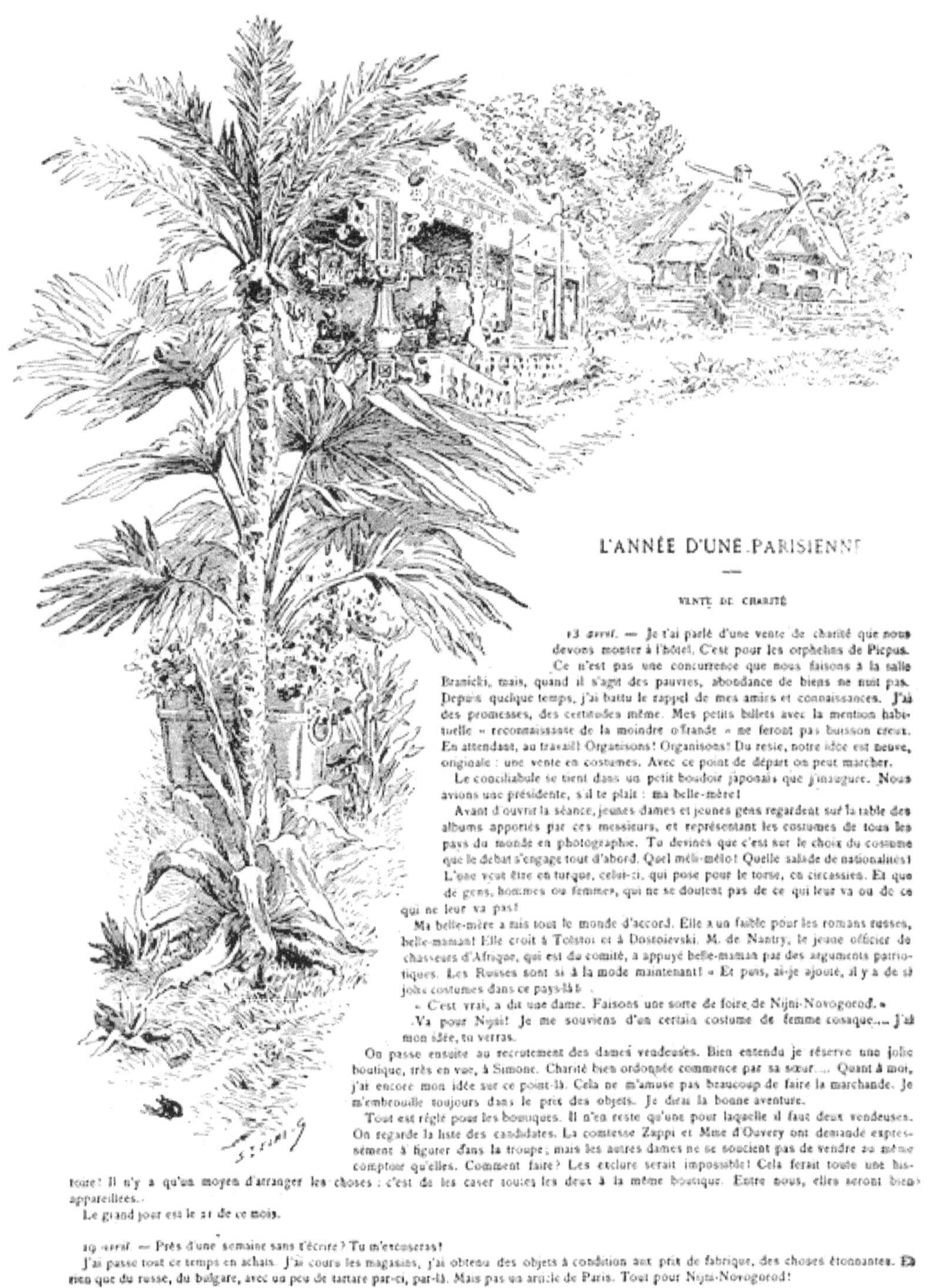

Pen drawing by St. Elme, decorating a page of a French journal, 9 1/2 by 13, showing a clever use of parallel lines, and a method of decorating a printed page, which will be considered later on.

{125} The best practice for you is to make drawings for your publication in any manner you see fit, and after you have had experience in printing the same, you can tell very well how much crosshatching is advisable, and how much clogs up in the printing. There are

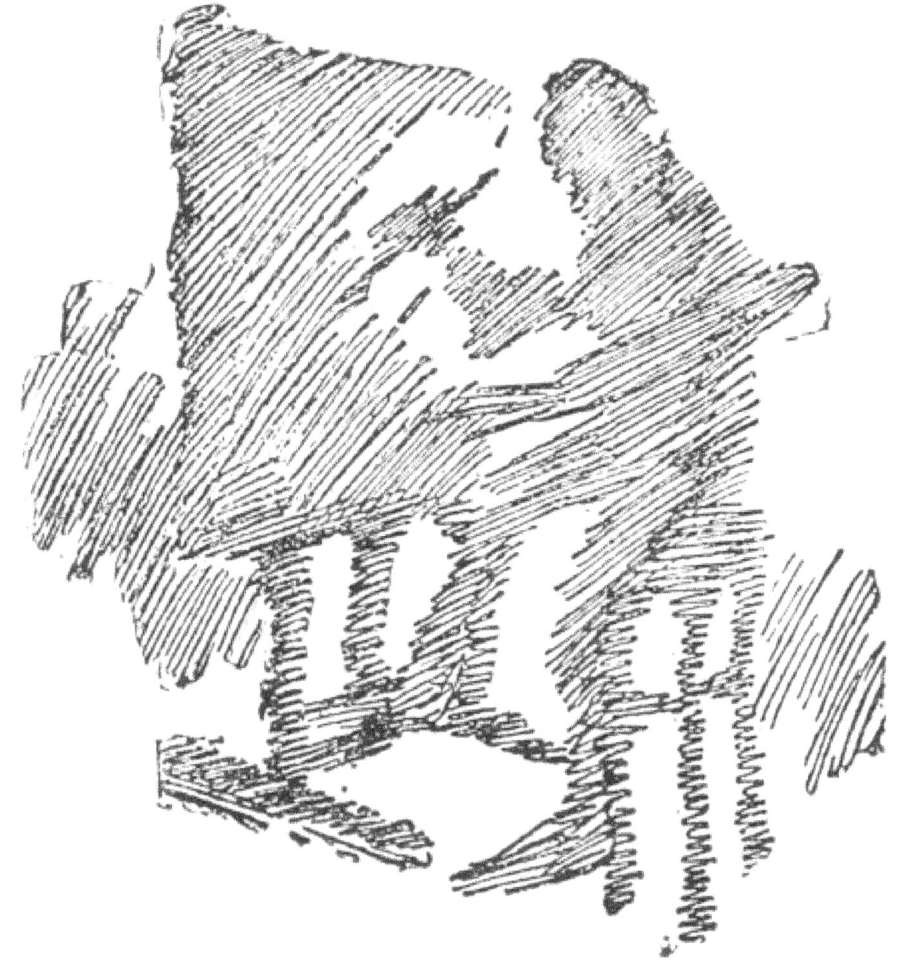

Caricature of the French painter (whose works are somewhat dark and misty in effect) Eugène Carrière at work. By Guillaume. From the French daily, *Gil Blas*.

several caricaturists in this country whose work is printed in daily papers in a thoroughly satisfactory manner, and yet they use a great deal of crosshatching, but of course they know just how open to keep the lines, for they know just what results their printer can {126} get and what not. But we would say it is a good principle, to begin with, that the less crosshatching in your work the better it will print. Hence the Marchetti and St. Elme drawings are given as examples.

In the portrait of the painter Carrière, we have an amusing example of the effective use of parallel lines. Instead of giving us a black silhouette, the artist—Guillaume—has given us a gray one, which suggests the subject seen through a fog. Had the artist wished to represent the palette as being of dark wood he could have pressed on his pen lines and thus given us that effect. Had he wished to show that the canvas was lighter than the figure, he could have refrained from pressing so heavily on his pen lines, or, better still, distributed his lines farther apart and thus obtained the effect of a lighter tone. Bear in mind, however, that I used the term pen lines in speaking of this drawing because the original was made in that medium, but the same graduation or contrast of lines is applicable to nearly all methods of line drawing; to etching and chalk plate as well. You will, perhaps, have a better grasp of the subject by thinking of it as—the theory of tone imitation by lines.

When you have grasped the theory of this pen technic, *alias* the representing of tone by lines, you will be prepared to make your own deductions from various specimens of illustration.

Some of our friends, for example, who might have been interested in our first chapters and the specimens of caricature given therein, may have been disappointed {127} that we have given so much attention to portraiture recently, so we have made an effort in this chapter to give a *mélange* that will cover many fields of newspaper illustration. In the Forain we have a splendid example of such work. It was printed on very poor paper stock, but it came out admirably, harmonizing with the type, which is larger than that used in this country, long

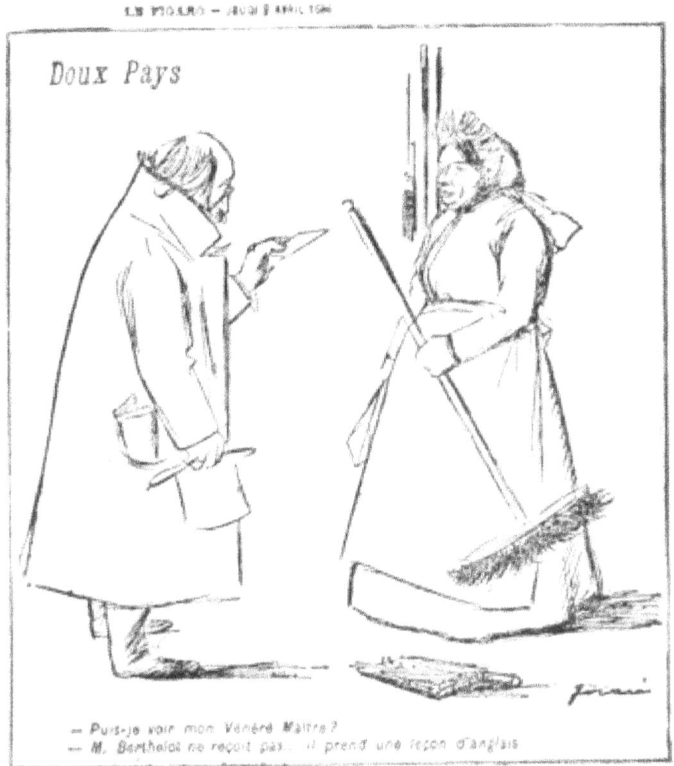

NEWSPAPER CARICATURE.

By Forain, from *Figaro*. This composition evidently makes fun of Mr. Berthelot, who has had, or expects to have, some dealings with England, for the visitor says, "May I see my honorable master?" and the maid responds, "Mr. Berthelot is not receiving; he is taking an English lesson." The cut in *Figaro* was 8 by 8, and it represents an excellent method of newspaper drawing, and one that could be easily imitated in chalk plate. We would also call attention to the drawing of the broom. Our readers who followed the directions of our first chapters will see that the silhouette of the broom is indicated in a masterly manner.

{128}

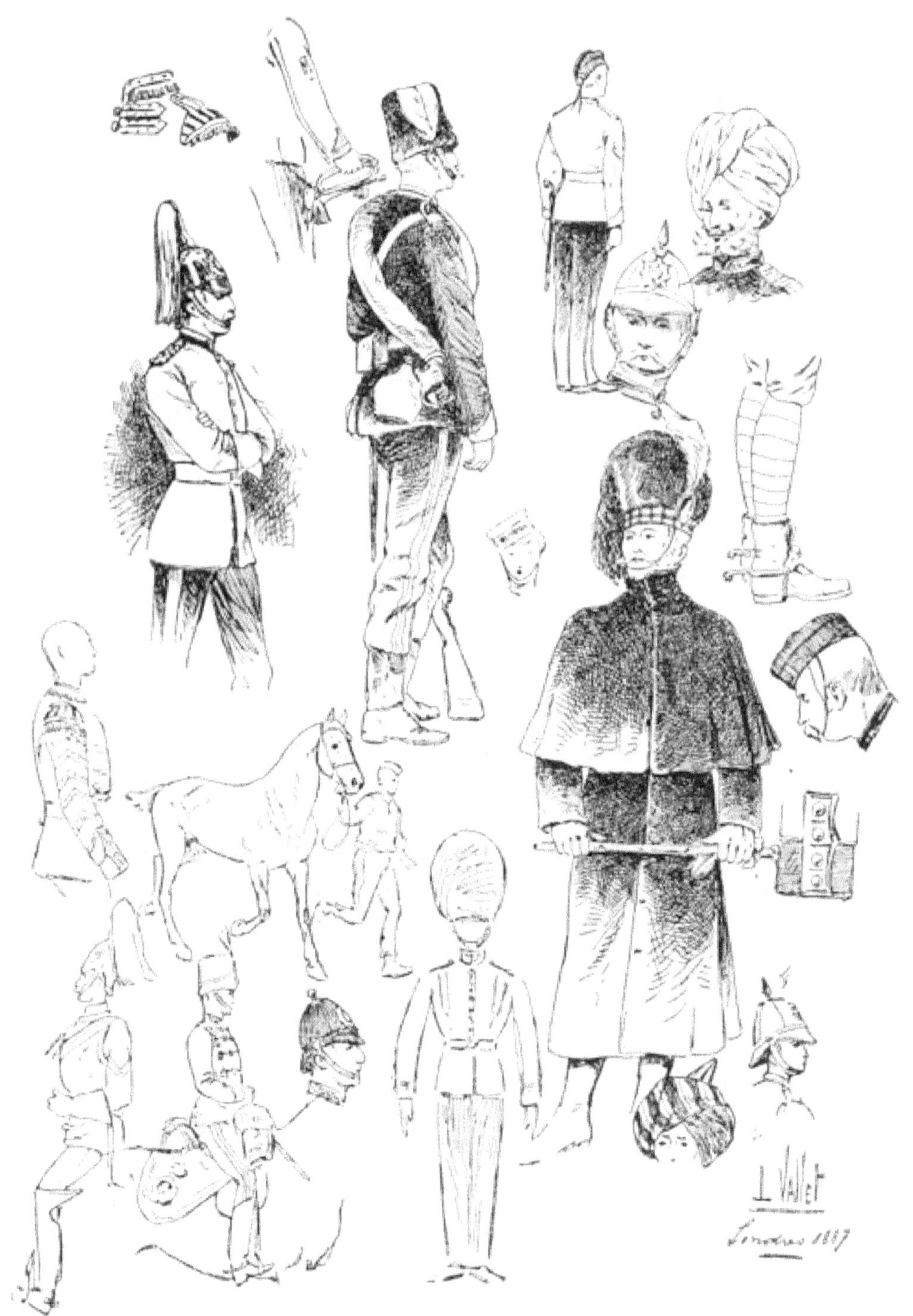

Example of news drawing, by L. Vallet, from a French periodical.

{129} primer predominating. The drawing of the still-life objects is particularly interesting. Look at the duster the woman holds: is not its form exactly what you would see if it were held up against the window and viewed in silhouette?

A good example of a news illustration is given in the Vallet page, which could easily be imitated in chalk plate. The artist viewed a collection of English army costumes, or witnessed a drill, and he shows us in very simple lines the style of accouterment. Any newspaper editor who could sketch tolerably well could do the same thing for his county fair.

In the Moullier we have a specimen that is well-nigh as amusing as the artist in the fog, for here we have a pen drawing that is not made by lines, but by a series of stipples. While the newspaper tyro should not employ this technic too frequently in his practice, still, realizing that the tone effect is graphically gained without the use of the conventional line, it must quickly dawn upon him that there are many technics, and, having practiced drawing mantelshelves according to the instructions in our early chapters, he will also appreciate the fact that the artist was in front of this mantelshelf, as the horizontal lines do not tip, and that the shelf was higher than his eye, as the top of the mantel is not shown. This knowledge gathered allows the student to see that various technics may represent the same truth in nature.

A good method of practice for pen work is as follows: Take a wood engraving or half-tone from some

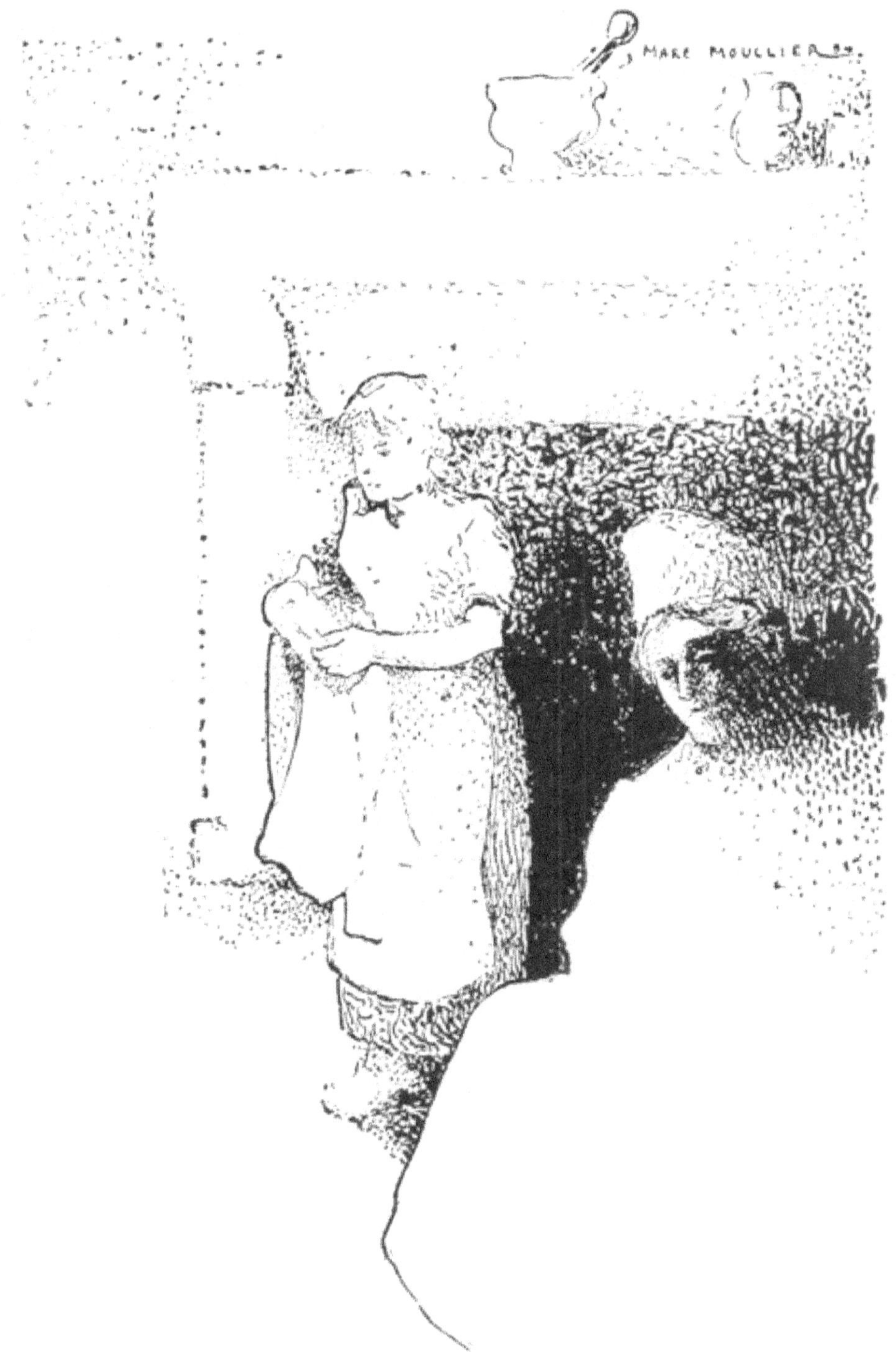

Pen drawing by Marc Moullier, for *La Plume*, showing a clever and eccentric use of dots. It may be remarked that since the mantelpiece is above the eye we cannot see the top of it. It is parallel to the artist's eyes, and so is represented as a horizontal line. So far as correct drawing is concerned, it makes no difference how that line is made. One artist makes it a thick line with a blunt pen, another a thin line with a fine pen, and another, like Moullier, makes it with a series of dots, but each of these methods is a matter of technic, and the rules of technic are arbitrary, not fixed as are the rules for drawing. You may invent your own technic, but you cannot invent perspective.

{131} periodical, the larger the better, go over the back of it with a blue pencil, lay it on a sheet of bristol board or paper, face upward, and go over the outline with a hard pencil, using such a pressure as will transfer to the bristol board a blue outline. The object in using blue is, that you do not have to erase it, but may work over it with a pen, as the blue does not photograph. Besides transferring the outline it is also advisable to outline the shape of any of the shadows you intend to introduce. You then endeavor with the pen lines to imitate the delicate shadows of the half-tone or wood cut. Perhaps instead of saying imitate, we would better say approximate, for you must not expect to be able to imitate with pen the extreme delicacy of a half-tone.

{132}

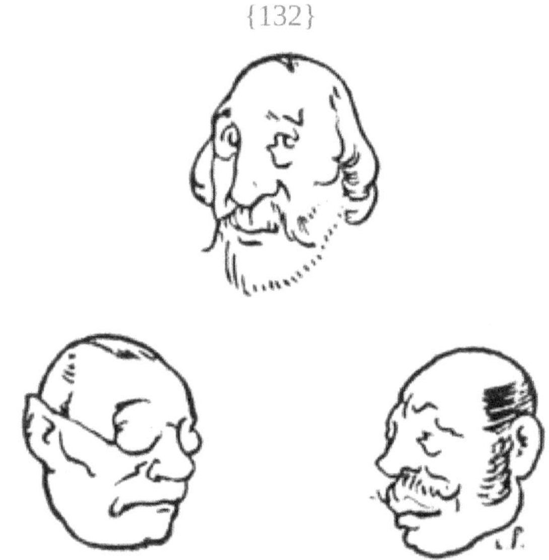

DES GUEULES (STUDIES OF MOUTHS, JAWS) BY HERMAN PAUL.

CHAPTER XIV.

A CHAPTER OF ILLUSTRATIONS AND A RÉSUMÉ — VALLOTTON HEADS ONLY UNDERSTOOD BY THOSE WHO CAN SEE LIGHT AND SHADE UPON OBJECTS — ME-DALLIONS BY DAVID D'ANGERS SHOWING THE PLANES OF THE FACE — THESE PLANES BROUGHT OUT IN SOME OF THE VALLOTTON HEADS, AND IN MEDALLIONS BY LORMIER AND D'ILLZACH, AND IN DRAWING BY CHAUME — LANDSCAPE BY LE ROUX, CARICATURE BY FORAIN — THE LE ROUX AND THE PAUL DRAWINGS INDICATE THE FORCE OF OUTLINE — EXAMPLES OF DIFFERENT KINDS OF TECHNIC.

THE definite character of our illustrations to the last two chapters should have made so strong an impression upon the reader (*if* he practices drawing) that there ought to be little necessity of further letterpress explaining the different technics of pen drawing. {133} So please permit us to introduce a large number of illustrations in this chapter, with slight comment; it being surmised that the reader will, however, give a fuller consideration to the drawings themselves than we do. Each one should be studied again and again, the reader not copying it, but making a drawing in the same style of some similar object. This chapter, moreover, must serve as a general résumé of our instruction in freehand drawing and pen drawing; it virtually ends the first part of our text-book; the succeeding matter will be confined to the consideration of different methods of decorating title-pages, and of designing chapter headings, tailpieces, etc.; and the third part will consist of the consideration of different methods of engraving, chalk-plate, wood engraving and color printing.

Now for our résumé.

In order to learn to draw you must first learn to discern the outline of objects, which you may do by seeing them in silhouette.

To draw the hair in outline, as in Vallotton's third Nietzsche, you must first see the hair as in the first Nietzsche; that is, see it in mass or in silhouette in nature. Before Vallotton took a brush in hand to put on the solid black of the hair in number one you may be sure he drew a pencil outline like the outline in number three; but before he drew that outline he saw the mass as in number one.

The Vallotton drawings may be further studied from two very different view-points. The third Friedrich Nietzsche is pure outline, like the examples of Engström

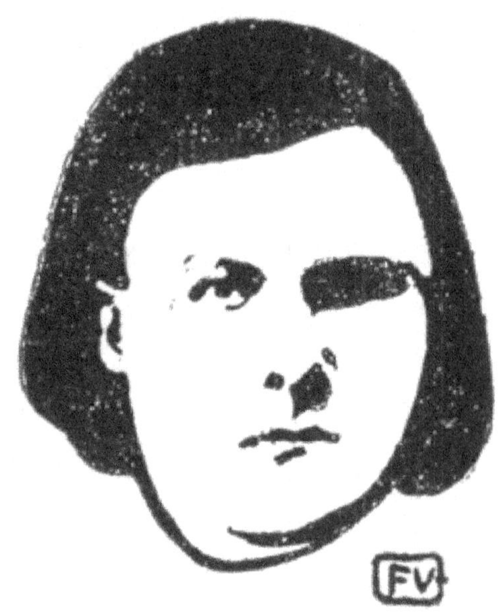

FRIEDRICH NIETZSCHE.

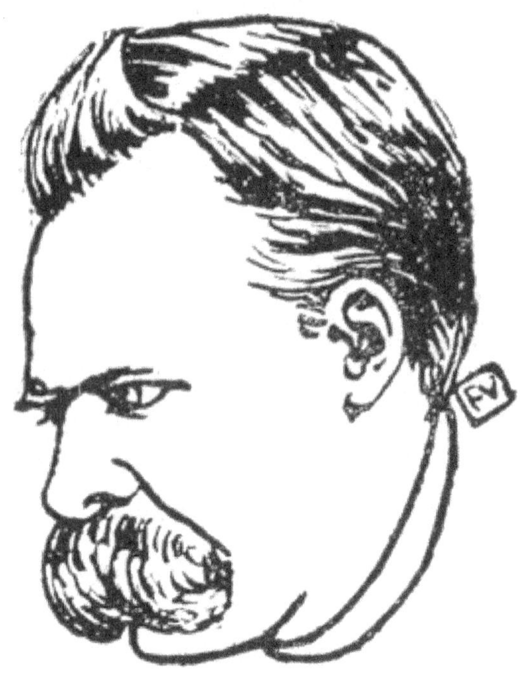

FRIEDRICH NIETZSCHE.

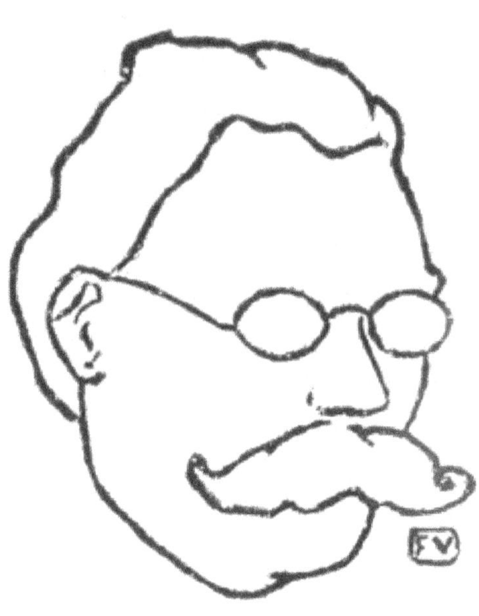

FRIEDRICH NIETZSCHE.

HEADS DESIGNED BY F. VALLOTTON.

{135}

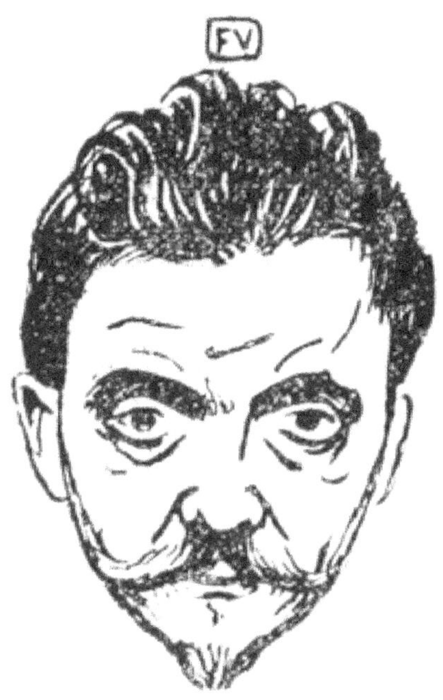

FELIX VALLOTTON.

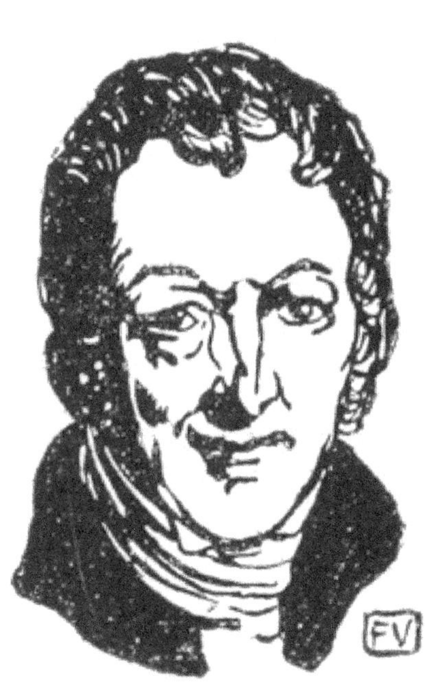

MALTHUS.

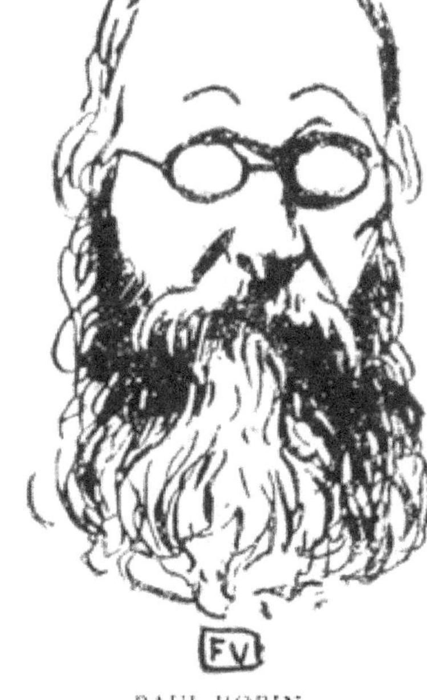

PAUL ROBIN.

HEADS DESIGNED BY F. VALLOTTON.

Vallotton has made it a practice to engrave a great many of his own designs. We do not know whether these heads were engraved by him, or merely drawn by him and photo-engraved, but the manner in which they are designed—that is, with great economy of line, and a few simple, telling spots—is one which is the outgrowth of his practice in wood engraving; he would work exactly like this if drawing on wood. (We shall treat of wood engraving for printers in a future chapter.)

{136} given in our early chapters, and is very simple and easy to understand, though not by any means easy to draw. The drawing of Malthus, on the other hand, is not easy to understand, for in addition to the outlines it is modeled—that is, it contains masses of shadow which bring out the different planes of the face. And it is necessary to study light and shade, as indicated in Chapter VII, before we can fully understand a drawing of this kind.

In order to model, you must learn *to see the light and shade upon objects*. When your eye is trained to see light and shade, you can draw the hair as in the second Nietzsche, and you can see planes in the face, as in the Malthus.

Although the David d'Angers diagrams were drawn to show the general masses of the head as they are brought out in successive stages by a sculptor, yet they become very interesting to the printer who has not had the benefit of an art school education, for they show him at a glance how much of the character of the human head is dependent upon the different planes of the face, and it explains better than words what is meant by planes. Chapter VIII should be read in connection with it, and the Vallotton portraits, especially that of Malthus, may be examined critically with this in mind, for you will then see that Vallotton has introduced masses of black with the idea of suggesting planes in the face.

We introduce the de Chaume to accompany the David d'Angers, Lormier and d'Illzach medallions, to emphasize the matter of the planes of the human face.

{137}

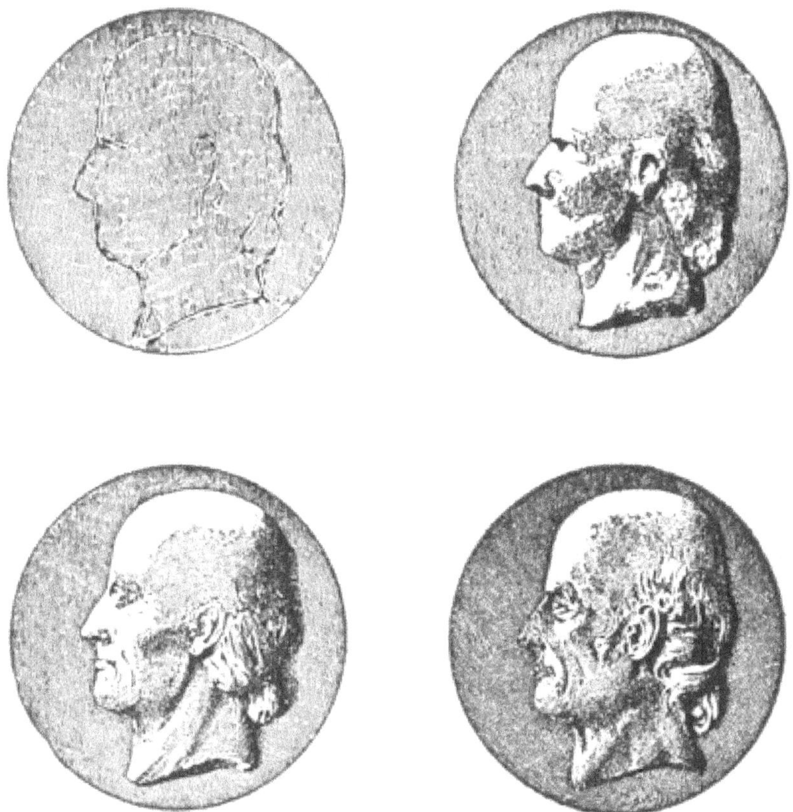

Medallion portrait of Hahnemann, after David d'Angers. Drawing by Carl Robert. Showing successive stages in modeling, from the flat to the relief.

We do not want our readers to think that the shadows we have pointed out in our text are the only ones to be noticed in the human face. Under certain circumstances, notably when an actor's face is illuminated by the footlights, there are shadows upon it quite different from those we have analyzed in previous chapters. But the shadows we have pointed out are those most prominent in a photograph, and those most frequently employed by the artist, but if your drawing is to be very extensive you must learn to look for new shadows in new aspects; and the de Chaume shows some such shadows, yet in the case of the naso-labial line it is easy to see that

{138}

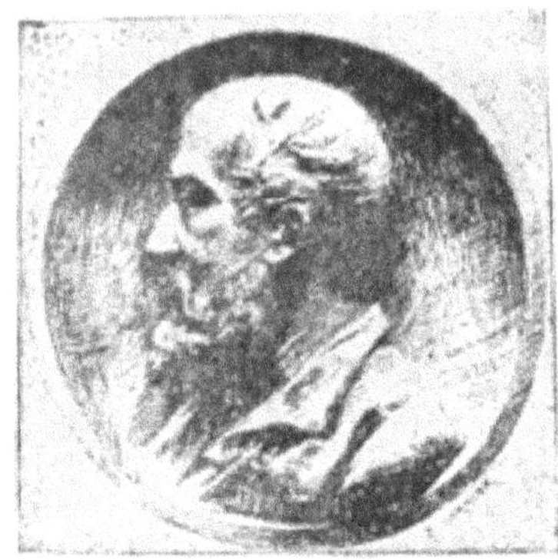

Crayon drawing, from a medallion of Alf. Leroux, by E. Lormier. Drawn on stipple tinted board; or else on plain paper, and the mechanical stipple added to the same after the drawing was made.

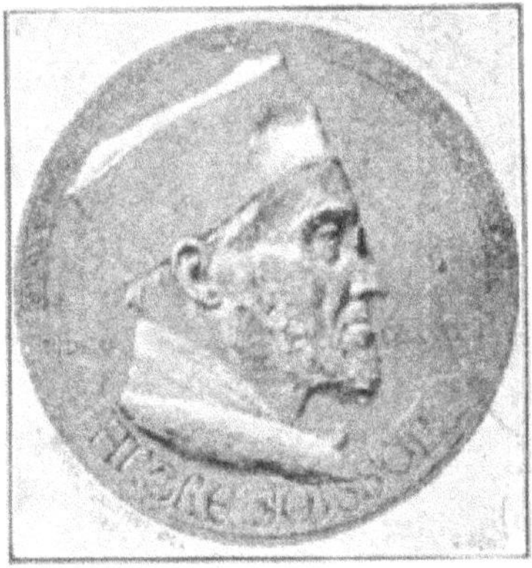

Medallion portrait of M. A. Soisson, by Ringel d'Illzach. Drawn by the sculptor on scratchboard with horizontal line tint, the blacks drawn with crayon, the whites scratched out with a penknife. As in the Monet, our engraver, instead of reducing the cut by the direct process, reduced it by half-tone, through a screen with diagonal lines, hence the horizontal lines have disappeared. (See page 148)

{139} it is not far different from other naso-labial lines which we have considered.

Again, much of our instruction has been given using the human face as a basis of study; but it is not for a moment to be surmised that the study of drawing should be limited to the human face. We have intended only to suggest a process of study; this process may be

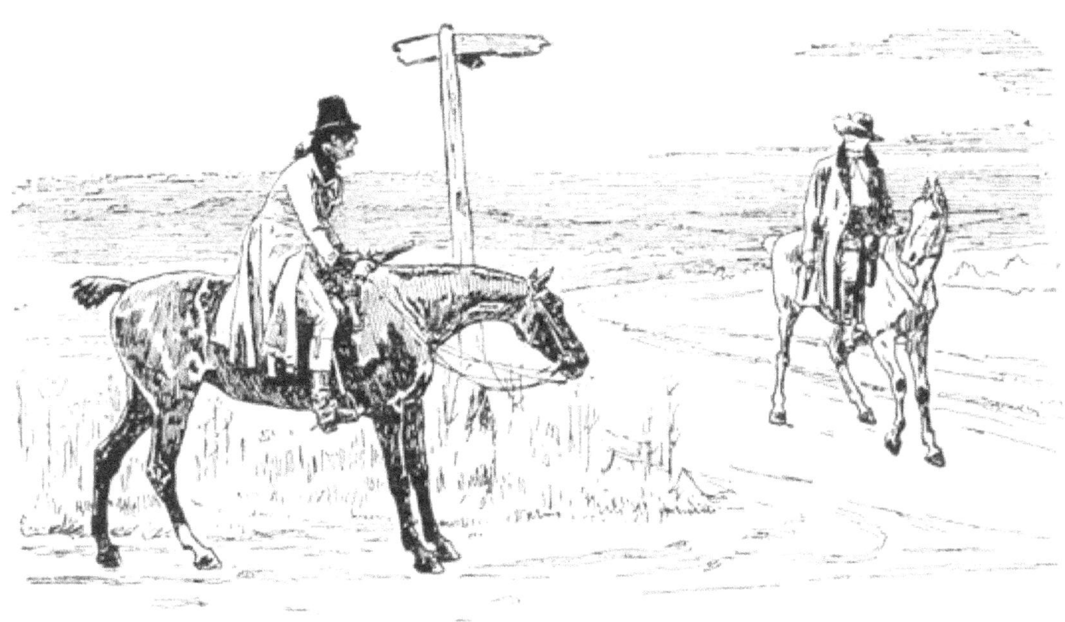

"HAWKS DINNA PIKE OUT HAWKS' EEN."

J. C. DOLLMAN, R.I.

Pen drawing from the artist's water color, made for an exhibition catalogue. This cut shows an excellent style of newspaper drawing, consisting of outline, and a gray got by parallel lines, without crosshatching.

applied to anything under the sun. Hence we give the Forain and the Le Roux outline to portray still life and landscape. And it is worthy of note that still life need not be circumscribed to mere drill; on the contrary, it is very frequently introduced into drawing—much to the perfecting of the composition. The dishpans, pots

{140}

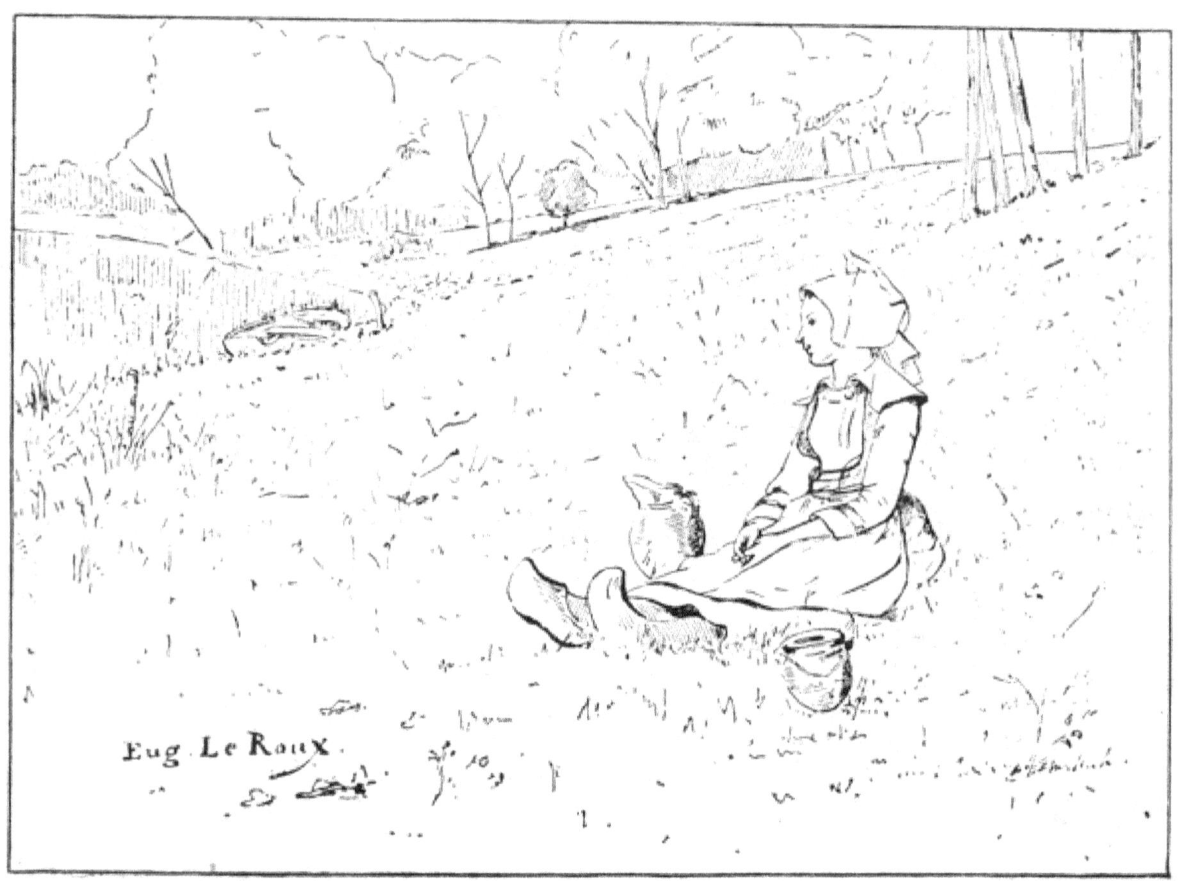

ON THE BANKS OF THE ISOLE. BY E. LE ROUX.
Pen drawing by the artist from his painting.

{141}

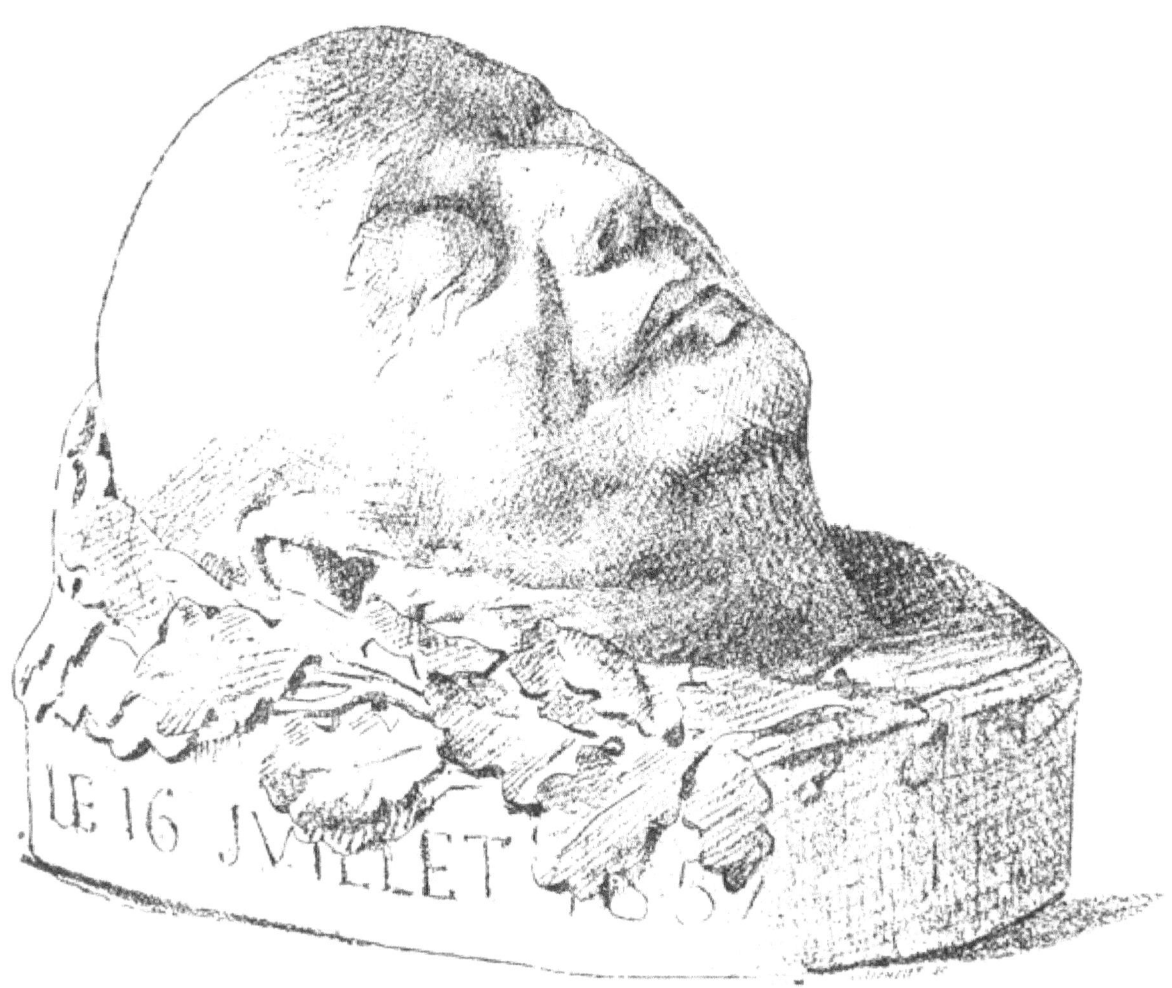

Mask of Béranger. Drawing by Geoffroy de Chaume. Drawn by the sculptor from his model, with (lithographic) crayon, on grained paper with a specially prepared tooth.

{142}

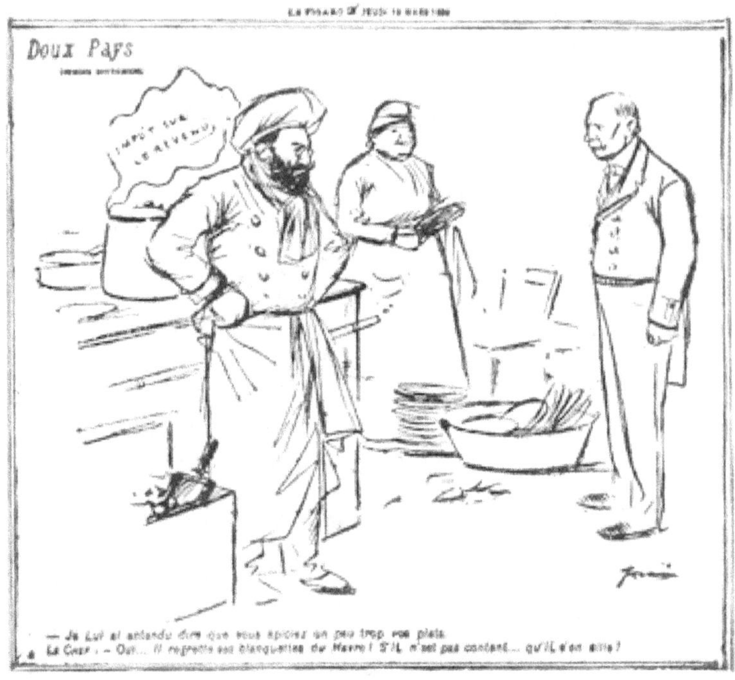

Newspaper caricature, by Forain, from *Figaro*. The butler says: "I have heard him say that you spice your dishes too much." The chef says: "Yes, he misses his Blanchette du Havre." (Some local hit, blanchette in cookery being a wrapper of pastry, bacon, etc.) "If he is not satisfied why doesn't he leave?" There are few draughtsmen in the world more expert in the use of line than Forain. He is most wonderful in his construction of forms; every line means something. The French do not mind a free line—one that runs a little too far out—if it has meaning to it; hence we see a line through the butler's nose, and his mouth extends to the right of the naso-labial line in quite an unnatural fashion, but since the line of the cheek is beautifully attached to the eyesocket and upper eyelid, it does not annoy the French at all.

{143}

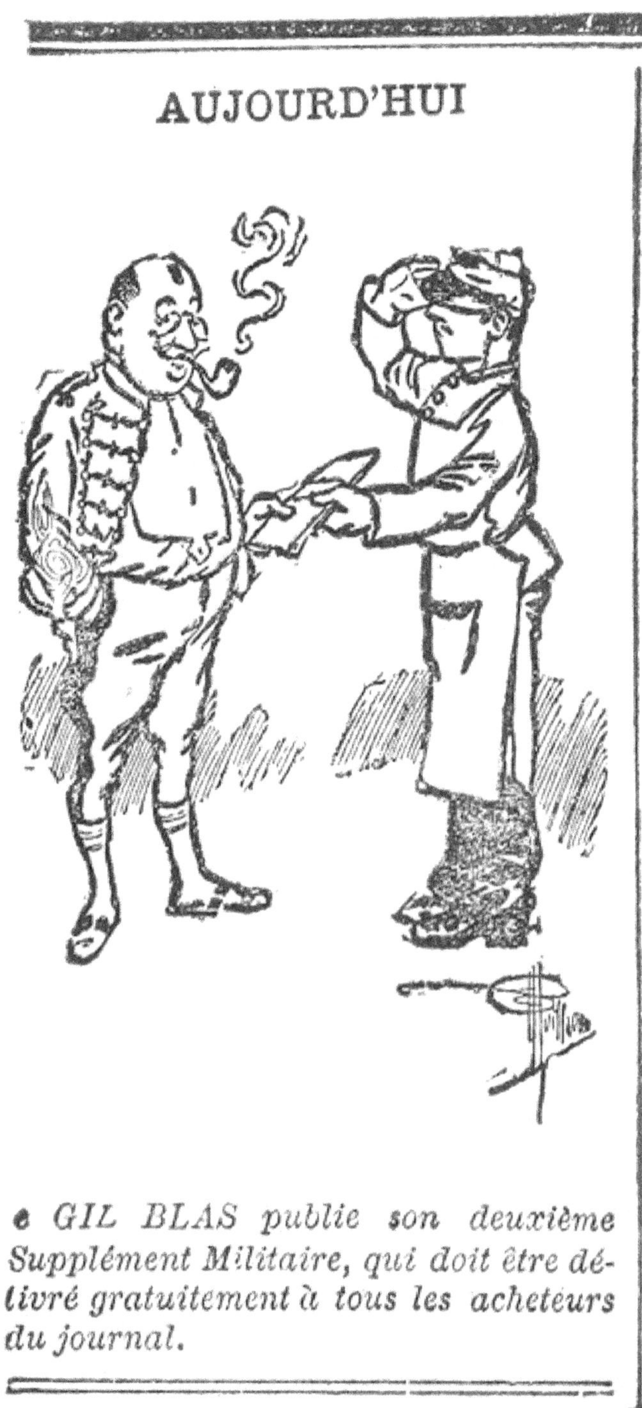

e GIL BLAS publie son deuxième Supplément Militaire, qui doit être délivré gratuitement à tous les acheteurs du journal.

Pen drawing by Guillaume, from the French daily paper *Gil Blas*. This is given as a good example of newspaper work of a kind that could be easily imitated on chalk plate. It is reproduced with adjacent head-line and type that you may get an idea of the typographical appearance of the French newspaper. The legend says: "Today *Gil Blas* publishes its twelfth supplement, which should be delivered gratuitously (by the news agents) to all the purchasers of the paper." The cut, then, is merely a little joke to call attention to the more important supplement inside, which supplement in itself is a pictorial one; French readers are fonder of illustrations than American readers.

{144}

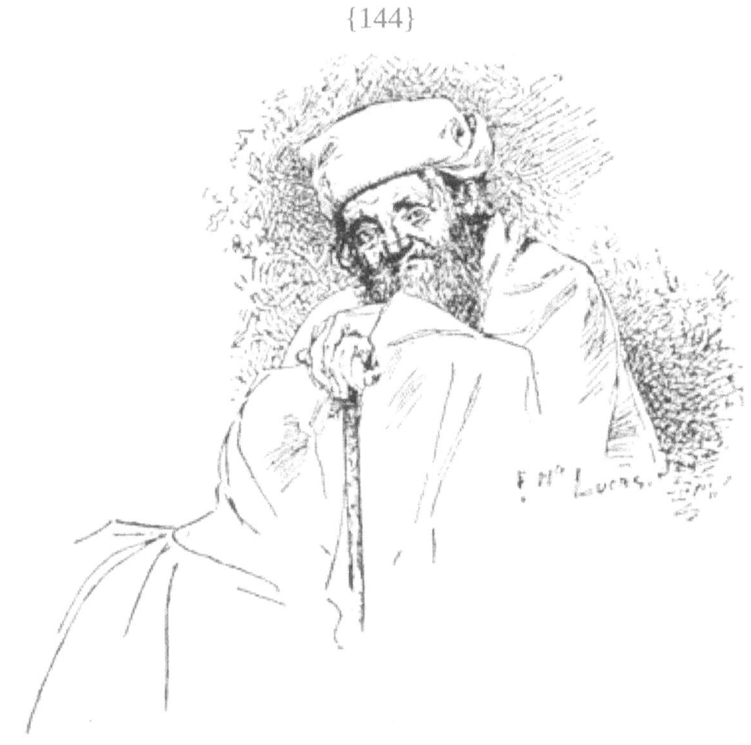

An example of pen drawing. Book illustration, by F. H. Lucas. This shows splendid modeling with very delicate pen work, and a certain amount of variety in the background. It is less adaptable to newspaper work than our other illustrations. It is given as a specimen of eccentric line work as regards the background, which is not unlike the Moullier.

and coal shovel, in the Forain, are particularly suggestive from this view-point. The Le Roux is given in order that our text-book may include an example of landscape, and also that the pupil may realize that drawing is frequently a matter of the right line in the right place. As we said in Chapter XIII, just as we studied the matter of the naso-labial line, and the orbicular muscle, one should study the direction of the wickers of a trash basket, so the artist has studied here the characteristic lines of tree trunk, foliage, hillside, and grasses. If you will study a city street or a shipyard in the same spirit—that is, search for the characteristic lines—you will be able to make a drawing which, even though it lacks

{145}

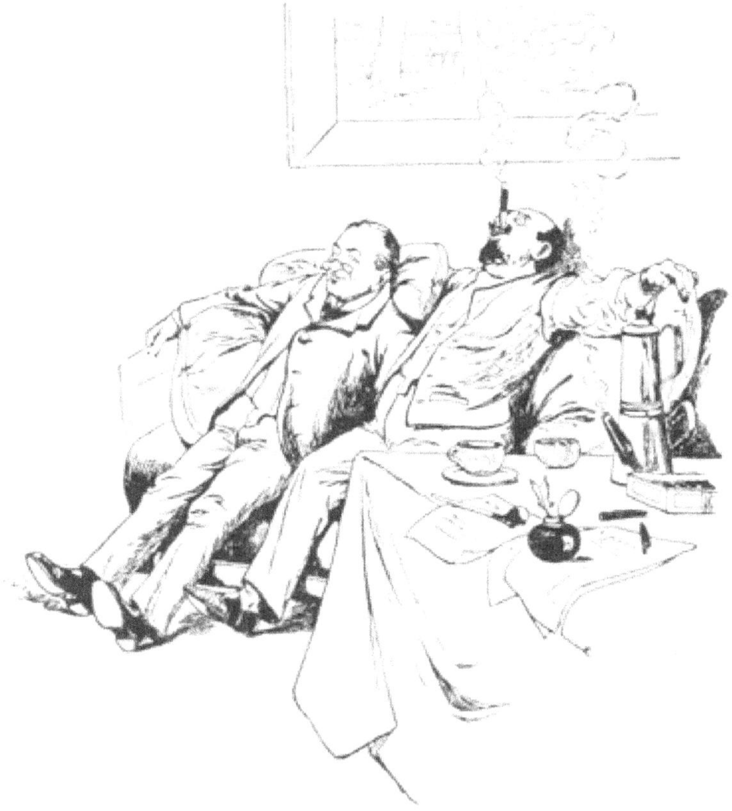

Illustration from the *Paris Illustré*. An example of combined use of outline, parallel lines and solid black, with very little crosshatch. Mainly interesting because of the introduction of still-life objects, which hint at subjects suitable for practice. The novice would do well to select a group of similar objects and endeavor to render them in a similar manner.

artistic finish, will have a certain graphic value; and for this very reason (we mean, to show that outline may be graphic) we purposely introduce into this chapter the Paul caricatures, consisting mainly of outlines, like those we gave in our first chapters, and we bid you harp upon them with the fact ever in your mind that they are not arbitrary, but each line stands for some prototype in nature; and that we may go a little farther in the analyzation of the face, we publish some models in relief in which the planes of the face are brought out. These planes were considered in Chapter VII, and you must

{146}

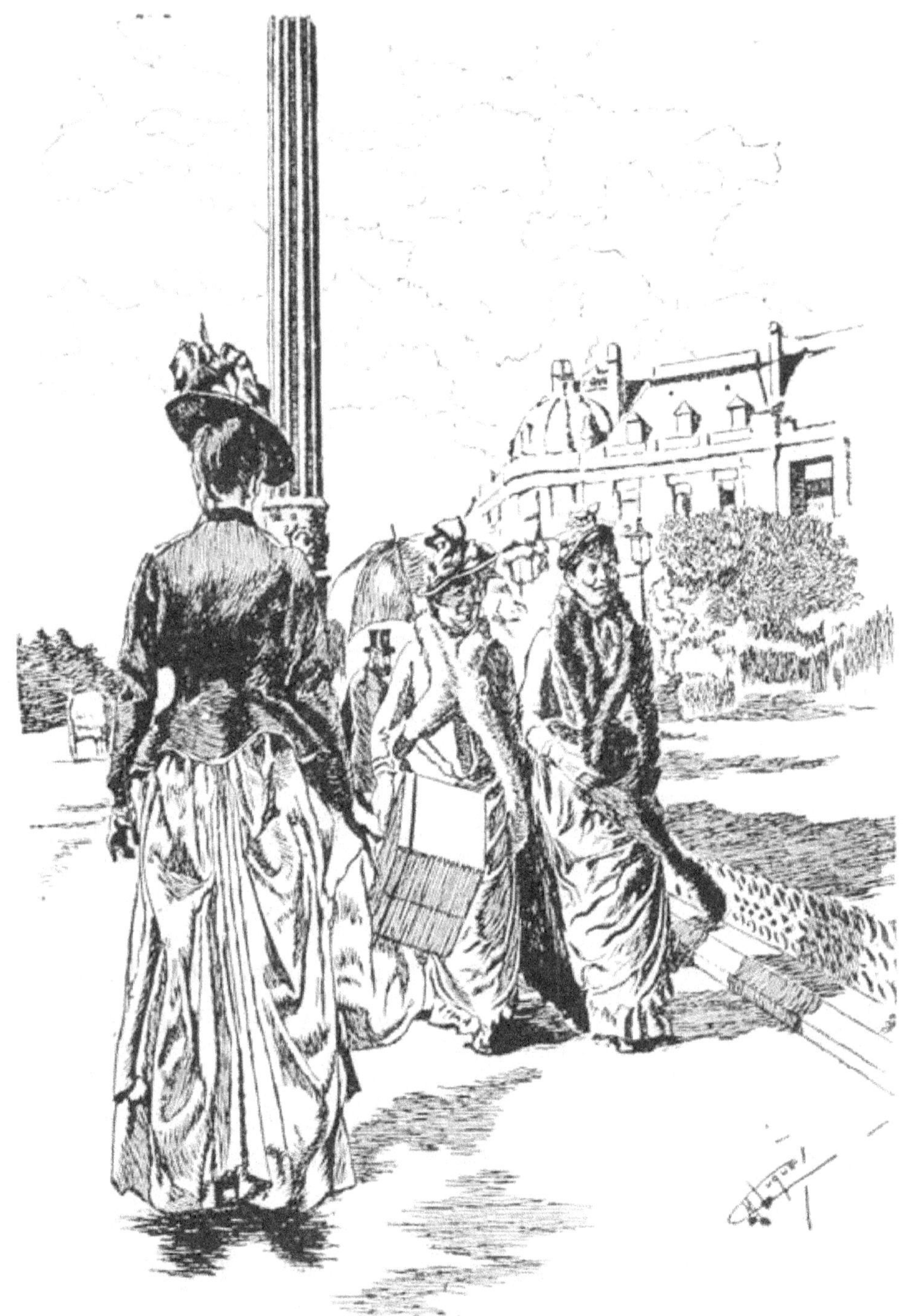

Illustration from *Paris Illustré*. Pen drawing, by M. Luque, evidently from an instantaneous photograph, containing all the elements of pen drawing without crosshatch. This has been reduced too much; the shadows in the building seem black because the lines have run together. In the original illustration the lines on the building were separated, and the effect was one of gray, which is the right tone for shadows seen at a distance on a clear day. The outlines of the clouds were probably drawn with an unbroken line, and after they were engraved were rouletted on the plate, and hence print as a series of dots.

A Practical Treatise Of Designing And Illustration

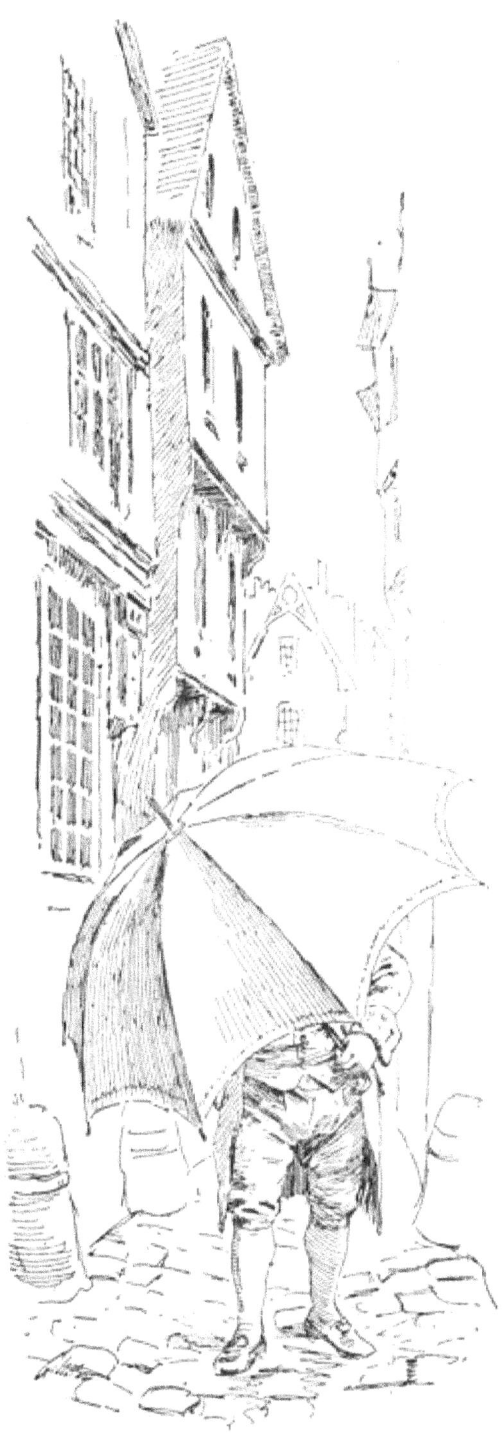

Pen drawing, by Maurice Leloir, showing admirable effect gained by use of parallel lines without crosshatch; a splendid example for the novice to study.

{148} look at Fantin-La-Tour's cast head in order to understand them. Do so, and then let your eye jump to the Vallotton heads, and we think you will grasp their characteristics immediately, for you will see wherein they differ from the Engström drawings. They differ in this: that in addition to pure outline, they mass the constructive shadows found in the David d'Angers. In other

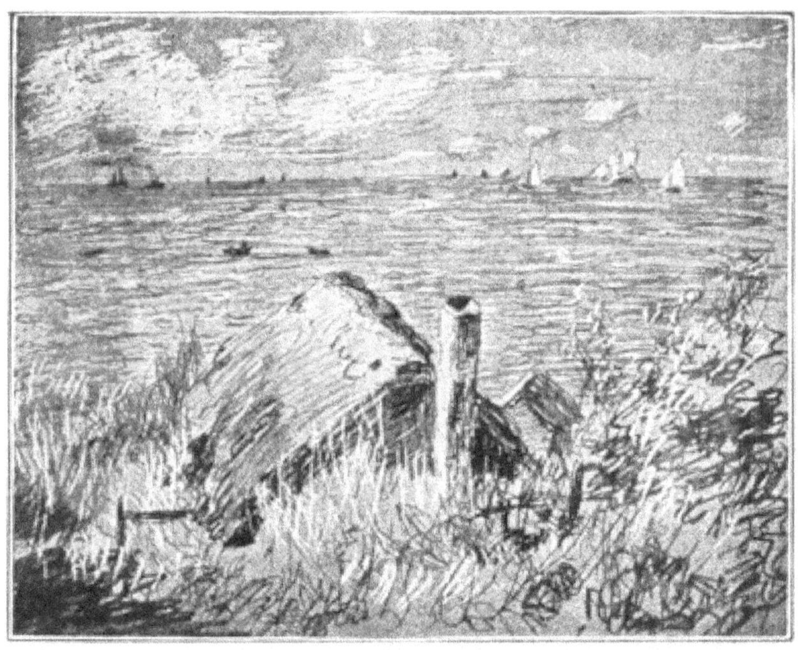

Marine, by Claude Monet. Drawn with lithographic crayon on scratchboard, the lines running perpendicularly, instead of horizontally as in the d'Illzach, the lights scratched out with the penknife.

This cut has a peculiar interest technically. The foregoing was dictated with the original in hand, which was a direct process cut in which one set of lines ran perpendicularly. Our engraver, however, instead of reducing the cut by the direct process, reduced it by half-tone, through a screen with diagonal lines, hence the perpendicular lines have disappeared.

words, the black under Vallotton's eyebrows does not mean that his eyebrows are abnormally thick, but it means that he has deep sunken eyes, and that there is

{149}

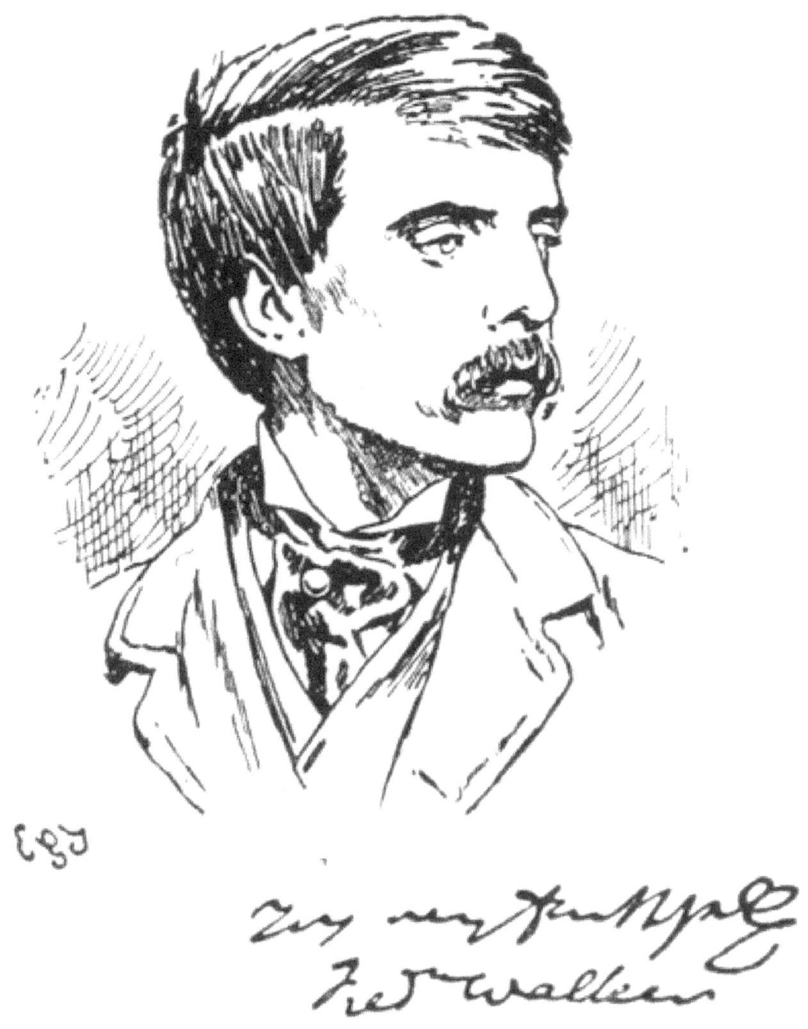

Portrait of Fred Walker, by E. G. T., from an English periodical. Reduced to a smaller area than when given in Chapter XI. By comparing this with the cut on page 102 we notice that the drawing is so simple that there is very little difference in the general aspect of the two, but here and there, as under the jaw, the lines have run together a little more in the smaller cut, giving a darker effect than in the larger one; the lesson is obvious.

a shadow under the eyebrows and in the plane of the superior orbicular muscle, which recedes, and Vallotton wishes to emphasize this. And in the Malthus he does not mean that Malthus had a triangular birth-mark on his right cheek, but he means that he had a prominent cheekbone, and a sunken cheek beneath it; hence the shadow, which is what we call "a modeling shadow."

{150}

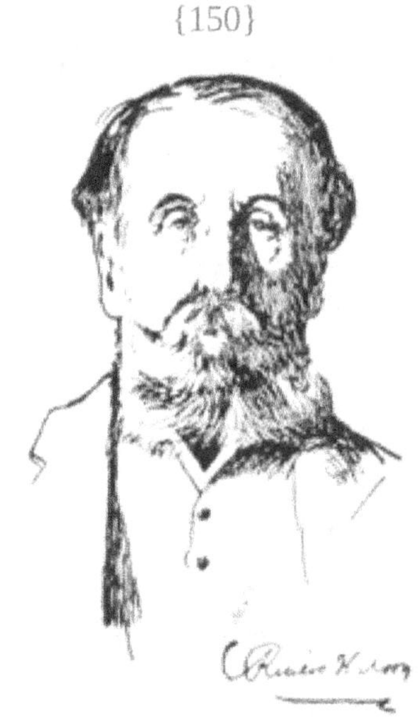

Portrait of C. Rivers Wilson. Pen drawing by Walter Sickert. From *The London Whirlwind*, 1890. Reduced to a smaller area than when given in Chapter XII. By comparing this with the cut on page 119 you will see that many of the lines, especially in the shadow of the nose, have run together, and we do not find as strong a contrast between the black accents on the nose and the gray half-tones produced by the open lines in the larger cut. It is often the case when a drawing is too greatly reduced that it loses snap, because the *graduation* from the grays to the blacks is not so perceptible as in the original. Still the lines were so open in this drawing that the present cut is a very fair one. The result is much better than could have been got from so fine a drawing as the Renard. (See page 114.)

We cannot complete our chapter without mentioning that the styles of drawing we have suggested by no means exhaust the different methods at your disposal. While it is well to confine yourself to outline, or outline and solid black, or outline and slight shading, yet you may experiment in many more complicated methods, as seen in the Monet, and the Ringel d'Illzach, for even if you do not use these methods for illustrations they help you to observe the capital lights and darks in nature.

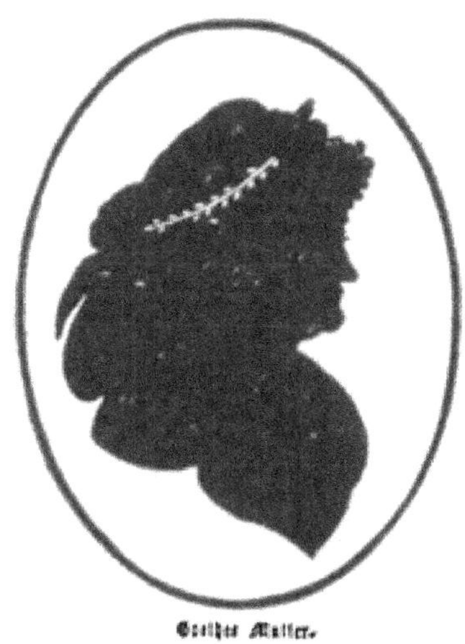

GOETHE'S MOTHER.
Old-fashioned silhouette. See chapter on wood engraving.

CHAPTER I.
INTRODUCTION TO PART II.

INSTRUCTION IN DRAWING ABANDONED AND DESIGN CONSIDERED — THIS INSTRUCTION LESS ABSOLUTE THAN INSTRUCTION IN DRAWING — THE PRINTER TO USE AS MUCH OF THE SUBSEQUENT MATTER AS SERVES HIS PURPOSE — IN THE STUDY OF LETTERING ALL STYLES HAVE TO BE COVERED, THOUGH ONLY ONE OR TWO MAY BE OF VALUE TO THE PRINTER — WOOD ENGRAVING VALUABLE BECAUSE IT TEACHES CONCENTRATION AND ECONOMY OF LINE — THE PRINTER IN AMERICA NOT ABLE TO BE ALWAYS ARTISTIC, BUT MUST INTRODUCE ART FROM TIME TO TIME AS OPPORTUNITY ARISES.

THE READER is asked to view this second part of "Drawing for Printers" differently from the first part. In the first part the writer aimed at establishing {154} recognized rules for drawing rather than giving his individual opinions.

He thinks that very little of the first part of the book can be questioned. For example, it is not a matter of personal opinion that the horizon line is on a level with the spectator's eyes, or that a mantelshelf on such a level should be drawn with a straight line; it is a matter of fact, which he merely reiterates as the writer of a grammar reiterates the indisputable facts of a language, that a noun is a name word, a verb an action word, an adverb a word which qualifies a verb. But when the writer of a literary text-book has exhausted his rules of grammar and takes up the subject of rhetoric, although he endeavors to give only such examples of writing as are excellent, still his own personal taste is apt to guide him in his selections, and he may claim as admirable that which is to be criticised. A rhetoric of the eighteenth century would necessarily contain much artificial, sentimental and Latinized English which a teacher of today would not put before his students.

So it is that in the following chapters I may advocate,

(1) That which may not meet with the approval of my readers.

(2) That which may not suit my readers' customers, and even

(3) That which is wrong.

You therefore may use as much of my advice as you find practical in your daily work, and discard that which is impractical. {155}

But do not forget that that which may be impractical today may come in handy some time next year!

That there will be much that you will find impractical goes without saying. It is absolutely necessary that the student of the arts (as the writer of these papers) acquaint himself with that which is classical; he then becomes fascinated with it and recommends it. But the classical covers an immense field, embracing that which is best in many ages and in many different lands, and it is utterly impossible that the practical worker in the arts should utilize all the classical styles at one time. Hence only a fragment of any text-book built upon the study of the classic can be practical at any given time.

Let us be more specific. Let us take the department of lettering alone. If an author publishes a work on lettering, and he is a cultivated man, he must examine the many styles of the past. He examines the monumental letter of classic Rome and the monumental letter of the Renaissance; the Caroline letter of 700 A. D., as well as the Gothic and the Visigothic. It is not his business to place one above the other, but to explain the beauty of all. If, however, you are a printer of today, and the Morris style of type is most in vogue, and you have stocked your cases with it, it is the Gothic letter you are most interested in, because it is what you are using and what your customer has just been trained to like; so the most practical part of a book on lettering would be that which would treat of the Gothic letter, and its offspring, the Old English; while the chapter on Visigothic, with its twisted letters, would seem quite

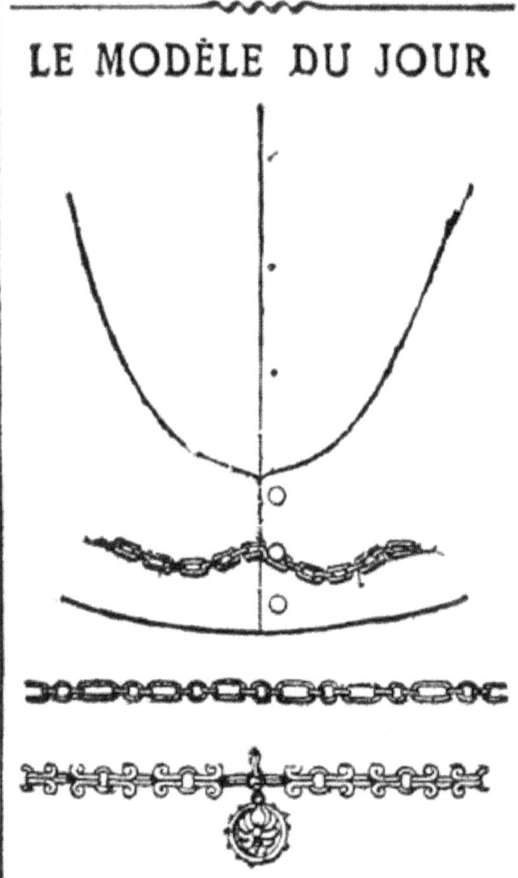

LE MODÈLE DU JOUR

Un peu de modes masculines.
Depuis un certain temps, la chatne de montre avait disparu. Elle était proscrite. Pourquoi? Par une de ces fantaisies de la mode qui ne s'expliquent jamais.
Par une autre fantaisie la chatne revient en faveur. Je donne aujourd'hui le modèle exact du gilet avec la coupe, dernier genre, et la chatne, telle qu'il est de bon goût de la porter.
Pour les chatnes, deux types. A l'une d'elles se trouve un pendant dont les enroulements rappellent notre agrafe moderne. L'autre est une chatne simple sans agrément et qui semble destinée à obtenir la préférence.

C. Duhamel.

NEWSPAPER ILLUSTRATION.

From the Paris *Figaro*, showing harmony of drawing, type, and rules—a method of drawing that could easily be imitated on chalk plate.

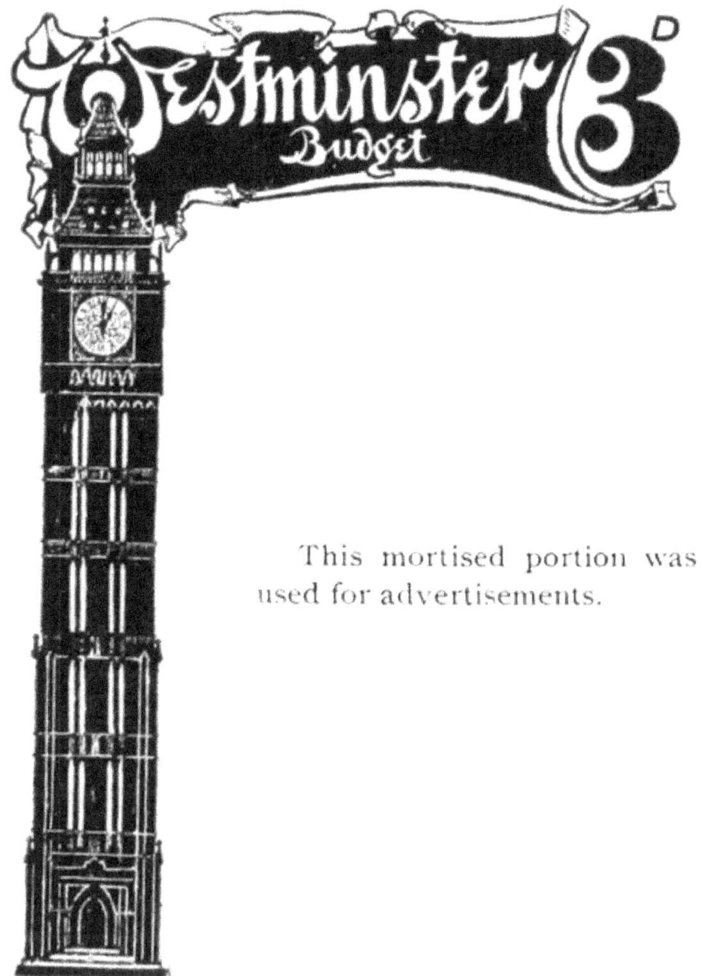

COVER DESIGN OF THE WESTMINSTER BUDGET.

Printed on light weight yellow paper, 10 by 13. An excellent example of the use of silhouette in design.

{158} impractical to you as you could not use the examples given. Yet it would be the business of the writer on alphabets to analyze them thoroughly, otherwise his work would be incomplete.

Now then, I shall try to be practical, and in the chapter on lettering bear in mind that the modern fonts are the Morris, Caxton, Jenson, Erhard Ratdolt, Old English and Touraine. I shall try to give a little more attention to the letters after which these are patterned than I shall to the Phœnician or Etruscan, the Visigothic, the Aldine, and the Irish text letter. But, on the other hand, no printer can be educated without knowing something about these latter alphabets. And so you must bear with me while I analyze them, though they may not be practical.

Once more, suppose you do agree that a style of lettering not now in vogue is a pleasing style, and one worth imitating, the question arises, How much time can you give to the study of it in order to use it? Nearly all artistic work requires hand labor, and hand labor is slow.

In our chapter on wood engraving, we shall recommend the study of that art, both because it can be used and because it trains you to appreciate good designing; but how many printers can neglect their business in order to spend hours and hours in practicing an eminently slow art, when rapid and cheap photo-engraving will serve the purpose almost as well? Very few, I fear.

So, also, when we come to the matter of taste, we come to the question of what should artistic printing {159} look like? Even if you are convinced that coated paper and the half-tone do not belong to ideal printing, how many can afford to attempt a piece of rough printing with heavy type, coarse paper and an outline device, and expect to retain his customers, when his rival, Smith, is using coated paper and half-tones that almost equal photographs? Very few printers, I fear, would be able to pay expenses by such a course. There are very few merchants but would have their catalogues printed by Smith with half-tone illustrations of photographs of their wares. Or even if the printer does not apply his art methods to job printing, but to his own publications, he will probably find few buyers who are cultured enough to appreciate his rough printing, so between the amount of time necessary for preparing artistic productions and the poor chance they have of receiving patronage, it is very difficult for a cultured printer to attain his ideal.

The writer has followed our art periodicals for years and knows too well that nearly all of them have failed. If artistic periodicals advertised for years to art-loving people have failed, how little is the chance of art methods succeeding with the people! We must, then, bear in mind that I may recommend methods because I know them to be artistic without expecting them to be accepted or put in practice.

The practical printer's course must be a compromise. He introduces an artistic principle here, another there, without ever reaching his ideal.

Sometimes it is his own circular, sometimes a literary pamphlet, or {160} sometimes a poster that allows him to experiment, while his average printing is commercial, nothing more.

But, let us say in parenthesis, that while we deprecate the lack of artistic culture that prevents our printers from turning out artistic work, we do not for a moment claim that that which is not artistic is poor, or that all printing that is not rough is not artistic. The half-tone and coated paper have their use. If, as a matter of news or information, exactness is required, any sensible printer will turn to the half-tone for assistance. Even Mr. Walter Crane, in publishing his book on "Decorative Illustration," though he uses 303 pages of rough paper to exemplify the superiority of the simple wood cut of the past, employs eleven sheets of highly calendered paper to reproduce delicate facsimiles of old manuscripts! He felt that the purpose of these supplementary pages was to illustrate and not to embellish the book; so he sacrificed artistic harmony for science. So, also, a printer does well, when getting up a catalogue of houses, horses or chickens for sale, to insert a frontispiece of coated paper and print on the same a half-tone which gives an adequate idea of the house, horse or chicken to be sold. That is a scientific piece of work. The point is, that a catalogue printed on cheap paper with an insert of a half-tone printed on coated paper can never be an artistic unit, can never be exhibited as a piece of artistic printing. The French, who are extremely artistic people, have carried delicate printing as far as it will go, and the French printer will get you up a catalogue with a half-tone {161} frontispiece, but everything will be in harmony with it; the paper of the body of the book is coated paper, the type is delicate, the initial letters are equally fine, and the printing of the entire brochure is so delicate that it is in keeping with the frontispiece. That is the right principle for bookmaking, that the work be harmonious. There is no objection to fine type (so long as it is not so fine as to tire the eyes) if it is printed properly. The main reason for recommending such heavy type as Morris' is, that it is pretty sure always to print well. When a French printer turns out a cheap newspaper he uses large type and heavy headlines, accompanied by illustrations that harmonize with such type and headlines.

Our examples of Forain's work (see previous chapters) show the style of the French drawing made for the daily newspaper in harmony with the typography and in a suitable manner for printing on poor stock. The clipping from the French newspaper we give with this chapter, showing different styles of watch chains, is an excellent example of good taste in this direction. The type, the drawing, and the rules all harmonize. With a chalk-plate outfit a clever printer could supply such diagrams for his paper each week without feeling that he was transgressing the canons of the highest form of art.

From this example it will be seen that one of the requirements for a good newspaper drawing is that it harmonizes with the type page. You may feel then that it is not required of you to make a finished drawing for {162} a newspaper—in fact, the more finished it is the less likely it is to be a good newspaper design.

Another example of good newspaper designing is the *Westminster Budget* cover. The original covered a folio 10 by 13 inches. The paper being a cheap stock (yellow) and the design being bold and effective, serves as an admirable example of what we choose to call a poor-paper design.

This design will in future be again considered in connection with wood engraving and lettering; and in the next chapter we shall consider similar headings and covers.

CHAPTER II.

THE MATTER OF TASTE AGAIN UNDER REVIEW — "MAGAZINE," "CITY NEWSPAPER" AND "COUNTRY NEWSPAPER PRINTING," ARBITRARY TERMS — A STYLE OF DESIGN APPROPRIATE FOR CERTAIN KINDS OF PERIODICALS MAY NOT BE APPROPRIATE FOR OTHER KINDS — SOME GENERAL PRINCIPLES OF DESIGNING — A BROAD, BLACK LINE DESIRABLE FOR LETTERING, "DEVICES" AND DESIGNS IN GENERAL; A FINE LINE MAY BE USED FOR ILLUSTRATIVE CUTS — BOLD MASSES OF LIGHT AND DARK APPROPRIATE FOR ROUGH PRINTING — THE APPROPRIATENESS OF THE DESIGNS FOR JUGEND, PAN, LA REVUE ENCYCLOPÉDIQUE, ETC., CONSIDERED.

I SUPPOSE a very orderly writer would have finished his introduction in the last chapter, beginning in this with definite instruction. But I feel so overwhelmingly the importance of the subject treated of in the last chapter —that is, the matter of taste—that I must before proceeding add a few more words to the subject. Besides, further review will strengthen the reader's understanding of my principle of instruction, which is that the fitness of things, the taste which you display in following a certain kind of design, is as much a matter of study as is the drawing of an object.

For example, I used the words in the last chapter, "printing on rough paper." Now, of course, that {164} term is indefinite, and, like our terms "magazine," "city newspaper" and "country newspaper" printing, can stand only for some style of printing agreed upon

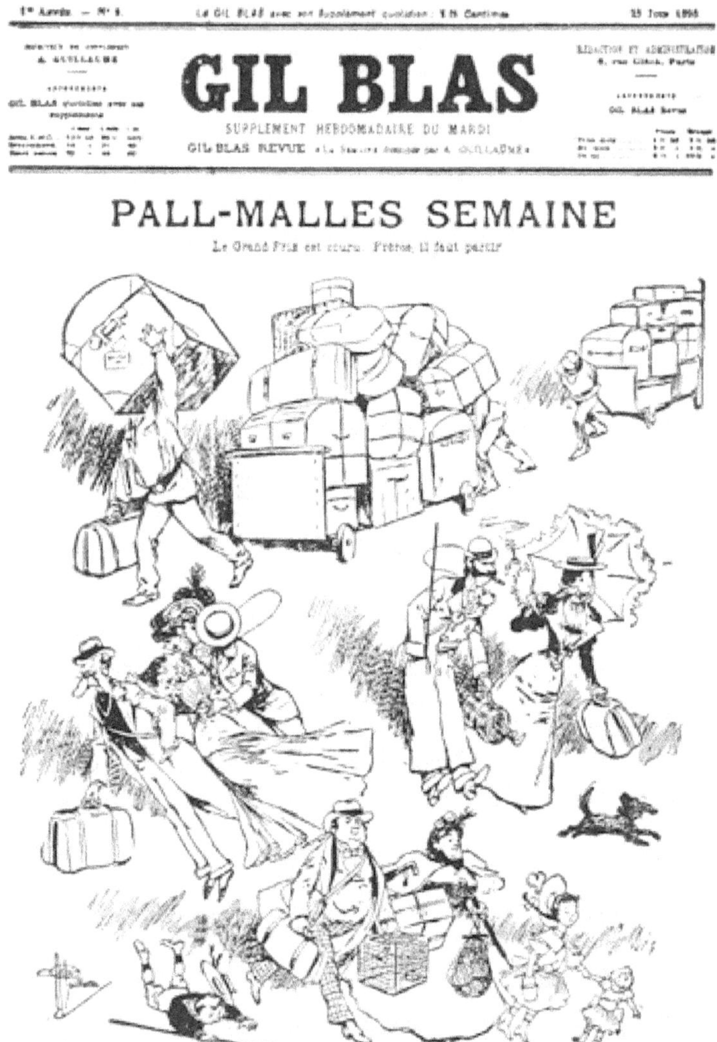

Front page of the French weekly, *Gil Blas*. Originally 10 3/4 inches by 15 3/4. This shows an excellent arrangement of type for the heading and subtitles. Also, the front page cartoon, done in excellent style, shows the use of outline and solid blacks on the main objects, with a little parallel lining behind the objects. The title means, "The Week in Pall Mall," i. e., in London. "The Grand Prix [that is, the Spring race, the Derby] has been run; brothers, we must depart."

by the writer and reader. Therefore, if you will allow, the term "rough printing" will stand for printing corresponding to all that done prior to the introduction of {165} coated paper, and where the type used was long primer or larger. And I choose, as a matter of taste, to insist upon it that all printing is bad that is not done in this way. Now, do not set me down as a faddist. I am not thoroughly converted to Morris' printing, because in his matter the words are so closely run together that they are not read with ease, and, above all things, I do not consider the so-called "deckle-edge, handmade paper"—which in all probability is never handmade—such an "artistic" cloak to cover a multitude of sins as many printers consider it. The very fact that it is artificial and imitative makes it as objectionable as coated paper, which also is artificial and insincere.

The matter can be explained in this way: We may have no objection to a dress suit and high silk hat. We recognize in it as legitimate a style of dress as the workingman's overalls; but we do not like to see a man working in a ditch clothed in a dress suit and silk hat. With this objection almost everyone will agree. But there are those who, wishing to follow the dictates of society, do not like to see a man, even if he is a lecturer or a bridegroom, disporting himself in a dress suit and silk hat at any hour of the day earlier than six o'clock.

Now, there are two distinct lines of judgment. The first is drawn so broadly that nearly all will agree. The second line is drawn so finely that but few may agree. But it is a fact that in either case the question is a matter of taste. So, then, when I claim that the title of a newspaper should be in heavy type, and not in such script as would be appropriate for a lady's visiting

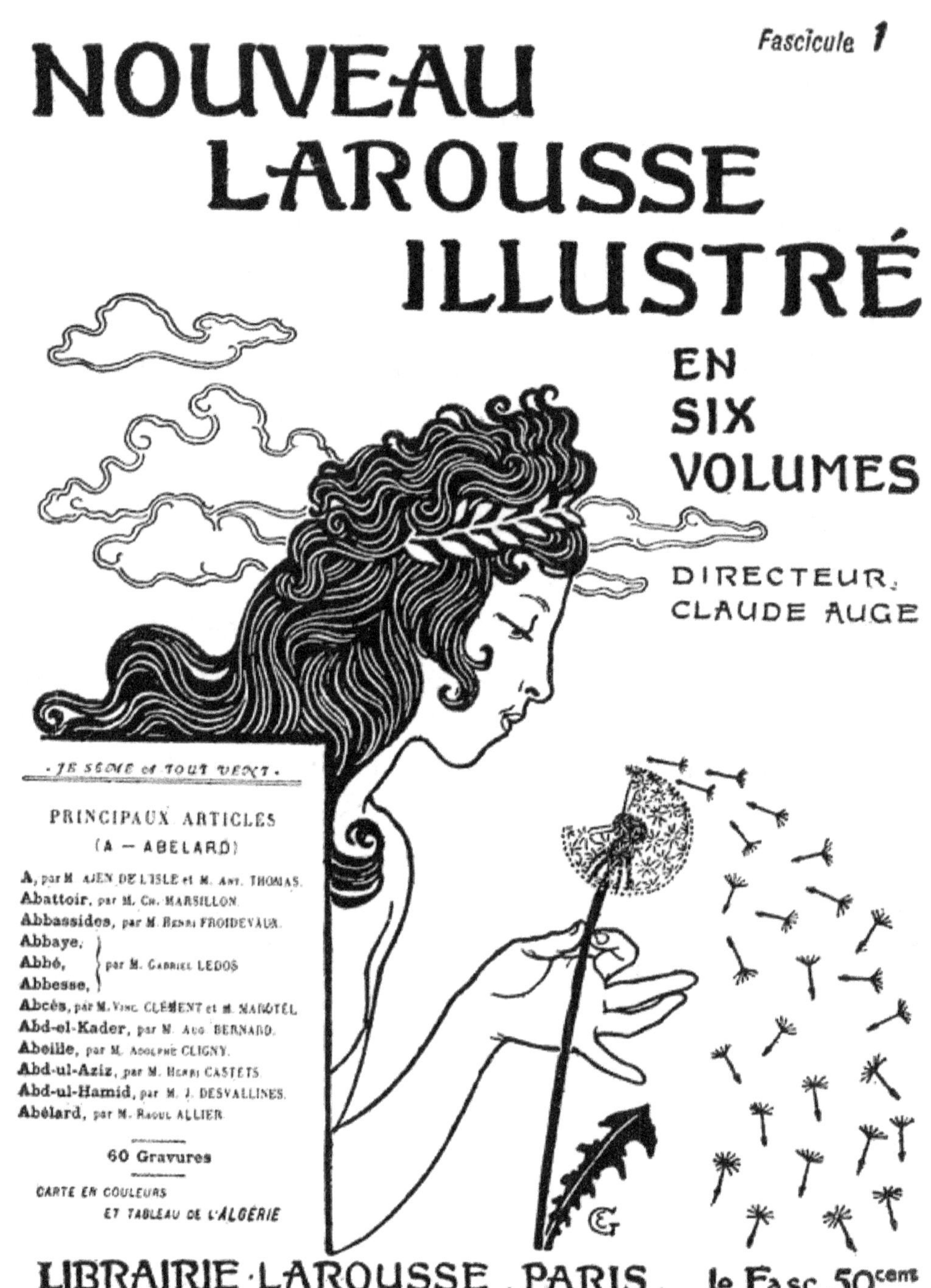

DESIGN FOR THE COVER OF A DICTIONARY, PUBLISHED IN PAPER-COVERED PARTS.

By Eugene Grasset.

Admirable lettering (more closely following the Caroline manuscript than the design for *La Revue Encyclopédique*), united with harmonious design, the artist not being contented merely to introduce a girl with poster-like hair, but bringing out an idea—that of the expansive distribution of knowledge, signified by the dandelion seed, which is freely distributed by the wind; see motto "*Je seme a tout vent*." I sow (or spread) seed with every wind.

{167} card, most of you will agree with me. But when I claim that the title should be in very heavy block type, and not in French Old Style, I shall not have so many followers. Of course, it is true that circumstances alter cases, and while I think it quite necessary that a "Daily News," "Journal" or "Press" should have the heaviest of type, I will acknowledge that a dainty little weekly in 8vo, called "The Needlewoman," or "Embroidery Notes," might be properly printed with a pica italic heading.

I think the reader now understands the object of the second part of "Drawing for Printers," and will see that nearly all the illustrations in it are selected with a view to their appropriateness for rough printing, simply because it is therein that you need to study the subject of designing for printing. It is self-evident that to print a half-tone cut you need calendered or coated paper, and that with this a little half-tone initial letter could be used, but as we study printing on poor stock, familiarity with the styles of the past is necessary to acquaint you with what is best in pictorial, or rather decorative, effect.

This much said, let us fall to considering some principles of designing. Other things being equal, a broad black line is best if there is any shadow or detail in the drawing. But if there is no shadow the outline need not be very heavy, but the drawing may partake of a diagram effect, as in the watch-chain illustration from the *Figaro*, given in a preceding chapter (page 165). Such a thin line harmonizes with the type and does not {168} attract too much attention. It is also well suited for the unimportant elements in a heading design. But if you wish to introduce in a heading an important element like the American eagle, the coat-of-arms of a state, or an emblematic design for a class paper, then a strong line or a solid black is preferable. Strong lines and blacks are also preferable for an initial letter that is to form part of the decoration of a page.

Therefore, if we consider the front page of a paper or catalogue consisting of a heading, an initial letter and an illustration, we may treat each design according to the following principles. If the illustration is to be the main thing, the heading and initial letter would best

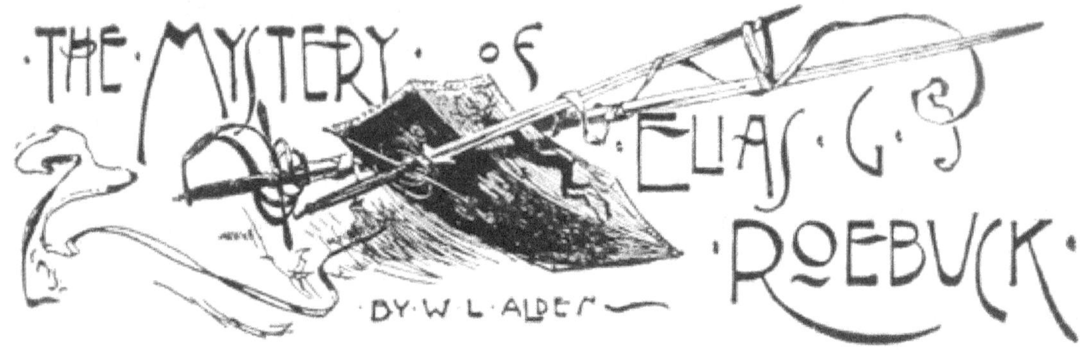

Heading to a novel in *The Pall Mall Budget*, an example of free-hand lettering and device, showing elements suggestive of the subject matter. The lettering is not heavy enough for the title-page of a periodical, nor is it so heavy as to interfere with the effect of the illustration on the same page.

be mostly in outline, as in the *Figaro* watch chains. But if there is no illustration, and we wish the heading and initial letter to be decorative, a heavy outline and solid black may be used. As an example of heavy outline and solid black we have selected the dictionary cover by Grasset. This is strong enough to serve as a heading for a newspaper or periodical, but in the case of a {169} chapter heading such heavy lettering might not be desirable, and the lighter *Pall Mall Budget* design might be preferable. So, too, as in the *Jugend*, since

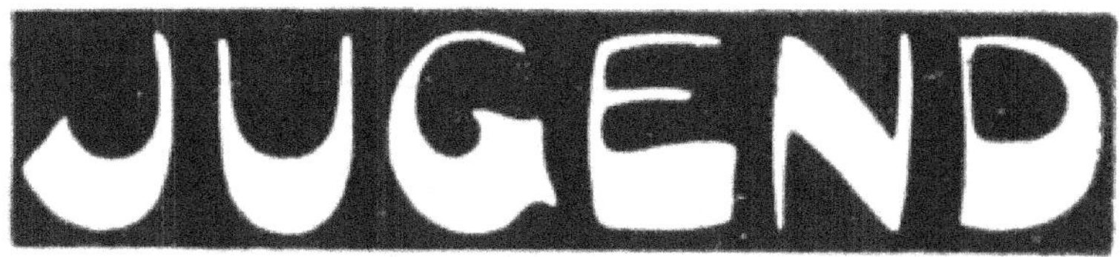

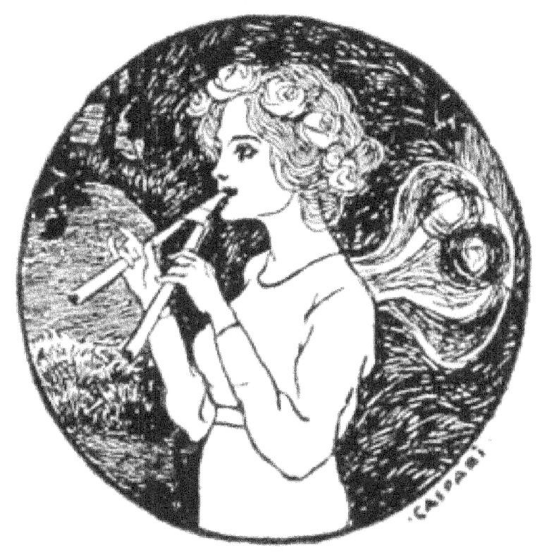

TITLE-PAGE TO VOLUME II OF JUGEND.
Designed by Caspari.
Showing harmonious uniting of free-hand designed letter, type, and device. The device, however, is a little too pictorial; it would be better if its background were simpler.

the illustration is not the most important thing, heavy blacks may be used; it is an excellent example of the {170} proper heaviness of the heading contrasted with an unimportant illustration. Here, however, the black is around, not upon, the letter.

Perhaps one of the most enjoyable features of the printer-designer's work is that of designing covers for booklets and pamphlets. If he does not have to confine himself to a definite idea, he may choose a motive from a thousand and one different elements. Of course, he must be more or less logical in his choice of motive, and not put a Pierrot upon a church fair programme, nor a bunch of violets upon a stove manufacturer's catalogue, though we frequently run across such designing. One of the enemies to good designing is the prevalent taste for photographic half-tone covers, where the stove manufacturer requires the reproduction of his stoves on the cover. Now, we are utterly opposed to this; not on the ground that the picture of a stove is not a fit emblem for a stove manufacturer's catalogue— for it certainly is quite proper—but we object on the ground that the printing of it requires coated paper, which often is not tenacious enough for a cover; and, secondly, on the ground that the delicacy of the half-tone, which has no strong outlines or masses of light or dark, does not make a picture that can be seen at a sufficient distance to warrant its being a cover. The brevier that you use in the body of a book is not the proper type for its cover, and so a delicate half-tone that is appropriate for the reading pages of your catalogue is not appropriate for its cover. The specimens we give in this chapter, therefore, are nearly all of them

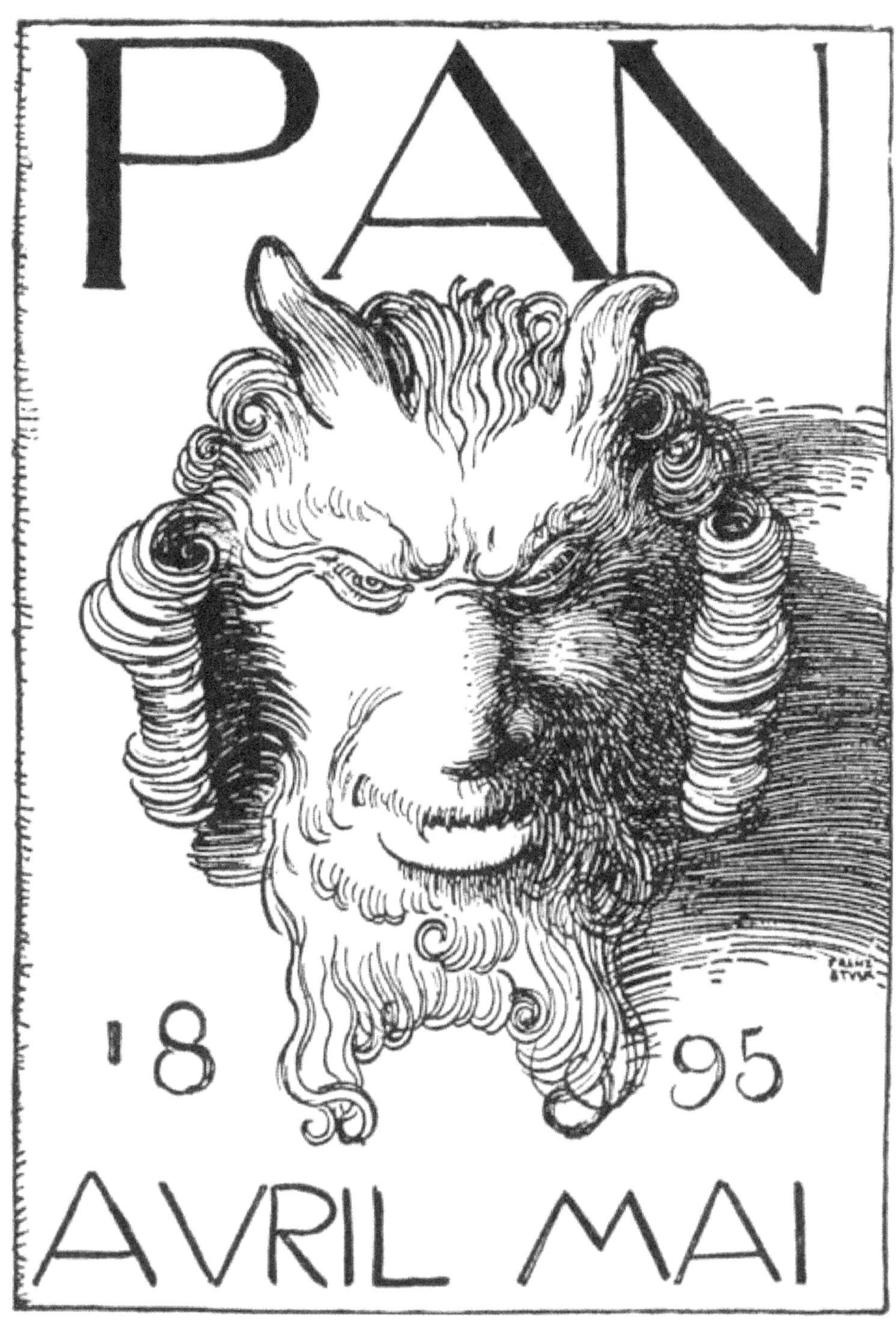

Cover design for a German periodical entitled *Pan*, by Franz Stuck. Original, 8 by 12. Printed in black on heavy green cover paper.

{172}

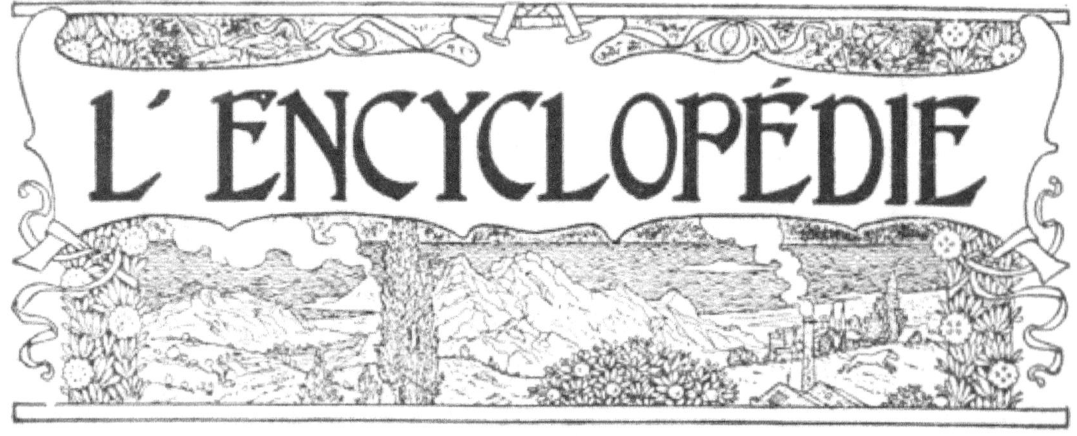

Department heading designed by Eugene Grasset for *La Revue Encyclopédique*, showing an excellent style of lettering (founded on the Caroline), also an admirable decorative outline made to give a finished effect, or an effect of delicacy.

adapted to rough, heavy paper, which will make a durable cover.

The design for *Pan*, by Franz Stuck, is a particularly good example. Possibly the shadow thrown by the head is a disturbing element in the composition; it makes the right-hand side heavy and is not in itself decorative.

The spacing also between the P and the A is greater than between the A and the N, without, so far as we can see, having a valid reason for so being. But the design was for the cover of a publication of artist's sketches, and it was consequently more permissible for the artist to draw with freedom than had he been designing a more conventional cover. Stuck is one of the best letterers in Europe; and, in his more serious moments, is most exact in his spacing. The two most interesting characteristics of the design are the elegance of the letters and the boldness of the drawing of the head; {173} substitute more commonplace lettering as in the "Roebuck" heading (page 168) and such delicate drawing as in the Grasset "Encyclopédie," and the design would lose force as a pamphlet cover.

The *Westminster* design, given on page 157, recommends itself because of the silhouette steeple, which could be easily engraved on wood, and also because of the lettering, which is as good an example of "pen-hand" as is the *Pan* of "monumental" lettering. It also suggests effects to be got by white on black, as does the *Jugend*.

The "Roebuck" (page 168) lacks the elegance of the *Pan* and the robustness of the *Westminster*, but it shows a good style for such newspaper lettering as has to be made quickly; as, for example, drawn on the chalk-plate in half an hour, when perfect spacing and proportioning is out of the question. There are times also when a letter is needed that is not truly elegant. It seems sacrilegious, as it were, to design a heading for "On the Diamond and Gridiron" with letters from a Lucca Della Robbia monument, or the Mazarin Bible. Therefore, some such lettering as the "Roebuck" comes in appropriate for the light departments of a paper.

Akin to the *Pan* design is the *Jugend* (page 169), though it is not nearly so good. It would be better with a border about it, and still better if the *Jugend* letters were not quite so narrow, and if the background behind the girl were more simply drawn; but the letter is good and strong, and the figure, being in outline, {174} might be printed upon the roughest paper. The whole page is interesting also as showing recent movement in type design in Germany. This is the result of the William Morris movement in England. It will be noticed that the type letters are broad and well proportioned; they are virtually modernized Jenson.

HEADING DESIGN BY GEORG AURIOL.
From *La Revue Encyclopédique*.

CHAPTER III.

SOME MISCELLANEOUS ILLUSTRATIONS APPROPRIATE FOR DIFFERENT PURPOSES — THE RIVOIRE APPROPRIATE WHERE EXPENDITURE IS UNLIMITED — HALF-TONES USED FOR NEWS-GIVING OR INFORMATION-GIVING PURPOSES — THE HASSALL OUTLINE APPROPRIATE FOR POSTERS AND DECORATIVE PRINTING.

LET US RESUME the consideration of some miscellaneous illustrations for the sake of investigating the different styles of design and the principles which underlie them. As we said in Chapter II, the French, who are the most ready to use simple designs printed on rough paper, also are experts in preparing with most exquisite workmanship most delicate designs. Let us cite the cover of the *Paris Illustré*—you will see that here a half-tone and a wood engraving have been used, and that each is virtually a picture. The type of the title is very fine French Old Style (by fine we mean thin), and while, of course, the hair lines in the a and e are due to our great reduction of the cut, yet in the original these lines were very fine, and therefore by no

{176}

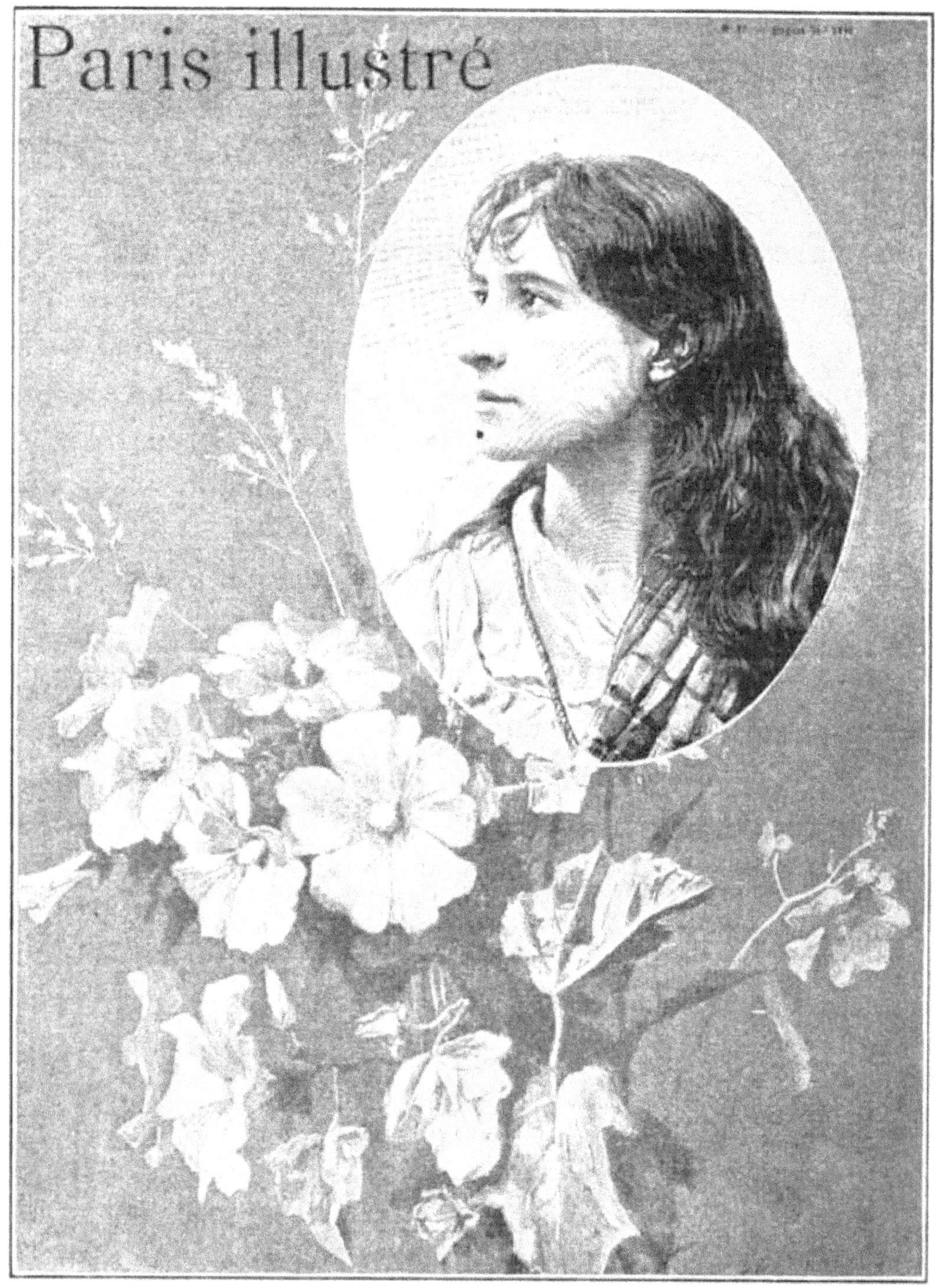

Cover design, by Rivoire, for a summer number of *Paris Illustré*, the flowers printed in slate color, in half-tone; the portrait, of Mlle. Weber, a wood engraving, and the title, printed in black. The original 11 1/2 by 15 inches.

{177} means as well adapted to ordinary printing as the Grasset, Caspari (*Jugend*), and Stuck designs given in Chapter II. Yet I consider the present design an admirable one. But what are the facts in the case? The art editor, in getting up this design, had plenty of money at his disposal. The cover was of heavy calendered paper, the flowers were printed in half-tone in color, and the woman's portrait, printed in black, was beautifully engraved on wood, a very costly process. This single cover may have cost as much as the entire sixteen pages of the body of the weekly.

The Auriol heading of this chapter is French also, and is no less artistic than the realistic flowers on the *Paris Illustré* cover; but on account of its simplicity it is far superior to the *Paris Illustré* as a floral design for ordinary printing, simply because it can be printed on cheap stock and can be cheaply and quickly reproduced. There ought to be no mistake, then, about my attitude in recommending one style of designing above another. I do so from a practical point of view.

A third example is found in the two Burns cuts. Surely, when I found the half-tone among the news columns of an English art periodical I did not object to its realism; on the contrary, it gave me a very good idea of what the original statue was like. But think of the expense of having a half-tone made large enough for a poster! Also, how vague it would appear from across the street if the poster were in half-tone.

But, turning to the Hassall, see how admirably the artist has given us the impression of Burns, how

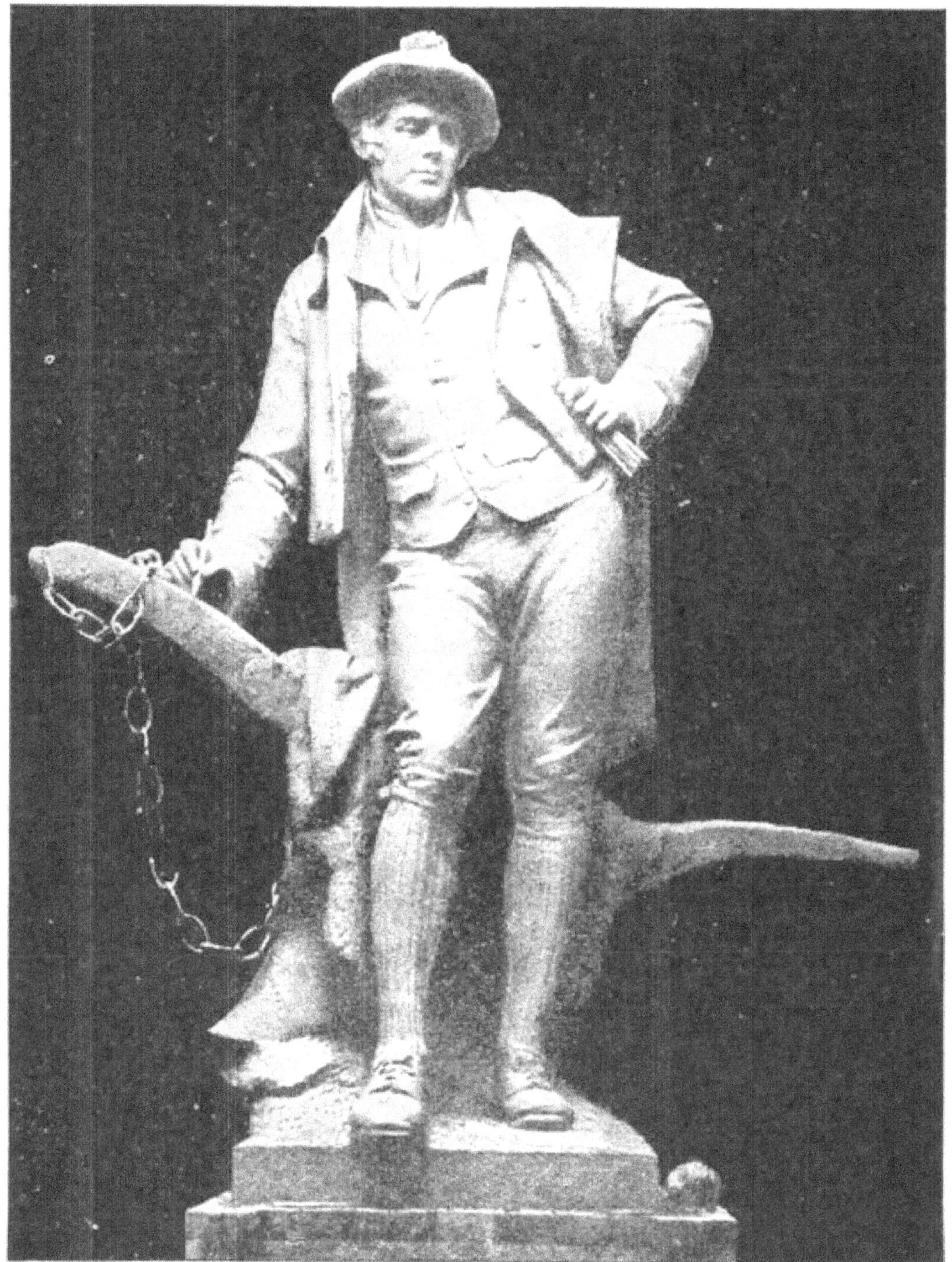

BURNS STATUE.

By F. W. Pomeroy. Recently unveiled at Paisley. Half-tone from a half-tone from a photograph, published in the *Magazine of Art*.

A Practical Treatise Of Designing And Illustration

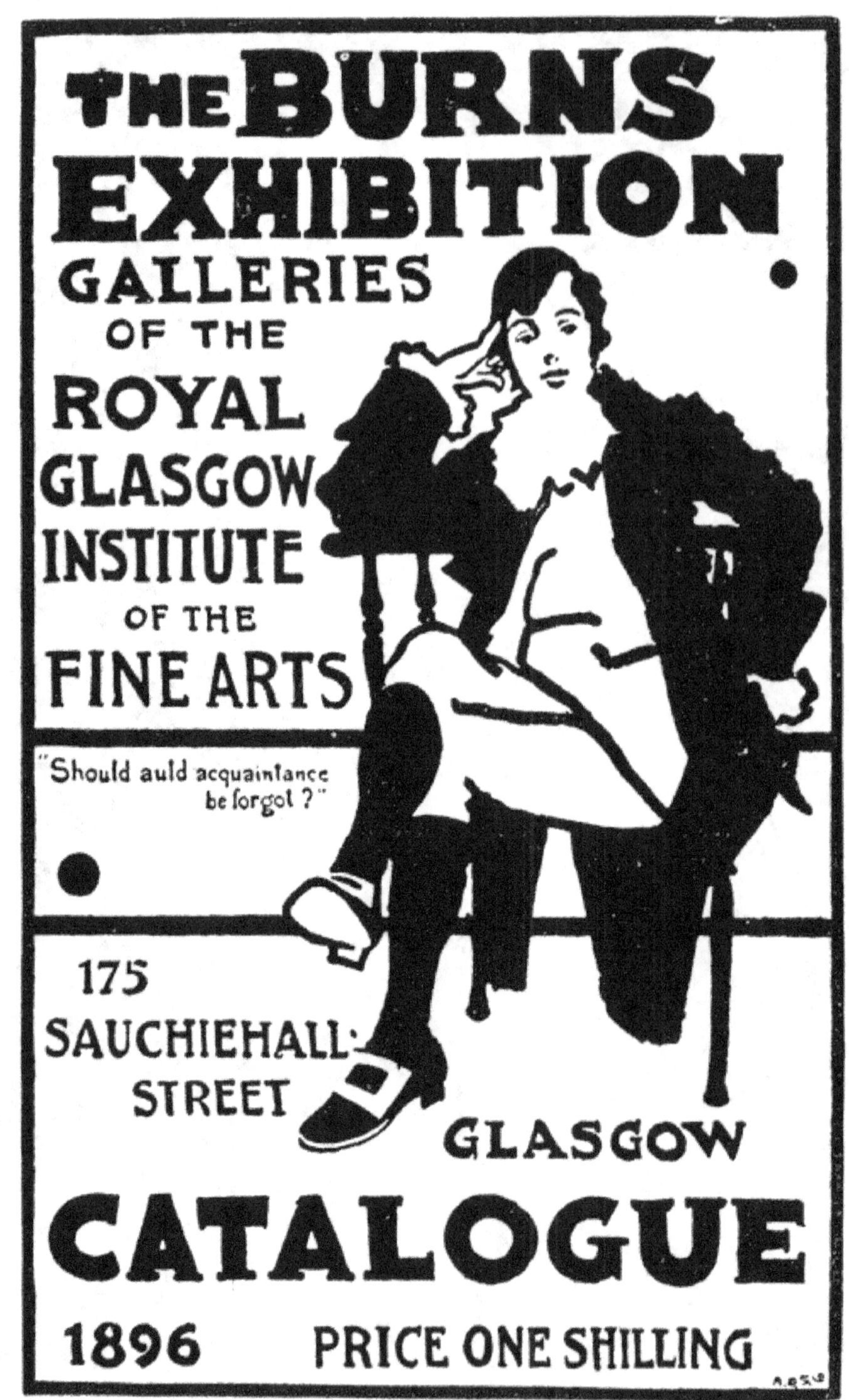

POSTER DESIGN FOR THE BURNS EXHIBITION, GLASGOW.
By J. Hassall.

{180} well his design would appear from across the street, and how cheaply it could be reproduced. Therefore, what an excellent style his is as a guide for my printer readers.

Hence, if the printer readers wish to make a cover design containing a portrait and flowers, I advise them not to follow the Rivoire—not for the reason that it is inartistic, but because it is too expensive for ordinary printing, and for cheap printing a poor imitation is abominable; while a design like the Caspari (*Jugend*, see page 169), where the portrait would be an outline and the lettering broad so it could be quickly read like the word "Jugend," and in which the floral form should be decoratively treated like the dandelion design in the Grasset "Larousse," or like the Auriol, page 175, would be just as pleasing to the eye, would print on the cheapest kind of stock, and would, therefore, appear to the critical as an artistic design.

CHAPTER IV.

AN IMPORTANT CHAPTER ON LETTERING — LETTERING CAN NEVER BE WHOLLY ORIGINAL, IT MUST FOLLOW HISTORICAL MODELS; MUST BE BLACKLETTER OR ITALIAN — THE STUDENT ADVISED TO MASTER THREE OR FOUR STANDARD ALPHABETS — STRANGE'S BOOK ON ALPHABETS RECOMMENDED — MONUMENTAL LETTERS CONSTRUCTED UPON A GEOMETRICAL BASIS — MR. GLEASON WHITE ON CHARLES RICKETTS AND THE VALE PRESS QUOTED — IT IS RECOMMENDED TO COPY A MONUMENTAL ALPHABET, AND TO GIVE SOME STUDY TO THE COMPLEX GOTHIC ALPHABETS, THAT THE STUDENT MAY UNDERSTAND THE PRINCIPLES OF THE THICKENING OF DIFFERENT PARTS OF A LETTER BY PEN PRESSURE — IT IS RECOMMENDED TO PRACTICE THE CAROLINE HAND FIRST, AND THEN THE GOTHIC.

This and the following chapters devoted to lettering give much practical information to the printer which may be enhanced in value if, before reading them, he will proceed as follows: Let him turn to the advertising pages of some printers' magazine and copy, *as best he can*, three or four lines of ornamental lettering of three or four different fonts. After he has done this, then read this chapter and the next, and *follow the suggestions therein*. We think he will then get a fuller benefit from them than if he reads our suggestions first and then proceeds to letter according to our directions.

A GREAT deal of time is wasted by the beginner who attempts to letter because of his impression that he can originate new styles of letters. Now, a critic sometimes speaks of "original lettering," meaning that the lettering shows individuality in treatment, and is not the mere slavish copying of some conventional form. {182} But in comparison to the other branches of art there is no such thing as originality in lettering. Your letter must be, broadly speaking, either Gothic (or blackletter, thus 𝔄) or Italian (or roman letter, thus **A**); that is, it must be built upon Gothic or Italian principles. The best thing for the beginner to do is to obtain some examples of good lettering and master two or three alphabets of Gothic or Italian style. After he has done this, he will see how all other alphabets he may come across in printed books will conform to the same general principles of the alphabets he has mastered. He will see how certain minor changes may be made, and if, in the end, he is anxious to be original he will, by broadening a letter where it may be broadened, or bringing its cross-bar down a little lower than usual, give a suggestion of originality to his work. (The chances are, however, that he will prefer to prove himself a good workman, and be content to combine, place and execute traditional letters.)

Strange's "Alphabets," published a few years ago, is an excellent book to study, and we shall give several alphabets from it. The old books on the subject are apt to be too ornamental for the printer, and the example we give from Niedling's "Book Ornaments" is of far less practical use than the Strange examples we shall give. But the Bauernfeind alphabet is valuable for study. It shows the construction of the capitals on a geometrical basis, giving an idea of how monumental letters are made. It is easy to see that with such a guide as this, made by an architect, the commonest workman, with the aid of the

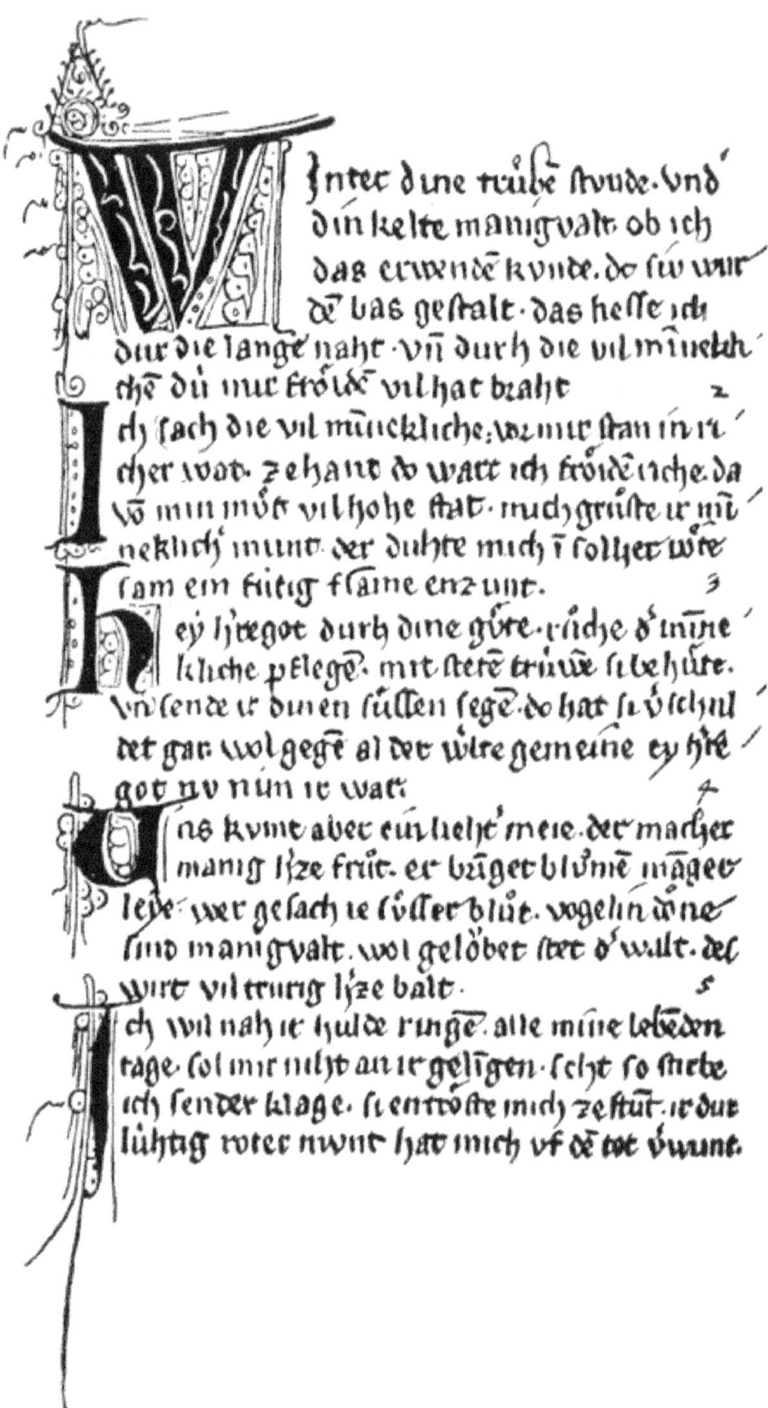

Page from a Minnesingers' song-book in the University library at Heidelberg. Example of Gothic letter. The initial letters were in black and terra cotta. The letter W was half black and half terra cotta; the U, H, and I were terracotta; the ornamentation was black. In all probability the letters were half an inch or an inch high. If you examine them under a magnifying glass you can understand their construction better than as they now appear. The first verse reads as follows:

> "Winter, dine trüben stunde
> und din kelte magnivalt,
> ob ich das erwenden kunde,
> daz siu wurden has gestalt,
> das liesse ich dur die lange naht,
> und durh die vil minneklichen
> diu mir froeiden vil hat braht."

{184} square and compass, could cut in marble an immense dedication of a building or archway, though the letters might be two or three feet high. A little study of this alphabet will give you the ability to understand anything written upon the subject of roman letters, so that the following quotation from an article by Gleason White, taken from the *Magazine of Art*, will immediately become intelligible to you. Mr. White was writing of Charles Ricketts and the productions of the Vale Press. He said the Vale Press had its own type, its own paper with its own watermark, but the printing was done by Messrs. Ballantyne. The type designed by Mr. Ricketts was "based on the precedents of the best Italian alphabets."

Mr. Ricketts believes that the plan on which all letters should be based is that of the perfect circle or the perfect square; it matters not which geometrical form you choose, since a certain number of letters—M, L, H, and the like—demand a parallelogram, and others—C, G, Q, O—an ovate or circular plan. If to draw this distinction between types based on the oval or the circle appear a mere quibble, we must remember that the difference between the Byzantine and the Pointed styles, which divide architecture into two great sections, is one of similar limit. There is all the difference in the world, to a specialist in types, between a small "b," "g" or "o" that follows the circle (O), and one that is planned upon an oval (O)—I wish to emphasize this point, because I know that the designer regards it as vital; and I, for one, agree entirely with his estimate of its importance. The question of "ceriphs" and the angles of certain strokes; whether a W consists of interlaced V's, or of two connected only by the ceriph; whether the ceriphs of a capital T are vertical, or slant divers

{185}

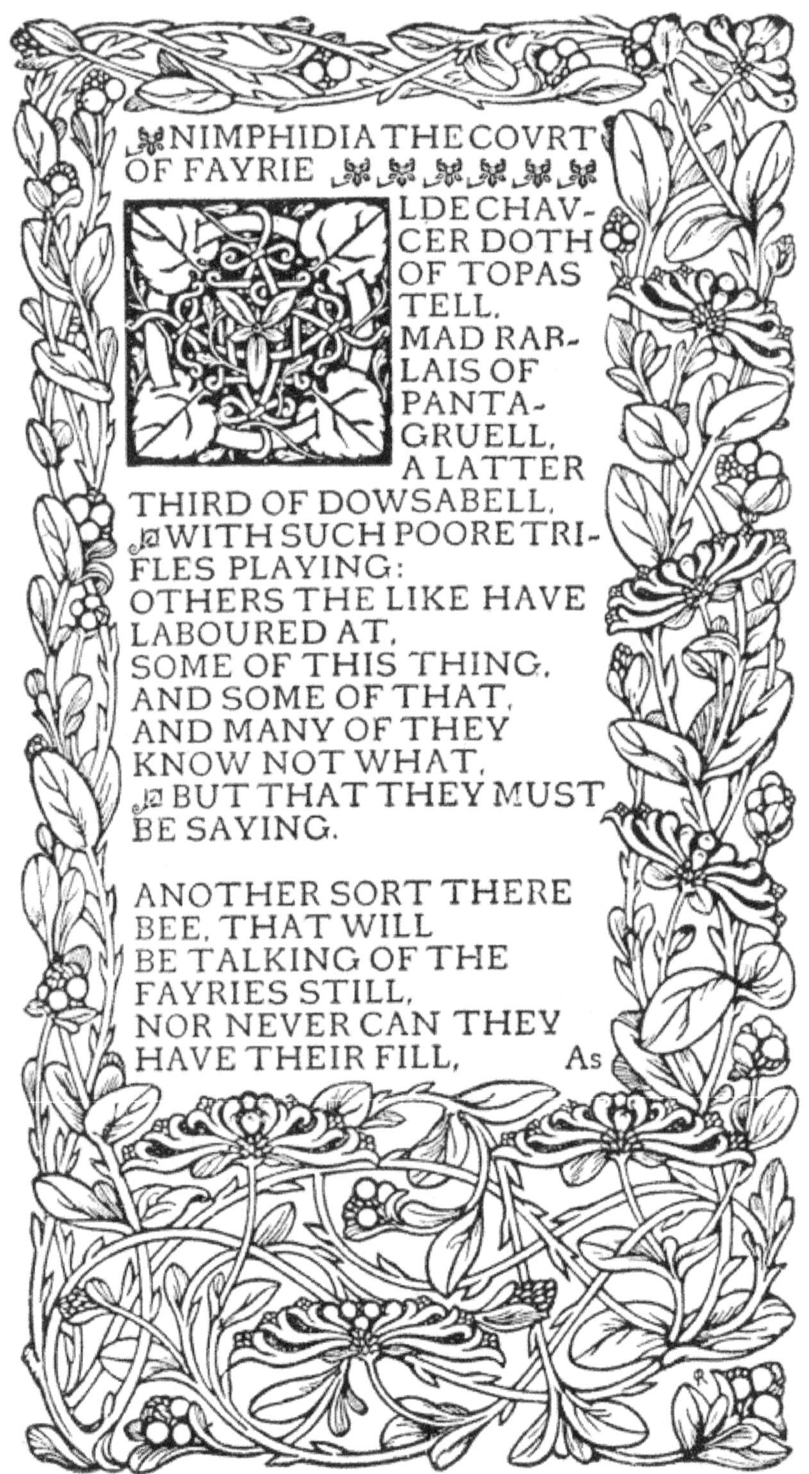

Reduced page from "Nimphidia," by Michael Drayton; design and lettering by Charles Ricketts. Lettering to be compared with the Italian "Lucidario."

A Practical Treatise Of Designing And Illustration

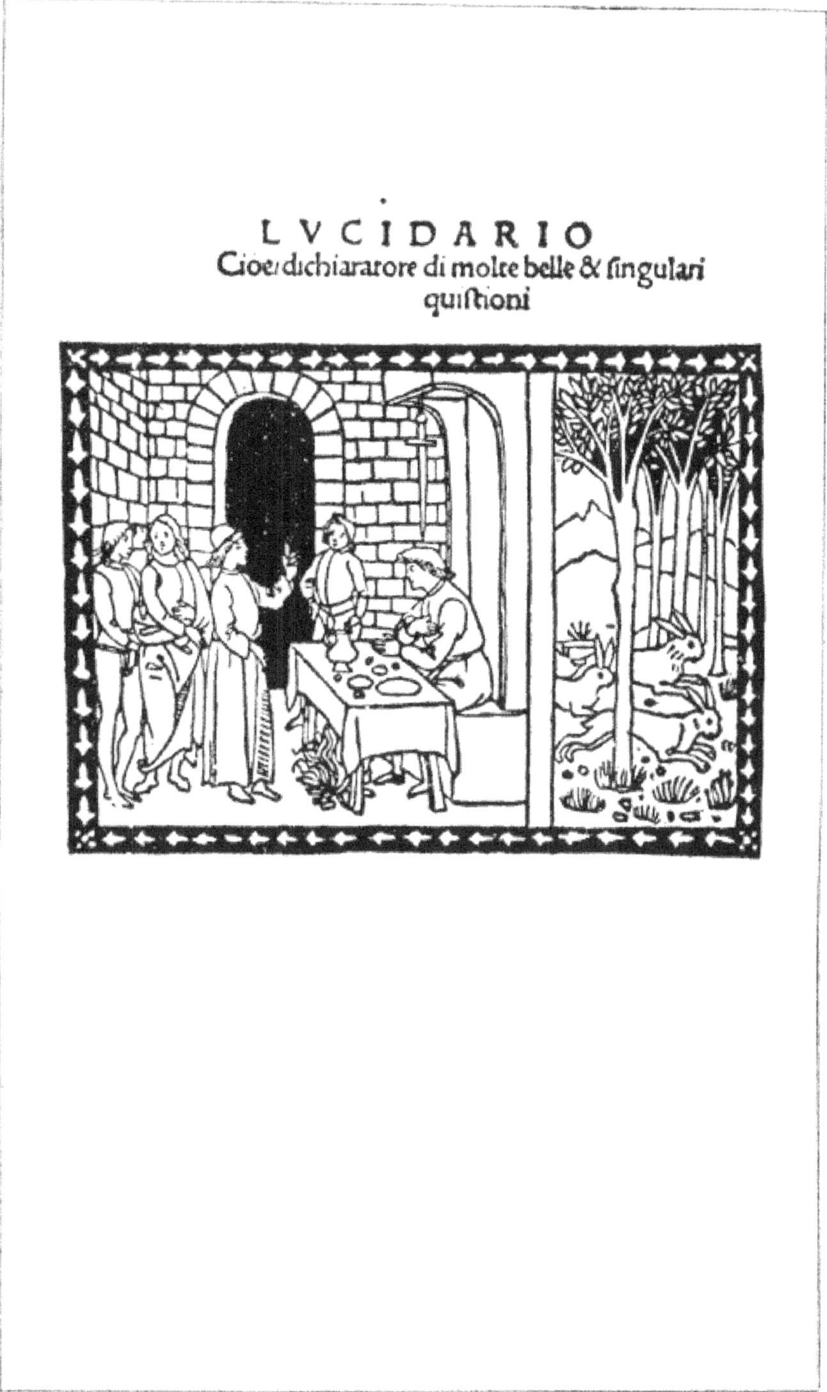

Facsimile of the title-page of the "Lucidario" (A. Mischomini: Florence, 1494). Original size of rule, giving proportion of page, 4 7/8 by 7 7/8 inches. Showing early Italian type letter and wood-cut design in harmony with same.

{187} ways, or parallel—all these are secondary matters, but the plan of the letter is not secondary.

In the beautiful Kelmscott type, as in the famous Foulis fonts and other notable instances, the O is ovate, and all other letters agree with it. In Mr. Ricketts' "Vale" type, the square and the circle dominate every letter. If this distinction be passed over as unimportant, further contention is useless. But on this point no compromise can be entertained. If it be unimportant whether the arch is a semicircle, or planned, like Euclid's first problem, upon the intersection of circles, then it matters little. But so long as architecture is separated by such structural difference, it follows that an O based on a circle, or an H based on a perfect square, must be entirely unrelated to the ovate O or the oblong H. When taste is in question, one allows the adversary equal vantage; but when geometry comes in, axioms must be observed. Therefore, the ill-founded assertion that Mr. Rickett's type copies any modern font cannot be allowed. You may dislike his symbol for the ordinary "&," or dispute over the beauty of his ceriphs and the oblique strokes of certain letters; but if you maintain that a circle and an oval are practically alike, the question of these nicer points need not be raised.

We give a reproduction of a page from the Vale Press, and for comparison the Lucidario printed in Florence in 1494. The similarity in the style of lettering is evident.

An evening or two spent in copying the Bauernfeind alphabet, and then making up one upon the principle that most of the letters should be contained in a square will lead you to understand the monumental letter, or what you recognize as upper-case Roman. You might then begin to collect pictures of mediæval and classical monuments, and you would at a glance be able to see {188} the principles upon which their inscriptions are constructed, and you would see that though the letters of certain monuments differed in proportion from others, yet the letters themselves of all the classical monuments would be virtually the same, and most of the Italian mediæval inscriptions the same in character. An Albrecht Durer alphabet given by Strange (on page 174) is particularly interesting, being constructed in the same manner as the Bauernfeind.

The Stimmer and Rogel Gothic alphabets are almost worthless for printers' designing, but it will not be without profit for you to realize that they are built upon the principle of the swell made with a quill pen, and this will lead you to the study of what you recognize as Gothic letters which grew out of the pen hand of the middle ages. Whether in solid black or white, any Gothic letter must have more or less the principles of the Stimmer and Rogel alphabets. Space will not permit of a full analyzation of the matter, so let us take the letter L only. In its simplest form it consists of two lines (or "limbs") at right angles—one perpendicular, the other horizontal. Both lines may be the same length; but conventionality has ordered that if either be the shorter, the horizontal should be. The irregularity of the ends of the letter, as in the monumental letters, is not a necessary characteristic of an L (which may consist of two simple lines); but it is the most frequent form in the monuments and is associated with our idea of a capital letter. When made with a pen in the middle ages it was sometimes customary to give the two lines

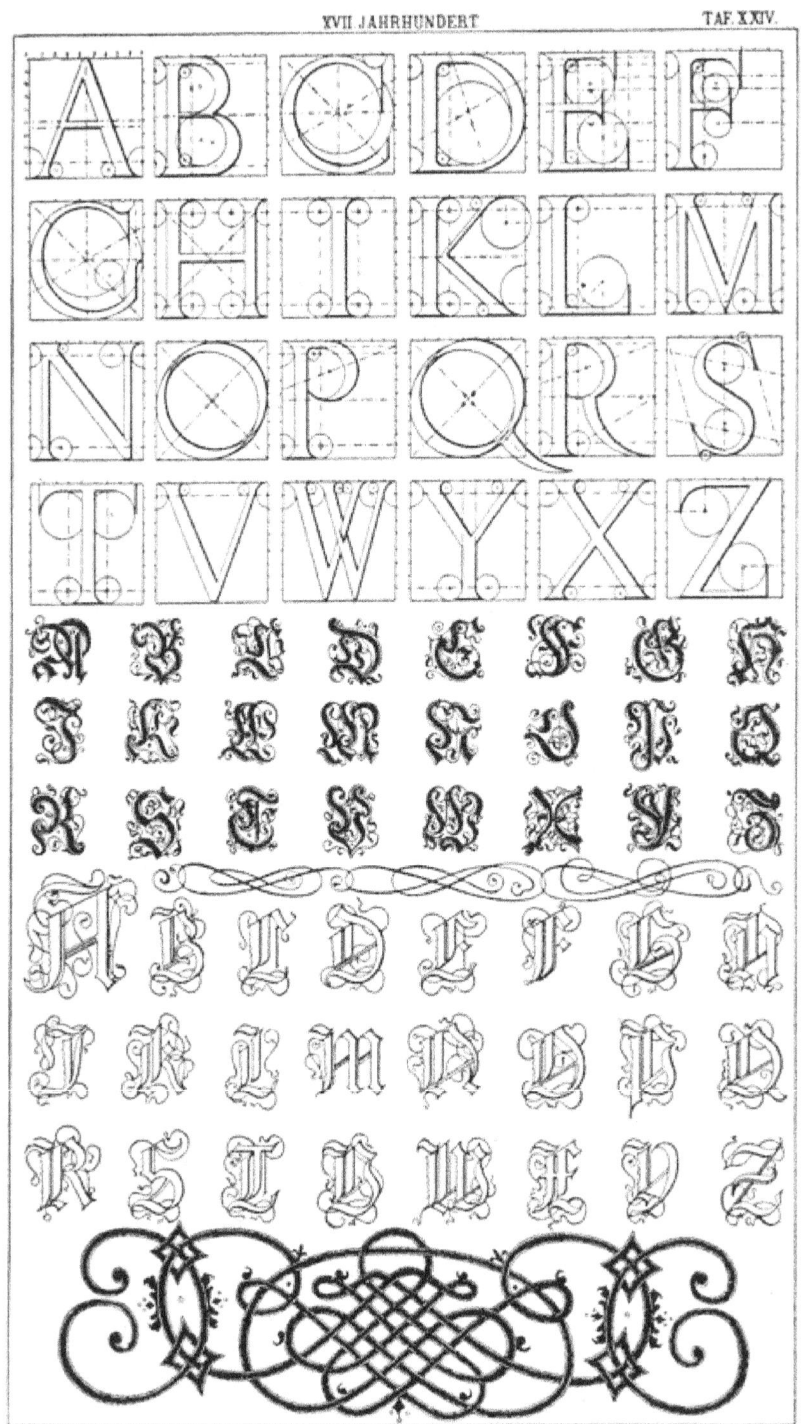

Examples of seventeenth century alphabets. From "Bücher Ornamentik," by A. Niedling, Weimar, 1895. B. F. Voigt. The first alphabet, after Michael Bauernfeind, is a monumental letter based upon the square, the margins of the letters being obtained by segments of circles. With such a diagram a letter ten feet high could be made as easily as one an inch high, and by an ordinary workman. The printer would not advisedly map out his letter with such exactitude, but it would be well to copy several of the letters, if not the whole alphabet, that he may study the character of the monumental letter. The second alphabet is after Chr. Stimmer; the third after type, the dies of which were cut by Hans Rogel.

{190} an undulatory character, and there is hardly any kind of twist or curve that has not been given to them. In making initial letters, in order to fill up the space it became the practice to make two lines of the upright shaft, and sometimes three lines were used. Cross-bars were also introduced, so that in Caxton's initial letters the L looks like the monogram P. E. L. Almost nothing restrained the caligrapher; and if he chose to make a dozen or two upright shafts, each getting smaller than the other on either side of the letter, the whole ending in some such Celtic interlacing as the base of the Niedling plate, he could do so. But none of this is an organic form of the letter L; and additional curve is pure ornament. The distinction between the superficial ornament and the organic lines of a letter is easily understood by first practicing the Caroline hand and then the Gothic. In the next chapter we shall be more explicit as regards details.

CHAPTER V.

THE DISTINCTION IN LETTERING BETWEEN SUPERFLUOUS ORNAMENTS AND ORGANIC LINES — A SOLID FOUNDATION FOR THE STUDY OF LETTERING — STUDIES, WITH THE QUILL PEN, OF THE CAROLINE ALPHABET AND ITS MODERN REVIVAL IN FRANCE BY GRASSET AND AURIOL — THE MINNESINGER LETTER NOT VERY ORNATE BUT MORE COMPLEX THAN THE CAROLINE — THE MINNESINGER CORRESPONDS TO THE STIMMEL AND ROGEL ALPHABETS — THE BERGOMENSIS LETTER MORE COMPLICATED AND MORE REGULAR THAN THE MINNESINGER — THE ITALIC LETTER MORE SIMPLE AND ROUNDER THAN THE MINNESINGER.

IN the last chapter we said, "The distinction between the superficial ornament and the organic lines of a letter is easily understood by first practicing the Caroline letter and then the Gothic." Let us explain the benefit of this practicing; the keynote to the matter is found in our Caroline example. Draw the second I and you will find that it is virtually a simple shaft with a little spreading at the top and bottom. If you draw with a quill or reed pen it is very easy to get this swell by a little extra pressure as you begin to draw and as you finish; and in almost all Caroline writing the I is made freehand and the shape depends upon pen pressure and varies a little each time the letter is made. It is not mapped out beforehand. The thin curved line on top of the first I is superfluous ornament; that line is made by a second stroke. We find several such ornaments in the first two lines which form the head of a chapter, just as we find much ornamentation of the initial letter; but we {192} do not find any ornamentation of the I's in the eight lines of text. There the I's are all made with a single stroke of the pen, so that the top and bottom of each one is a trifle different from that of the others. In the first line of text there is superfluous ornamenting of the T's, and of the H. Otherwise this is a true pen hand; the I made with one stroke, the C, D, L, O, P, Q, U, X, etc., with two strokes, the A, B, E, M, N, R, S, with three. The reader is advised to copy this alphabet with as large a quill pen as procurable, making the letters from half an inch to an inch high, and then, turning to the Grasset "Nouveau Larousse Illustré," it will dawn upon him that he knows exactly how the letters there were made; and he will have little trouble in imitating almost to perfection the three words, "En Six Volumes." When he tries the words, "Nouveau Larousse Illustré," he may have some trouble with the A, the S and with the O, which does not show its separate halves as in the Caroline: the horizontal line of the L also is more difficult to make than if it were the same width throughout. The I, R, N and V he will find quite simple. As he familiarizes himself with the Caroline M, D, V and I; with the H in the second line of the text under the ornamental H; and with the P, S, C, he will begin to realize that upper and lower case letters were originally the same. He will also be surprised, if he next falls to studying the Minnesinger letters (last chapter) under a magnifying glass, to find how like they are to the Caroline. Is not the capital I somewhat clumsier than the first I in the Caroline top line? Are not the c, d, h, i, o, p, s, u, v and y clumsier, more angular drawings of the same letters as in the

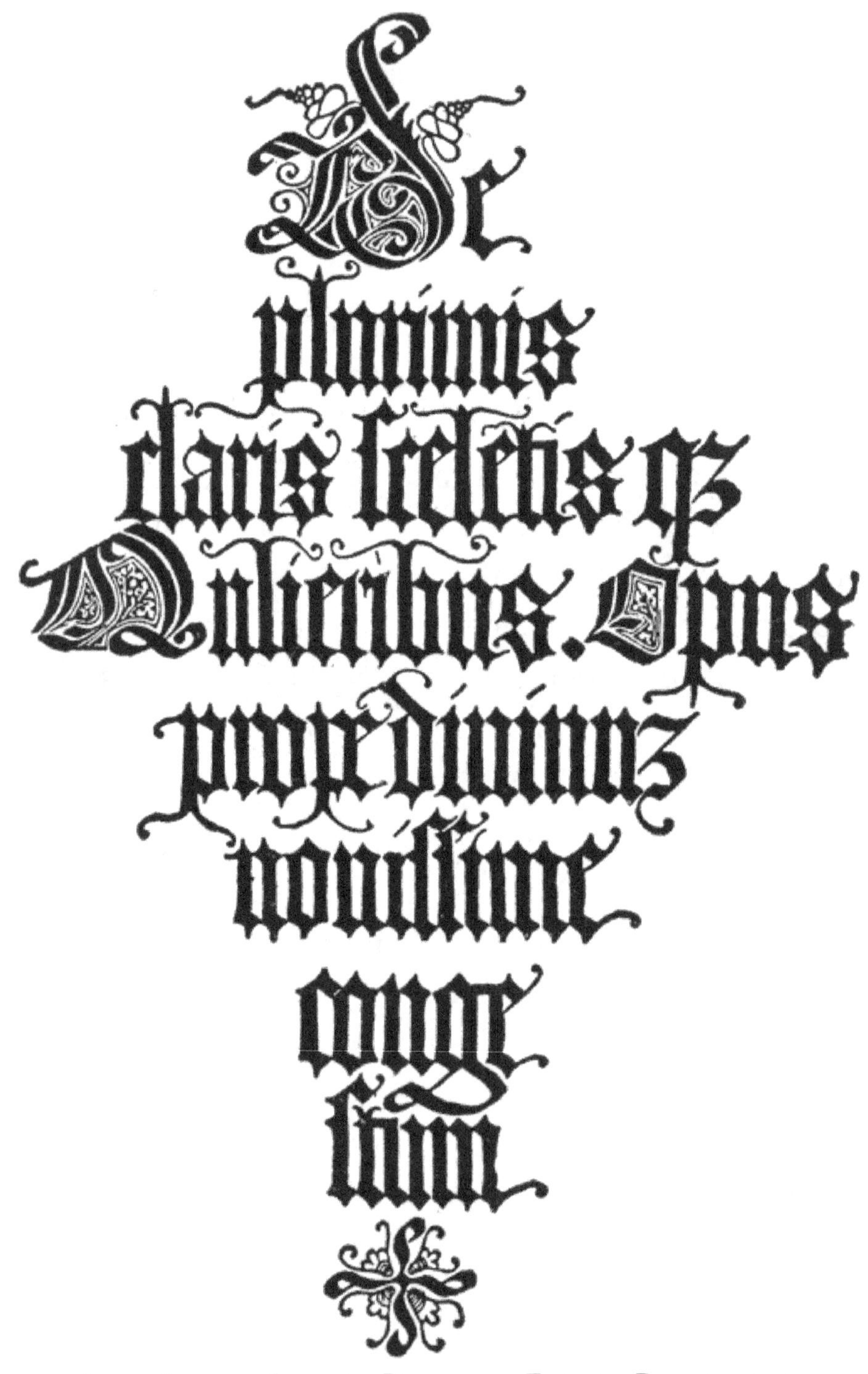

TITLE-PAGE BY JACOBUS PHILLIPPAS FORESTI BERGOMENSIS.
(Ferrara, 1497.)

A splendid example of Gothic lettering. It is to be remembered that this was originally designed with a reed or quill pen, and the ornamentations are such as may be easily made with that instrument. But its regularity is also due, in a small measure perhaps, to its having been engraved on white metal. In an entire book written in this style the letters would be less regular—a little more like the Minnesinger letters.

{194} Caroline alphabet? You find the s more decidedly four strokes, while in the Caroline it may be considered three. You find the m slightly different: turn to our last chapter and note the Hans Rogel m, which is upper case, and see how it corresponds to the Minnesinger lower-case m.

The Caroline e you think, differs from the Minnesinger e, but if you will look at the e in *erat*, third line of text, you will see how decidedly the e there is a lower-case e.

Now turn to the Bergomensis letters and recognize that they have certain characteristics. One characteristic is that the final letters and several others are ornamented with the same kind of curved lines as in the first Caroline I. Then that the letters are made with a pen stroke, but that three strokes are frequently used where one is satisfactory in the Caroline. This is plainly seen in the letter I. And of these three strokes, one is the shaft of the letter, which is long, the other two are the top of the shaft, which extends a little to the left, and the bottom which extends to the right. And these three strokes become the basis of the letter i, of u which is a double-i, of n which is a double-i, and of m which is a triple-i. The o is made of the main shaft and the right-hand base, and the left-hand top and the main shaft. So you will then see that the Bergomensis is nothing less than a more complicated and more regular letter than the Minnesinger, which in turn is nothing less than a more irregular letter than the Caroline! In order to make the Bergomensis letter you must have your pen cut to a comparatively blunt point the exact width of the letter—a letterer uses such a pen almost always. {195} When you study the Italic specimen (see last chapter, "Lucidario" page), however, you find that the lower-case letter is very much like the Minnesinger, except that it is more simple and a trifle more rounded, but note that it is evidently written with a comparatively sharp-pointed quill pen. But it is not to be overlooked

✝INCIPIVNT·LECTIONES·INVICI
LIASBEATIPETRIAPOSTOLI
LXXVII   I

ETRVSAVTEMETIOHANNESASCEN
DEBATINTEMPLOADHORAMORATIO
NISNONA· ETQVIDAMVIRQVIERAT
CLAVDVSEXVTEROMATRISSVAE·
BAIVLABATVR QVEMCOTIDIEPONE
BANTADPORTAMTEMPLIQVAEDICITVRSPECI
OSA·VTPETERETELEMOSYNAM ABINTROEVN
TIBVSINTEMPLVM

Example of seventh century lettering from a Latin manuscript, reproduced from Strange's book on lettering. In this letter, freed of the curves in the capitals I, T, L, V, C, etc., we find the principles of a very simple and graceful style of lettering, virtually the Caroline, which is being revived by Grasset and Auriol in France today.

that the variety in the letters is still due to the pressure of the pen. The Italic letter is best practiced with a new quill; and then when it gets a little out of order it may be cut a trifle and be used for a Gothic letter, like the Minnesinger; and then when it spreads again it may be cut a second time and then used for a broader Gothic letter like the Bergomensis. {196}

Now, I do not claim that this chapter will be intelligible to a mere reader —I feel sure that it will not be—but to anyone who will put in practice all the exercises I have suggested, I feel sure that it will be intelligible, and that it will give him the foundation for the whole study of lettering so that he may pick up any alphabet and master its principles after a few days' practice.

CHAPTER VI.

USE OF QUILL FEN NECESSARY IN THE STUDY OF LETTERING — THE ORNAMENTATION IN LETTERING OF NORTHERN AND SOUTHERN SCRIBES COMPARED: THE ITALIAN, GOTHIC, VISIGOTHIC, LOMBARDIC, ROMAN, VENETIAN, ARABIC — THE FIRST PRINTED LETTERS: TYPE OF CAXTON, GUTENBERG, ALDUS — THE ITALIC (LUCIDARIO PAGE), MODERNIZED, BECOMES THE JENSON AND MORRIS TYPE, THE FRENCH OLD STYLE, ENGLISH OLD STYLE, AND OUR MODERN ROMAN LOWER CASE: THE ALDUS TYPE BECOMES OUR ITALIC — THE PRINTER MUST HAVE EDUCATED TASTE IF HE WOULD DESIGN CORRECTLY — APPROPRIATENESS OF CERTAIN LETTERS BECAUSE OF THEIR HISTORIC ASSOCIATIONS — THE BAD TASTE OF ORNAMENT AT THE EXPENSE OF CLEARNESS — AIMLESS, UNBALANCED ORNAMENTATION — OVERORNAMENTATION — GRASSET'S LETTERING STUDIED — IN AURIOL'S LETTERING THE SPIRIT OF PLANT FORM IS EXTENDED BY LETTERING, AS IN GOTHIC ARCHITECTURE PLANT FORM IS BUILT UPON.

IT is to be hoped that upon our advice the printer, after reading Chapter I, attempted to copy some font, and that, not following any special method, he found it pretty tedious work: that he then read Chapters II, III and IV, and found, with the help of our information about the Latin capitals in a square, and about the Gothic letter being dependent upon the spreading of a quill pen, that things seemed clearer, more intelligible. But we think that, with the help of the present chapter, he will make still more progress. If he, fully appreciating our reference to the quill pen, procured one, and set to work studying the Grasset letters {198} he must have made rapid progress; for it is only by using the quill pen that the Grasset and Auriol letters can be understood. So we say that if a printer will procure one and practice the Caroline alphabet given in the last chapter, next the Burgomensis, next the Minnesinger, and then the Stimmel and Rogel alphabets, he will find that he has a solid foundation on which to study lettering, and a clear idea of the genius of letters. He will begin to realize that the Caroline is the simplest, the Burgomensis and Minnesinger the more complex, but not very ornamental, though in them the caligrapher had begun to assert himself, using a flourish from time to time to ornament the letters. And he will notice that these flourishes are such as are made naturally with a quill or reed pen, and that upon these curves and swellings are based not only the Gothic capitals, but also what are known as lower-case letters.

It so happened that most of the southern scribes (Italians and Spanish) confined themselves to a very simple letter, while the northern ones took pleasure in variety. The southern style is called the Italian, or italic; the northern, the Gothic. There are many historical instances, however, where northern manuscripts are simple; and on the other hand, the letters of Visigothic and Lombardic writers, though southern, were more ornamental than those of their Roman and Venetian brethren; and our Burgomensis specimen we call Gothic, though it was originated in Italy. The true southern ornamentation was originated under the Arabic influence in Spain (at the time of the Saracenic conquest), and traveled up to France, where it is found in the elongated d, s and f in the French diplomatic hand.

{199}

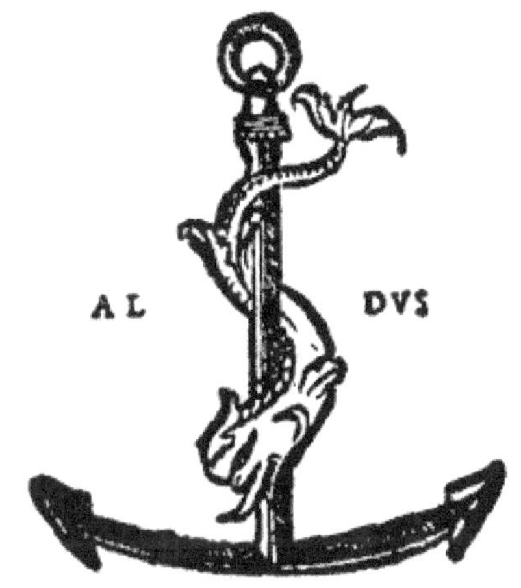

Facsimile of the title-page of an Aldine Horace, 1519. Showing Latin monumental letter now known as upper-case roman; and Italian cursive hand, now known as italic.

{200}

You, of course, know that when the art of printing was invented the types had to be cast, and the dies were naturally cut in the form of the letters of the manuscript of the country in which the printing was done. Caxton imitated the manuscript of the Low Countries and not that of England, when he printed the first book printed in English movable type. So, too, Gutenberg's type imitated the German manuscript, while that of Aldus, tradition says, was cast after the manuscript of Petrarch, and that form has been called Italian or italic ever since. We give a specimen of Aldus' "Horace": copy with a quill the lower case in it till you can write with ease, and you will be able to write as Petrarch did. It is harder to associate it with quill pen writing than to associate the Gothic with the pen letter. Nevertheless, if you will write for a little while with an old quill, lettering like the Minnesinger, and then with a new quill imitate the Aldus italic, you will soon see that the italic character depends upon the pressure of the quill pen, just as the Gothic does, though not to such a degree. Make lower-case a, d and s, or an m several times, and you will see what I mean. The other Italian form, which printers do not call italic, is like the Lucidario, which is less cursive than the Petrarchian form. When modernized, the Lucidario becomes the "Jenson" and Morris type (while the Aldus is our italic); it only needs a little investigation to realize how easily it became the French Old Style and English Old Style, and then our modern, roman lower case.

It will not be difficult for you, if you will really obtain the quill pen and practice as I propose, to realize the truth of the following suggestions:

A printer should show an educated taste in his {201} designs. Few people know this, and your fight will be continually against this ignorance, both in yourself

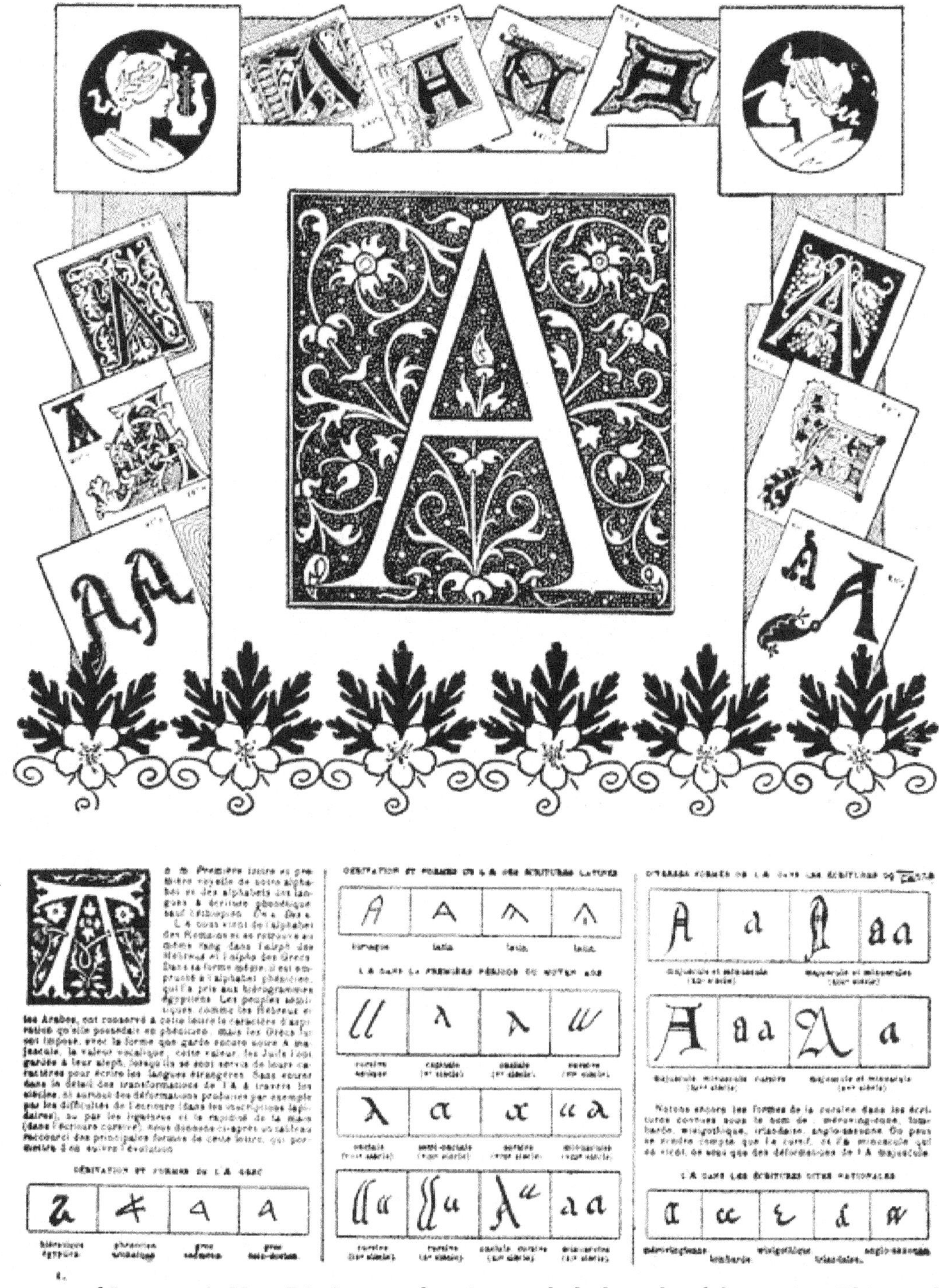

First page of Larousse's New Dictionary, showing a scholarly style of decoration. This can be best studied under a magnifying glass.

and your customers. You will think that anything you like is artistic and appropriate and you will be tempted {202} to undertake it. Your customers will say that they "know nothing about art" but they "know what they like";

so they will pick out some ill-executed and inappropriate job and insist upon your following it. But my business is simply with that which is established as standard, and not with what people like or dislike. Now, historic association plays an important part in designing for printers. The first page of the Larousse dictionary is a superb example of historic association introduced into a design. Here, to illustrate the letter A we have letters from many different periods, but they are all harmonious because of their ornament and their execution. And they are appropriate because they are historical. So if you are designing an announcement of the Ancient Order of Hibernians, a prospectus of a genealogical society, a book of early English poetry (earlier than the tenth century) you could use the sixth or seventh century A because that belongs to the very best Irish-English lettering used between the sixth and tenth centuries. The other letters that go with the Larousse sixth century ornamented A specimen you will find in an example from the "Book of Kells," given in Strange's "Alphabets," and perhaps in the "Durham Book." This identical A is probably from "The Rule of St. Benedict." Now, if you should obtain an Anglo-Saxon alphabet and master its style and apply it as we have suggested, it would be properly associated with these historic subjects; so you, as an educated printer, would know that you were right, and any criticism would not deter you from using it.

I take it for granted, however, that you use such letters as this A only as initials, or in designing a title {203} of a line or two; and that you would not let it occupy too much of the page: for it is not only necessary that a letter should be associated historically with a subject and that it be well designed, but it must also be associated with printing or bookmaking. It is true that some introductory pages in the sixth and seventh century Irish-English manuscripts were sometimes very ornamental, but the reading pages were, as a rule, quite

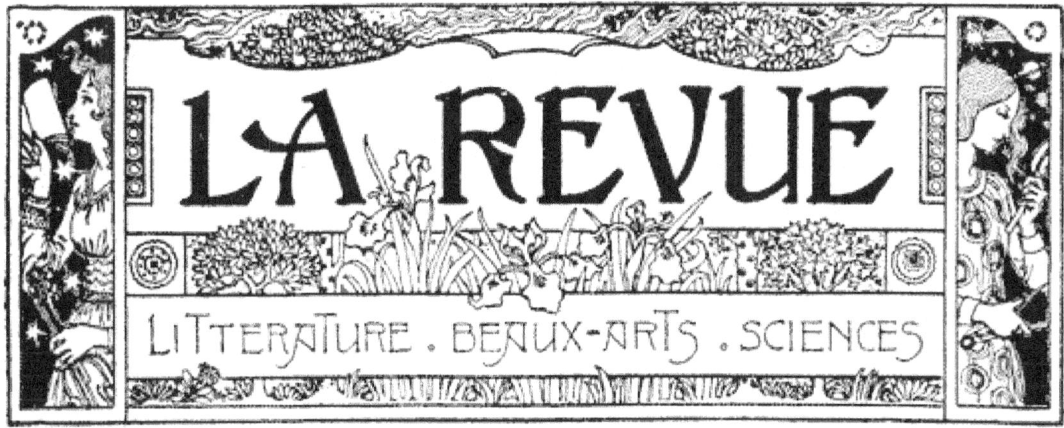

This is a design by Eugene Grasset for the heading of a department in "La Revue Encyclopédique." It represents French designing art at its best. It is free from conventionality, and yet orderly and well balanced. The Auriol design for "La Revue Encyclopédique" is bold and striking, but not as perfect as this.

simple. The good bookmaker never forgets his pages are for reading. So, a Gothic ornamental letter that might be appropriate in a stained glass window or on a hand-painted testimonial might be offensive throughout a printed book. I know of nothing more inartistic, more nauseating to critics, than the millions of lithographed mottoes, Christmas cards, etc., that the English lithographic publishers have put out for the last decade— overburdened with ornament that should be painted and not printed. And so the whites in this sixth century A, and the dotted outline around it, make {204} it in a way less appropriate for general printing than the solid black, twelfth century A.

The middle A is in the style of the wood-cut Venetian letter of the sixteenth century; and while on general principles a gray background like this is not so satisfactory as a black one, yet this is not a bad specimen of designing, for the stipple could be punched into the wood very deeply, and is so near together that if one hole did fill up it would not be missed. However, it, too, must not be used for general printing, but only as rich ornament. It is well balanced, mind you, and therefore the detail is not so worrying as would be as much detail put in freehand, aimlessly and unbalanced.

If you will now turn to the cover design of the Larousse given in the August number, you will find it a beautiful production by Grasset, wherein we see also some decorative elements that may be studied in conjunction with what we have written in this and preceding chapters about letters. For example, the use of line with silhouette—we find a dandelion leaf reduced to silhouette, and another laurel wreath like the one pictured on the head of Goethe's mother. But the lettering of the title is the most interesting part of it. Grasset has studied the Caroline letter, and reproduces it with very scholarly fidelity. Only when you have studied an example like the Caroline alphabet we give from Strange's book can you appreciate the workmanship and good taste in the Grasset. A companion piece to this is the heading by Auriol where we see a modification of the monumental letter and the uncial as in the d and the r. Here the initials J J and the initial L are Gothic in principle, and you will not fail to see how

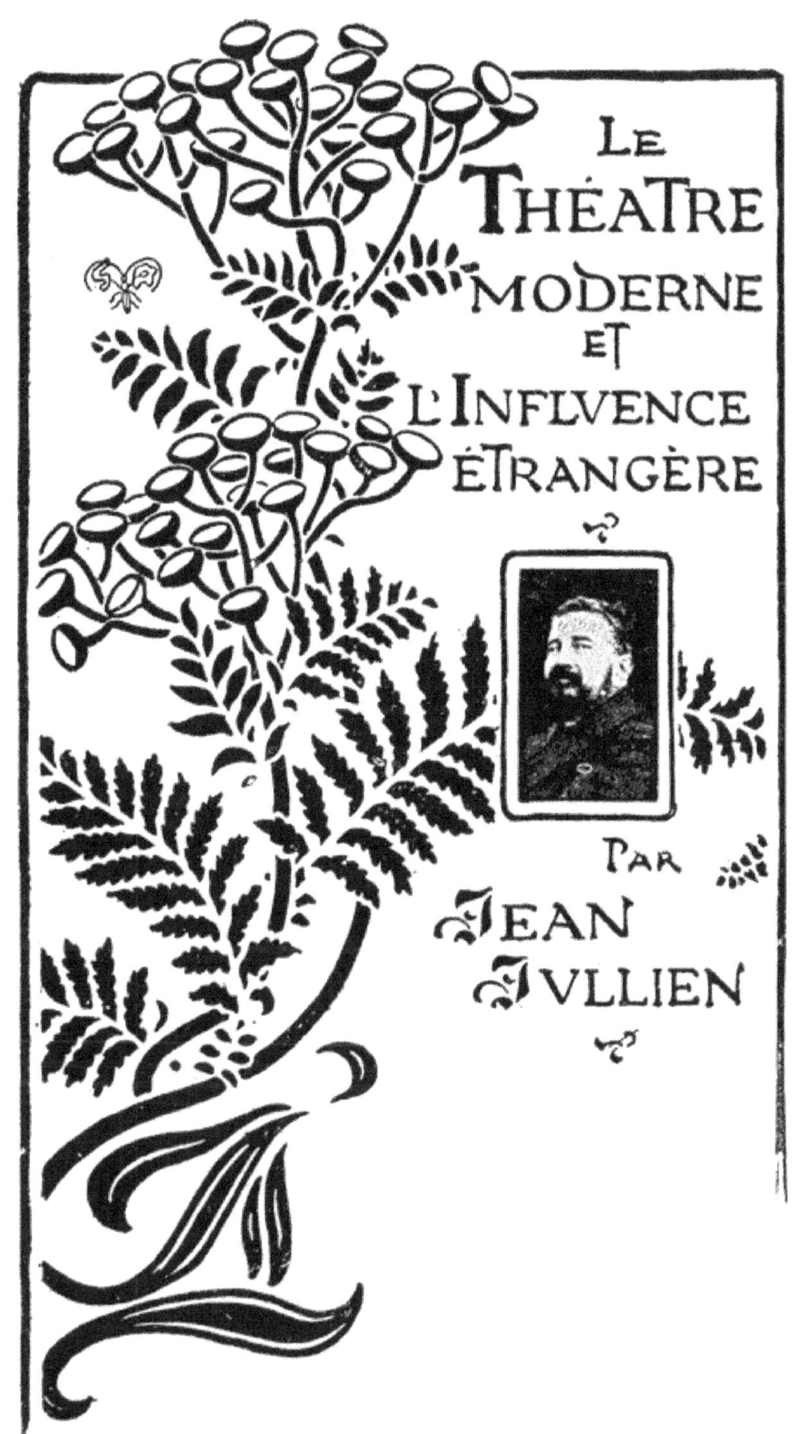

Design for an article in "La Revue Encyclopédique" on "Le Théatre Moderne et L'Influence Étrangère, par Jean Jullien," with an initial letter and design embracing a half-tone portrait of the author. A harmonious design, showing the use of silhouette; and Caroline lettering not so well understood as in the work of Grasset. Designed by George Auriol.

{206} harmoniously the L below the leaves extends the spirit of the plant design, so that if you have ever read essays upon Gothic art, like the writings of Ruskin, you will readily see the plant form is here built upon, as in Gothic architecture. What we have said so far ought to have prepared you for a historic survey of the topic of lettering. Our space is much too limited to make such a survey very extensive, but what we shall give in the next chapter will serve as a foundation on which you can build, by reading, a much more exhaustive study of the subject.

CHAPTER VII.

THE GROWTH OF WRITTEN LANGUAGE — SIGNS AND SYMBOLS BECOME HIEROGLYPHS — EGYPTIAN HIEROGLYPHS BECOME HIERATIC OR CURSIVE — THE HIERATIC BECOMES ANGULAR IN THE PHŒNICIAN — PHŒNICIAN ALPHABET A MONUMENTAL ONE AND THE LETTERS LIKE OURS — FROM THE PHŒNICIAN COME THE GREEK AND LATIN ALPHABETS, WHICH ARE USED THROUGHOUT EUROPE TODAY.

THE GROWTH of written language is briefly recorded as follows. Primitive man used signs and symbols, as does the North American Indian. Noah understood the symbol of the dove with the olive branch. Had he wished to record the event of the flood he would probably have drawn several waved lines to represent water, and a mountain peak underneath, to show that the water rose above the mountains. A second picture of a dove with an olive branch would have indicated that the waters had subsided. This method of writing was used by the Assyrians and Egyptians 5000 B. C. With the Assyrians the symbols developed into "cuneiform," or wedge-shaped signs, stamped on clay. With this form we have nothing to do, as it never influenced our writing; but with the Egyptians (as with the Chinese) the symbols soon took a written form called hieratic (used by the priests), which is the direct parent of our own handwriting. In hieroglyphs on monuments in Egypt, the sign for water was a horizontal zigzag, and for a mountain a silhouette of hill-like form. These {208} were painted, and sometimes partly incised on soft stone or stucco, and had a pictorial character. But when the priests had to write voluminous rituals, they used a reed pen on papyrus, and reduced the silhouette pictures to shorthand-like marks. The first example in the Larousse Dictionary (page 201), represents the hieratic shorthand of the hieroglyph of a bird. But not only did the Egyptians use their signs as hieroglyphic word symbols, but they also used them as phonetic signs, so that the sign for water stood for both water (*mu*) and the sound *n*. The Phœnicians and Hebrews are supposed to have borrowed their alphabet from the Egyptian hieratic writing; and in the transition the irregular character of the markings of the reed pen on papyrus disappeared and monumental regularity took its place, as nearly all of the early Phœnician and Hebrew writing was in the form of inscriptions on stone and metal. But in this transition the letters did not revert to the Egyptian hieroglyphic symbol, but simply became an angular, simplified form of the hieratic, so that the A became a V or caret-like form with a line crossing it.

With the Phœnicians and Hebrews the signs were never used for word signs, but for syllabic (or letter) forms, so that with them N was simply a phonetic sign (plus variable vowel accompaniments).

This alphabet was used by the Phœnicians, Hebrews, Moabites and other Semitic inhabitants of Palestine. It is supposed to have been carried by the Phœnicians to Greece, and possibly to countries farther west, but until investigation throws further light upon the subject it is well to suppose that all the other countries of Europe {209} received their alphabets from Greece, so that, virtually, all the alphabets of Europe—Latin, English, German and Russian-are simply modifications of the Greek (see the succeeding specimens in the Larousse Dictionary page). The Greek alphabet was modified in two ways: first, in the monumental form it became more regular —more right-angled—than the Phœnician; secondly, in the manuscript it became much more irregular—cursive in general, with angles not at right angles (see cursive examples, third row of Larousse Dictionary page)—so that in some third century manuscripts there is as much irregularity as in the Egyptian. This character, however, is more apt to be found in the late Greek manuscripts—that is, those written during the Christian era—than in classic Greek manuscripts where simplicity and regularity prevail. It is particularly interesting to the printer to realize this fact: for when he sees a difference in European lettering—as, for instance, the difference between Russian and German text on the one hand, and English on the other—he must remember that Russian and German are outgrowths of the late Greek or ornamental lettering; while English, Italian, Spanish and French are the outgrowths of the simpler classical Greek forms. To distinguish the two we have called the first (most of which is irregular) Gothic, the second (which is generally regular) Latin. But many an irregular manuscript was written by other than Gothic scribes, and there are some Latin manuscripts that are as irregular as the Gothic.

No matter how a letter may vary in ornamentation in a German, Russian, or English book, it is an outcome {210} of a Greek original. In the Russian, in one or two cases, a sign is a compound of two Greek letters, but in English each letter has its Greek prototype. Now anyone who stops to think will notice that monumental letters on stone are about the same in all countries. (The letters on Gothic brasses, however, are dissimilar to the usual monumental letters.) For the monumental letter is usually made by measuring, as in the first Bauernfeind alphabet, and is cut by an ordinary workman who follows a pattern, which should be simple. Therefore, an A is nearly always two oblique uprights and one horizontal crosspiece, like the sixth Larousse example. The two uprights are not always at the same angle, but they are nearly always oblique, though one may be very near the perpendicular. The crosspiece is sometimes oblique, but rarely at an angle greater than fifteen degrees. So a monument erected in Greece 600 B. C., one in Rome 60 B. C., one in Italy in 1400 A. D., and one in Paris today, have virtually the same letter A upon them as one written in Paris today, and a child who had just learned its letters could recognize it in each.

It must not be expected that in a short treatise of this kind we can cover the whole field of paleography, but our few notes on the subject may indicate to some readers a line of study that will repay anyone who undertakes it. The easiest method is to examine manuscripts of Bible text, where the subject matter is pretty well known, and, following the different styles of writing, acquaint oneself with the development of writing in different centuries and in different countries. A valuable handbook giving facsimiles of many Bible pages is "Bible Illustrations," published by Henry Frowde, New York—it costs but $1.

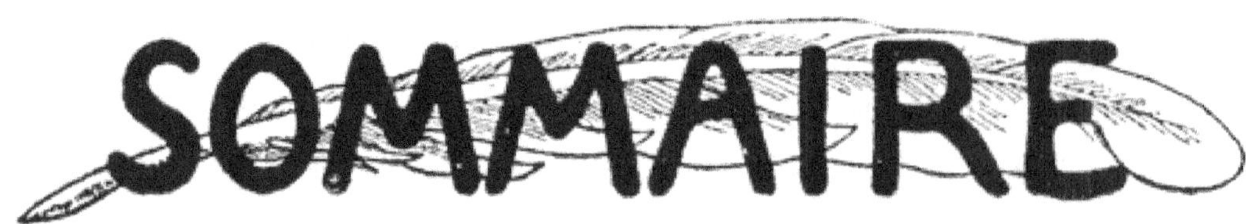

SOMMAIRE
Headpiece for a French periodical.

CHAPTER VIII.

SUMMARY OF METHOD OF INSTRUCTION GIVEN — PRELIMINARY "PLACING" OF LINES IN A SKETCH — THE RELATION OF A SILHOUETTE TO AN OUTLINE — DRAWING IN OUTLINE, IN SILHOUETTE, WITH PARTIAL SHADING AND WITH FULL SHADING — CUTS GIVEN OF VARIOUS STYLES OF BOOK DECORATIONS — ANALYSIS OF THESE STYLES.

Now for our summary. My method of teaching in this series has been one of suggestion, and very often I have seemingly gone off at a tangent, to hint at an application of some rule; in so doing perhaps the chapters seem to lack continuity, but I think several readings of them will show that there has been a logical development throughout. Perhaps the following summary will bring various parts together and fix all in the memory.

First, the student is advised to practice drawing from objects, and to learn to get something on the paper as soon as possible, and then by further labor to develop this something. There should be at first, lines and markings showing *about* where the different parts of an object should come. In the Lautrec drawing the lines are not meant for a bicycle or the calves of a man's legs, but the lines represent about where the bicycle and the man's calves should come. Anything that can be seen may be "placed" in this way —a tree, a house, a cloud. After the student has learned to "place"